DATE DUE

SCOTUS SPEAKS TODAY

1266 - 1966

seventh centenary symposium

APRIL 21, 22, 23, 1966

DUNS SCOTUS COLLEGE

Southfield, Michigan

1968

Dedication to

Friar John Duns Scotus,
    spiritual son of Francis of Assisi,

proponent of freedom and love,
    defender of man's dignity,

Subtle Doctor,
    master-molder of precision,

Doctor of Mary,
    her champion and theologian,

Herald of Christ the King,
    exponent of His Primacy,

teacher for our day
    in the treasury of his works,
    in the vitality of his teachings,
    in the richness of his spirit.

Foreword

As the seventh centenary of the birth of John Duns Scotus drew near, much thought was given at Duns Scotus College as to how the event might be celebrated in a fitting manner. Because of the conviction that the Subtle Doctor has a real message for the modern world—in his spirit as much as in his teaching—, the theme *"Scotus Speaks Today"* became the motif, and invitations went out to outstanding scholars to participate in a symposium. Speakers were sought whose intellectual interest in Scotus was coupled with a genuine love for him. Hopefully the papers presented would spark significant discussion.

The symposium was held at Duns Scotus College on April 21-23, 1966, with a roster of speakers and discussants from various parts of the United States and abroad. Discussions following the presentations proved lively ones, and several times extended long into the night. Regrettably, only the formal discussions could be published with the papers.

In the course of the symposium a petition was sent to Pope Paul VI begging his apostolic blessing upon the participants and proceedings. The Holy Father's blessing came by way of the following telegram . . .

WESTERN UNION TELEGRAM

April 28, 1966

Father Leander Blumlein
President
Duns Scotus College
Southfield, Michigan

Holy Father imparts to Father Charles Balic and participants in convocation celebrating seventh centenary of birth of John Duns Scotus, in pledge of abiding divine assistance, his paternal blessing.

Cardinal Cicognani
Vatican City

The proceedings of the symposium are published in this memorial volume with the hope that they might inspire further interest in, and love for, John Duns Scotus.

Contents

CONTENTS CONTINUED

FATHER PHILIBERT RAMSTETTER, O.F.M., graduated
from Catholic University, Washington, D.C. and
has taught in the Franciscan houses of study
of St. John the Baptist Province, as well as
at St. Bonaventure's, New York. He served
several terms as President of Duns Scotus
College, Southfield, Michigan, and at present
is teaching at St. Francis College, Fort
Wayne, Indiana. He is author of numerous
articles and has lectured widely on the topic
of Franciscan Spirituality.

Sermon:
JOHN DUNS SCOTUS

PHILIBERT RAMSTETTER, O.F.M., M.A.

Very Reverend Father Celebrant, Very Reverend Father Provincial, Very Reverend and Reverend Fathers, all my Brothers in Saint Francis, Christian ladies and gentlemen: This is as it should be, this celebration to give some publicity to, maybe even to add a little glory to, the goodness and genius of a simple man, a priest of Jesus Christ and devoted follower of that most unusual man of history whom Catholics and non-Catholics alike, with high regard and much affection, have dubbed the Second Christ (notice, not a second Christ, but the Second Christ). As for the celebrating institution, this seminary-college, it must be deeply grateful for the decision of its founders that it was to function under the inspiration, and to the honor, of a genuine Franciscan student and teacher, one highly gifted yet, if we may judge from his writings, thoroughly humble, . . . one who could cope with non-Franciscan brilliance but would gladly seat himself at the left of the lowliest of his Brothers.

Much too often great, virtuous minds are poorly known to those that come after them; few such, it would seem, have remained quite so unknown as he of blessed memory, John Duns Scotus. Only scanty details concerning his life have succeeded in coming all the way down to us. One might say, then, he lives with us today almost purely on the strength of his own powers, on the strength of his soul. Certainly, however, as long as there are thinkers on this earth, this man's passion for truth will never cease being a matter for wonder and a challenge to imitation. His passion was for truth, not for victory, for truth of any kind, always for truth in its high, clean sense. That is, whenever he went out looking for truth, he sought it for its own sweet sake, although in the same moment it would delight him to recognize in the particular item of truth before him a necessary, maybe a ravishing, prelude to goodness, the goodness that would eventually invite and lead to love. Moreover, breaking through the character of our times, technological, sociological, or whatever else the stamp, this man still lives among us by the very energy and warmth of his convictions. For example, how could anyone at all forget his illuminating insights and his zealous conviction regarding human freedom and, consequently, human equality? I think it no exaggeration to say that to few other intellectuals, even those of highest optimism, has freedom, the freedom of choice and decision, meant so much as to John Duns Scotus: <u>Of the essence</u> of man's grandest power, the will, is the ability to choose, to decide.

Too soon did death come to this man to permit him the time and effort needed to woo the approval of posterity, had that kind of ambition been in him. It was not even given him to set his manuscript-house in proper order. So, putting aside for the moment the fine research accomplishments of learned and devoted scholars, we may assert that he is with us today by the utter exactness and force of his mentality, by the progressiveness of his attitudes, but, above all, by <u>his sense of God</u>. This sense of God (admittedly rather <u>different from</u> that of his confrere, Bonaventure) shows through almost every proposition proceeding from his soul. I should not venture here to treat of this sense of God explicitly; I must hope that it will be realized as an implication of what I have to say.

I hasten to add: A sermon even, or perhaps especially, on an occasion such as this is hardly the time for apology or polemic. Therefore, in my illustration, though contemplating the picture of <u>goodness versus truth</u>, of <u>love versus knowledge</u>, I shall merely skirt the problem, or problems.

It ought to be clear from his works that, no matter what the controversy or question, John Duns Scotus never faltered in his loyalty to truth. Call him voluntarist, if you will (in one sense you may and must), he was intellectualist all the way, even as he vigoursly battled for the supremacy of goodness and love. Let it be declared, and proudly: For this man, to seek out the truth in any matter whatsoever was the same thing as trying to find out the <u>mind of God</u>--when all is said, truth is <u>what God knows</u>. And questing for goodness, the goodness of righteousness, was, for this man, trying somehow to take <u>hold of God</u>, the Infinite, and, at the same time, trying to know precisely what He, the Creator and Savior, <u>wants of us</u>, . . . of us human beings in general, of any one of us in particular.

This, to be sure, is critical matter in both the philosophical and the theological thinking of John Duns Scotus, namely, what He asks of us Who is the great and good God, our Creator, our Lord, our Owner, and then our Redeemer and our Sanctifier. For herein are implicated two duties that are comprehensive and all-pervading: first, to honor, worship, and love Him to the extent that He must be honored, worshipped, and loved by creatures rational as we are and baptized as we are; second, to carry out His exactly defined will in accordance with whatever state or condition or vocation in life may be ours and in any circumstance or set of circumstances in which we may happen to be. And it is only for the sake of completeness that the simple reasoning need be stated here: Since we belong to God totally, our obligations to Him are total. There are no others: As this man saw it, the binding of an essentially free power can come only from above; even charity, in its purest sense, is fulfilled in an obligation given, and accepted, from above. All of which means: Nothing more than the Divine will can be of duty; nothing less can be of sanctification. Just as that which exactly pictures God's mind is, and must be, true, so that which exactly answers His will is, and must be, good and therefore, a perfect fulfillment of duty.

My brethren, we should reach an even more refined appreciation of this man's sense of God when we consider his teaching on love, charity. The faculty of love is God's best gift to man as the Creator; it is his highest ability as a spiritual being, his greatest purely human function. Here we must set aside entirely all thought of what we at times call physical, bodily love, emotional love, even what is referred to as an enlightened spiritual self-love. To fit our context, we must have in mind only what John Duns Scotus thought of as unselfish love, unselfish devotion, what he preferred to call charity. This kind of love, it need hardly be mentioned, has meaning only when its object is a person.

One cannot be wrong in thinking that his most deeply cherished thesis with regard to human conduct is this: The Creator has endowed human beings with freedom, with the ability to choose and decide, to say "yes" rather than "no" in definite situations, to say "no" rather than "yes"

--the Creator has given us this kind of freedom to make it possible for us to love . . . and, of course, to hate. In other words, we are free so that we may willingly and unselfishly accept and be devoted to goodness recognized for what it is, that we may willingly and unselfishly reject and, if possible, eradicate, destroy recognized evil.

It stands to reason that our nature, in its highest spiritual reaches, tends to its own good, its own perfection, its beatitude. However, what we are here concerned with is man's ability to rise cleanly above and beyond self--his ability properly to evaluate goodness, particularly goodness in another person, and, accordingly, to love that person. Manifestly, this implies unselfish giving to another; to say the least, such giving is a sign of love. In this is contained the true glory of the human race: first, there is within us the possibility of heroic love, of one human person for another; secondly, there is likewise the possibility of complete, perfect surrender to Him Whose goodness is without end.

What a satisfying thought: The best within us moves us to the best in rational conduct, charity! In this sense, nature, our nature, and, for that reason, the God of nature, want us, seemingly beg us, to love and to hate: to love what by God's creation and implicit ordination is lovable; to hate what by God's eternal loathing is fit only to be despised and shunned by rational beings. They beg us, our nature, and our God, not only to give a willing recognition to goodness, which really is largely forced upon us by natural, necessary affection, but also, to give it a willing acceptance; and in every way to abhor whatever evil we face and recognize as evil. Thus, what might be called active love and active hate tell whether we are loyal to ourselves and to our Maker, eventually also to our Redeemer.

The thought of John Duns Scotus in this matter, while inspiring, is simple. Whenever we come to see goodness spiritually, intellectually--when we come to see in another person goodness precisely as goodness, then the affection of love (spiritual, to be sure) is immediately, implicitly made present within us, that is, the affection

15

of love rises spontaneously with, in the vision of value, of goodness; it is a given, inescapable, necessary. However, nature cannot, and the God of nature would not, force us to love, to consent to this presented love. The Creator would have the right to demand it of us, and to some extent He does so demand; yet He will never force us to the supreme act of opening the arms of our soul to admit the given love. In this is the large, significant, critical import of human freedom as John Duns Scotus outlines it; in the recognized presence of what is good, high good, perhaps supreme good, with our soul powerfully drawn by its high nature to accept and love that goodness--in that critical moment we are physically, actually free, completely untrammeled: We are able to say with full deliberation "yes" and open our eager soul to the goodness presented; but it is also within our power, just as deliberately, if almost unbelievably, to turn aside to some self-indulgence or to some mere stagnation or even to hatred.

Nature cannot force any one of us to be loyal to goodness; God will not. According to the Creator's arrangement the spiritual affection of love is presented to us in, and together with, the recognized presence of goodness; but the virtue of love is of free decision. Goodness and love are a present, acceptable, rejectable; however, personal goodness, that is, virtuous love, charity (in the supernatural order, God's Grace being granted)-- virtuous love, charity must be chosen, for it is a fully human act, not merely an affection. The perfect God will present, and does present, his own perfect goodness to us for our acceptance and love; He will not physically impose it upon any soul. Here, it would seem, is answer to the question: Why did love have to be a law, a commandment?

It is worth repeating: We have been given this freedom in order to be able to love . . . and to hate. Clearly, this ability to desire and choose charity is high dignity for a creature; indeed, as John Duns Scotus himself would say, herewith the human being approaches closest to his Creator: here the creature himself, in a sense, creates something, namely, an act, an existence, of charity by a free action of the one faculty on all this earth that can be, and is, free, the human will.

Still, we dare not forget: Herein is also the possibility, the danger of the greatest human humiliation, namely, choosing to hate something good as if it were truly some evil, choosing to love an evil as it crookedly wears the smile of gracious goodness.

Quite evidently, in the order of nature (my re-marks have mainly been in reference to that order) Scotis-tic thought is God-centered. In the order of supernature, as everyone knows, it is Christ-centered, with a special personal quality and intensity characterizing that thought. In truth, so thoroughly Christ-centered is John Duns Sco-tus' thought in matters Catholic that before Adam and Eve, before the world as world, no matter how many billion light years that world itself may demand--before any of all that Jesus Christ was in the Creator's mind; He was the Creator's very first thought as Creator, and everything else literally depended upon, hung on, that First Thought; everything else was to be created in and for Jesus Christ. Granted that this is correctly said, then, in the mind of this man, the world, all creation, is both actually and by nature centered in Him Who is God-Become-Man. In this same Scotistic mind of charity it also follows that the Blessed Trinity desired and foresaw only one adorer, a perfect one, only one servant, a perfect one, and only one lover, one creature that could and would love perfectly-- all other intelligent beings were to get their complete fulfillment in sharing, by free decision, in the God-Man's adoration, service, and charity. In our finest poetic de-sires we may long for the union of the whole of nature and supernature; if Scotus is correct, the wedding took place in eternity.

The "sense of God," which fills all Scotistic phil-osophy, is baptized into the "sense of Christ" just as soon as it crosses the border of theology. Thus, almost incidentally, it cannot surprise anyone to learn that he who could not bear the thought that Jesus Christ's becom-ing man was to depend upon sin could neither bear the thought that Christ's Mother was to be redeemed as merely another human being. Because of this loving insight never can the dogma of the Immaculate Conception be separated from the name of John Duns Scotus.

With this, my brethren, I hurry to my conclusion, which, as I think, ought be given to my fellow Franciscan teachers.

We face a large responsibility towards all this modern world; if not, there is no longer any reason for Franciscan existence. Evidently, we have an especial responsibility towards those who have an especial right to look to us for guidance and inspiration. For us as teachers there is much to inculcate, very much to explain. In any case, to justify our existence, we should be teachers of Franciscanism . . . to whatever extent and degree our devotion to truth, our love for goodness, and our Family character of simplicity will warrant. With all the urgency of practical logic and with all the zeal that might move us to give Jesus Christ's Good News to more and more of mankind, we must begin our proper influence with the childlike yet burning and deep wisdom of the Little Man of Assisi; we must drench our students with the Seraphic unction of Bonaventure; and we must expose them, for as much as they need or can bear, to the hot brilliance of the Doctor of High and Deep Charity, John Duns Scotus, for whom what finally counts in a man is his goodness and for whom, therefore, the Holy Gospel is the most practical thing in all this world. "Salvation News" is but a newer term for what the Subtle Doctor, some seven hundred years ago, liked to speak of as the word of God, meant to transform creatures, rational creatures, into children of the Infinite God. Here we have pragmatism at its loveliest best: Goodness and Divine childhood somehow grown into synonyms!

Goodness and love, freedom and human dignity, the unqualified Primacy of Jesus Christ and His Mother's fullness of Grace, and, through it all, God's law, God's will, the Creator's and the Redeemer's--that, as I see it, my brothers, is the heart of Scotism, the Catholic heart; and this becomes purest Scotistic prayer: "Not my will but Yours be done. I want only what You want, great, holy Redeemer, Infinite God--I want all that You want, and because You want it; and I find no joy except it be in accordance with Your will . . . for me."

What a singer for Psalm 118 the man we are celebrating would have been!

"I have chosen the way of truth; I have set Your ordinances before me.

"I run in the way of Your commandments, for You give me a docile heart.

"I will keep Your law continually, forever and ever.

". . . I will walk in freedom, because I seek Your precepts.

"How I love Your law, O Jahwe! It is my meditation all the day.

"Your command has me me wiser than all my enemies, for it is ever with me.

"I have more understanding than all my teachers when Your decrees are my meditation.

"Falsehood I hate and abhor . . .

"O Lord, I long for Your salvation, and Your law is my delight."

With that expression of intense joy, I ask the Almighty to bless all of you, the Father and the Son and the Holy Spirit. Amen.

FATHER CHARLES BALIC, O.F.M., is best known in
Scotistic circles as President of the Scotistic
Commission, Rome, critically editing the works
of Scotus. He is also President of the Pontifical Athenaeum Antonianum and in the Pontifical
Lateran University, Rome. He is Consultor of
the Sacred Congregation of Seminary and University Studies and of the Congregation of Sacred
Doctrine. He is author of many theological
articles, and he served as peritus for Vatican
Council II.

DUNS SCOTUS

in the Present Moment

of the Church

CHARLES BALIĆ, O.F.M., S.T.D.

Paul the Sixth said that the closing of the Second Vatican Council was to be considered "the beginning of many things."

It is necessary to form a post-conciliar conscience. This implies the implementation of the Council's teachings; it means the work of translating them into concrete forms.

In the fourth session of the Second Vatican Council, the Church has examined herself and her nature. She opened herself to the world. There is need of dialogue for searching out the solution to many problems and of realizing that aggiornamento and the renewal of the Church's life and teaching, so much hoped for by the Council.

In this atmosphere, in this post-conciliar situation, one of the first and most urgent tasks is this: the different Catholic schools and systems of theology and philosophy need a confrontation with the many decrees issued by the Council, so as to model their outlook and action on their inspired and undeniable authority.

The Franciscan School, with Duns Scotus at its head, celebrating precisely in this immediate post-conciliar atmosphere the seventh centenary of the birth of him who was called and is the DOCTOR OF THE ORDER, very gladly takes this occasion to study diligently the relationship between the doctrine of the Franciscan School, and in particular of John Duns Scotus, and the doctrine, orientation, and dialogue desired by the Second Vatican Council--dialogue vertical and horizontal in the ambient of Catholicism, and dialogue with the systems and the doctrine of non-Catholics.

In this symposium, held at Duns Scotus College, the only college as far as I know graced with this name, I would treat only some points of this confrontation, and precisely:

I.   Duns Scotus and the other Catholic Doctors in the light of the Second Vatican Council;

II.   Doctrinal positions of Duns Scotus and some conciliar documents;

III. Duns Scotus and the dialogue so much desired by the Second Vatican Council.

I. DUNS SCOTUS AND THE OTHER DOCTORS IN THE LIGHT
OF THE SECOND VATICAN COUNCIL

After the encyclical AETERNI PATRIS of Leo Thirteenth and various documents of Saint Pius Tenth; after the
well-known prescription of Canon Law, "Philosophiae rati-
onalis ac tehologiae studia et alumnorum in his disciplinis
institutionem professores omnino pertractent ad Angelici
Doctoris rationem, doctrinam et principia, eaque sancte te-
neant,"(1) there were not lacking authors who interpreted
this canon in an exclusive sense.

One of these authors arrived at statements like
this: "There is no question here of a free teaching, but
of a defined teaching"(2); with this canon the Church is
supposed to have imposed "en bloc the philosophy of Saint
Thomas."(3) Others reasoned in this way: "Because the
twenty-four thomistic theses are safe directive norms,"
and because "safe" means "certain," and certain is equal
to "true," one has to say that positions contrary to them
are not safe directive norms. In a few words, if the
Church recommends a teaching with insistence; in fact, says
that it has made its own the teaching of Saint Thomas; one
must conclude that "it is true," and consequently that the
contrary teaching is already condemned.(4)

As a doctrine contrary to that of Saint Thomas,
there was naturally pointed out not only that of Suarez,
but above all of Scotus. Festugiere, after having defined
Scotus "the zealous contradictor of Thomism." affirms: "Aux
'epoques passèes, les deux doctrines ont pu librement se de-
velloper dans l'Eglise. Mais, autres perils, autres be-
soins. . . ."(5) Briefly this means: Either with Thomas
and the Church, or with Scotus and Suarez against Thomas
and against the will of the Church.(6) Medium non datur.

This exclusivism was favored by two apocryphal
testimonies that unfortunately entered the encyclical
AETERNI PATRIS, where we read not only that Innocent Sixth
is supposed to have said that no one could ever attack the
teaching of Thomas without being "suspectus de veritate,"

but also that the Fathers of the Council of Trent are supposed to have placed on the altar, together with the Sacred Scripture, the SUMMA of Saint Thomas "unde consilium, rationes, oracula peterentur."(7)

And one is not to marvel if at the very beginning of the Second Vatican Council all this made itself seen again. Actually, in certain newspapers it was insistently requested that in the Second Vatican Council the SUMMA THEOLOGICA should be placed alongside of Sacred Scripture, forgetting that the Church has never identified human thought with the Divine Word, forgetting that criticism for some time now has shown the legend that at the Council of Trent, the SUMMA THEOLOGICA was enthroned next to Sacred Scripture to be without foundation. Criticism has proved this legend an invention of Gonet, in whose epitaph we read: "Plures fecit thomistas quam Thomas."(8)

I have pointed to these few facts certainly not to arouse polemics or to incriminate anyone, but simply and only to evaluate and judge the better what was said and determined in the Second Vatican Council on scholasticism and on Saint Thomas, and mainly for the purpose of seeing the place that Duns Scotus occupies among the other scholastic doctors according to the Second Vatican Council.

Knowing what had been said in the pre-preparatory phase as regards a certain project concerning the Angelic Doctor,(9) with great prudence and balance the Commission on Seminaries,(10) Studies, and Catholic Education wished to avoid the term "scholastic" and mentioned the Angelic Doctor once only in the Schema ON CHRISTIAN EDUCATION, and once only in the Decree ON THE FORMATION OF PRIESTS.

In the Decree ON CHRISTIAN EDUCATION we read that the Catholic Church wishes that universities, and the theological faculties depending on them, "organica ratione . . .singulae disciplinae propriis principiis, propria methodo atque propria inquisitionis scientificae libertate ita excolantur, ut profundior in dies earum intelligentia obtineatur et, novis progredientis aetatis quaestionibus ac investigationibus accuratissime consideratis, altius perspiciatur quomodo fides et ratio in unum verum conspirent, ECCLESIAE DOCTORUM, PRAESERTIM S. THOMAE AQUINATIS vestigia premendo."(11)

The Decree ON PRIESTLY FORMATION proposes the following methodology for the cultural formation of priests: "ipsa themata biblica primum proponantur," and then, "quid Patres Ecclesiae Orientis et Occidentis ad singulas Revelationis veritates fideliter transmittendas et enucleandas contulerint necnon ulterius dogmatis historia--considerata quoque ipsius relatione ad generalem Ecclesiae historiam--alumnis aperiatur." Thirdly, it speaks of speculative theology in these very moderate terms: "deinde ad mysteria salutis integre quantum fieri potest illustranda, EA OPE SPECULATIONIS, S. Thoma magistro, intimius penetrare eorumque nexum perspicere alumni addiscant." Lastly, it teaches that one must consider these truths also in the context of the liturgy and of the life of the Church and ever keep in mind the efficacy of revealed truths in the solution of the problems that regard the actual life of human society.(12)

If, instead of the expression "S. Thoma magistro," the same had been said as in the Decree ON CHRISTIAN EDUCATION, "Ecclesiae Doctorum, praesertim S. Thoma vestigia premendo," probably there would have been no discussion on this point in the Council Hall. In fact, the Fathers were few who requested that the name of the great Aquinas be passed by in silence where there is a question of dogmatic theology, because the Council should not propose any other teacher but Jesus Christ, and because "homines et systemata cum tempore transeunt," and lastly because "ansa datur ut de inobedientia vel de haeresi accusentur qui S. Thoma non sequantur, cum iactura caritatis."(13)

As one can easily grasp, there is already budding here the preoccupation of combatting that deplorable exclusivism which in the past centuries, and above all at the beginning of this century, showed itself now and again.

This preoccupation appears in the numerous interventions and from the numerous JUXTA MODUM, once the well-known "Timeo hominem unius libri!" was uttered in a general session by the mouth of a very eminent Cardinal.

The main JUXTA MODUM or modes for avoiding the exclusivism propose either putting the particle "especially" before the name of Saint Thomas, or adding the little clause "aliisque Doctoribus quorum laus est in ecclesia."

Some Fathers, suggesting that the name of Saint
Bonaventure be placed alongside that of Saint Thomas with
the expression, "S. Thoma, S. Bonaventura, aliisque Doctoribus, quorum laus est in Ecclesia," were thinking directly of John Duns Scotus, as one can gather from the
motivation of the proposed mode which says: "S. Thomas
princeps scholasticorum ab Ecclesia proclamatus est, sed
in eadem Encyclica AETERNI PATRIS legitur: 'Aliique scholasticorum Principes.' Deinde: 'Theologia scholastica
quam duo potissimum gloriosi Doctores, Angelicus S. Thomas
et Seraphicus S. Bonaventura . . .excoluerunt.' S. Pius
X, non raro locutus est de principibus scholasticorum et
de S. Bonaventura hanc adhibet expressionem 'Principes
scholasticorum alter.' -- Pius PP. XI, in Encyclica STU-
DIORUM DUCEM diffuse affert textus ex celeberrima bulla
TRIUMPHANTIS HIERUSALEM in qua sollemniter S. Bonaventura
inter 'primarios ac praecipuos' Ecclesiae Doctores adnum-
eratus est. Neque oblivioni dandus est Venerabilis IOANNES
DUNS SCOTUS, Dux Scholae Franciscanae, qui post Concilium
Tridentinum suas cathedras habuit in omnibus fere Univer-
sitatibus Catholicis Europae una cum cathedra Divi Thomae.
-- Haec omnia melius quadrant cum notissimis verbis Pii
XI in encyclica STUDIORUM DUCEM, nempe: 'neque enim in iis
rebus, de quibus in scholis catholicis inter melioris no-
tae auctores in contrarias partes disputari solet quisquam
prohibendus est eam sequi sententiam quae sibi verisimilior
videatur.'"(14)

But to all the proposals, to all the objections,
the Pontifical Commission constantly replied that "juxta
mentem Commissionis alii Doctores ab Ecclesia approbati,"
or, "alii Doctores minime excluduntur," without the word
"approbati."(15)

As a confirmation of this spirit the Council refers
in its notes to three pontifical documents: one of Pius
Twelfth, who said that "aemulatio. . .in veritate quaerenda
et propaganda per commendationem doctrinae Sancti Thomae
non supprimitur, sed excitatur potius ac tuto dirigitur,"
(16) and two documents of Paul Sixth, one of which assumes
a special importance: the allocution pronounced at the
conclusion of the International Thomistic Congress, in the
very last days before the opening of the fourth and last
session of the Council,--the eleventh of September, nine-

26

teen hundred and sixty-five.

In this discourse, the Holy Father, imitating his predecessors, exalts the Angelic Doctor as the most authoritative witness of the value of human reason, and thinks that the philosophy of Aquinas has "une aptitude permanente à guider l'ésprit humain vers la connaissance du vrai." This explains why the magisterium of the Church has recommended "l'oeuvre de Saint Thomas comme une norme sure pour l'enseignement sacré." That said, the Vicar of Christ went on to affirm that with these recommendations the Church does not wish "nullement amoindrir" the value it has recognized in the precious heritage of the great Christian thinkers of the East and the West, among whom shines with special brilliance the great Augustine. The study of the truth, as also the service of the Word of God, are certainly not "l'apanage exclusif du Docteur angelique." When the Church declared him the Common Doctor and made his doctrine the basis of ecclesiastical teaching, "le Magistére de l'Eglise n'a pas entendu en faire un Maitre exclusif, ni imposer chacune de ses théses, ni exclure la légitime diversité des écoles et de systémes, et encore moins proscrire la juste liberté de la recherche."(17)

Etienne Gilson, who was present, exclaimed: "This is a great day! This was known, but it needed to be said!" And he defined this discourse on the one hand "The Statute of Thomism," and on the other, "The Magna Carta of just liberty."

However, someone could ask: if the Council was persuaded that it was necessary to reject every exclusivism, instead of referring to these discourses of the Supreme Pontiff, why has it not placed the names of other outstanding Doctors alongside that of Saint Thomas, as many of the Fathers proposed in the modes?

To answer this question one must keep in mind not only the conciliar regulation, according to which generally a text approved "plusquam duabus tertii partibus" of the Fathers had to be retained, but especially the need of conciliating the demands and keeping in bounds the requests of those Fathers who wanted Saint Thomas mentioned by name not only where there was a question of dogmatic theology, but in a particular manner in the teaching of philosophy.

In the first sehema the following proposal was made by the Commission: "Philosophicae disciplinae ita tradentur, ut alumni PERENNIS PHILOSOPHIAE principia clare perspiciant eiusque cohaerentem synthesim acquirant; alia quoque systemata philosophica, praesertim moderna quae in propria natione maiorem influxum exercent, necnon recentiores scientiarum progressus cognoscant, ut suae aetatis mentem melius percipiant eiusque quaestionibus apte respondere valeant."

Around this article arose a very animated discussion in November, nineteen hundred and sixty-four.

In this regard an examination of the modes submitted by the Fathers proves very interesting and significant. One current, in different degrees and with different approaches, requested the insertion of the name of Saint Thomas. The majority of the Fathers went against this, believing it inopportune. From the various modes we can gather the reasons for this opposition. First the character of free study is adopted, distinguishing philosophy from theology; then the ambiguity of some generic terms such as PHILOSOPHIA PERENNIS and SCHOLASTICISM is denounced. And above all the distinction between philosophy and theology is highlighted. With the mind open to dialogue with the world they propose instead the study of those systems that especially interest the men of today and with emphasis on the actuality of an athropology inspired by Christian thought. As an exemplar of this, there were not wanting Fathers who proposed Saint Thomas himself as one who knew how to fuse in his time Aristotelian philosophy with Christian wisdom.(18)

Keeping in mind all these and many other observations, the Council did not name not only the Angelic Doctor where it speaks of the teaching of philosophy, nor the term scholastic philosophy, but much less perennial philosophy. It had recourse rather to a new phrase, PHILOSOPHICAL PATRIMONY PERENNIALLY VALID, urging at the same time the study of contemporary philosophy for accomplishing dialogue.

In two other paragraphs the Council ratifies the method of the study of the history of philosophy and inculcates the rigorous research of the truth "simul cum honesta agnitione limitum cognitionis humanae"; and then it insists that the study of philosophy pay attention to the problems of actual life and prepare the students for the search of truth revealed in theology.

The Commission could finally say justly: "necessarius dynamismus investigationis philosophicae et theologicae in textu emendato omnino ratus habetur."(19)

In this our examination we limited ourselves to reporting some of the modes, without referring to the direct interventions and to the many judgments expressed on our theme, whether in the discussion of the text in the Hall or in its preparatory phase. But from what has been said I believe it is possible to grasp the place the Council intended to attribute to Saint Thomas and the other scholastic doctors, whether in the teaching of theology or of philosophy, and among the doctors our John Duns Scotus himself.

The Council distinguished well between the teaching of philosophy and of theology, and the role of scholasticism in the one or the other field. The five ways for proving the existence of God are not found in a philosophical work of Aquinas but in the SUMMA THEOLOGICA. The scholastics cultivated philosophy, they wished to harmonize pagan Greek and Arabian philosophy with the Christian wisdom, the better to understand, the better to illustrate the MYSTERIUM CHRISTI and the MYSTERIUM ECCLESIAE. They did not give themselves to philosophical speculation for the sake of philosophy but to have a better knowledge of revealed truth, of the deposit of faith, according to the saying: "Fides quarens intellectum. Credo ut intelligam. Intelligo ut credam." Therefore, rather than philosophers, the scholastics were philosophizing theologians. Justly, then, the Council does not give to scholastic philosophy that importance many have attributed to it in our time, unfortunately identifying scholasticism with philosophy.

The council openly recognized the transcendent
character of Christianity in its relationship with human
cultures; it is not bound to a particular culture and much
less to a European occidental culture. It adapts itself
to every culture, using in place of philosophy the phrase:
PHILOSOPHICAL PATRIMONY PERENNIALLY VALID. The term "patrimony" recalls the German term "Gemeingut," or the French
expression "Le patrimoine commun," with which some modern
philosophers wish to model a definition of scholasticism
"ab intrinseco," that is, the sum of the elements common
to all the great scholastics by which they are distinguished from modern philosophers.

At any rate, the expression "patrimonium perenniter
validum" is much more extensive and embraces all Christian
culture. In this patrimony one finds the doctrine of a
St. Bonaventure, of a Duns Scotus, and in a special way
that of Aquinas. But, as Cardinal Seper observed well in
his discourse SCHOLASTICISM IN THE LIGHT OF THE II VATICAN
COUNCIL, to the expression "philosophical patrimony perennially valid" the Council has given a "dynamic signifi-
cation, and so it does not say that all that is 'perennially valid' has yet been reached, or that what different
thinkers have created in the past has been sufficiently
evaluated. Therefore, the Council--the Cardinal justly
observes--supposes that the future of scholasticism depends more on the truth and the vitality of its ideas
than on their belonging to this or that school."(20)

This dynamism, this vitality, this aggiornamento
or renewal, the Council demands also in the theological
field, where Aquinas was not able to be mentioned, but in
the sense in which he was always interpreted by the very
great majority of Church documents, by theologians and
jurists who never favored the exclusivism of Thomism.

In past centuries there was the controversy over
who was the greatest: Thomas, Bonaventure, or Scotus.
In the judgment of the Supreme Pontiffs, among all Aquinas
"longe eminet" and holds the first place. But if he is the
first, he is not the only one! From ancient Christianity
to the thirteenth century the first doctor was the great
Augustine; from the thirteenth century to the Council of
Trent, the Master Peter Lombard was the first; from the

Council of Trent on, it was Saint Thomas. However, alongside the chair of Aquinas, was that of Scotus in practi-
cally all the universities.

Cardinal Seper concluded the admirable discourse
already cited by pointing out the example of the Lateran
University, in which for many years, there have been established chairs for the doctrine of Saint Augustine and
that of the Franciscan School of which Duns Scotus is the
head. We hope that other Catholic universities, theological and philosophical faculties, will follow the example
of the University of the Eternal City. No one could doubt
that this would be in conformity with the spirit of the
Second Vatican Council.

II. DOCTRINAL POSITIONS OF DUNS SCOTUS IN RELATION TO SOME DOCUMENTS OF THE SECOND VATICAN COUNCIL

In presenting the doctrinal positions of Scotus in
relation to documents of the Second Vatican Council, I will
limit myself necessarily to the two Constitutions strictly
doctrinal, occasionally pointing to the doctrinal part of
the Constitution ON THE PRESENCE OF THE CHURCH IN THE MOD-
ERN WORLD. The two Constitutions are the dogmatic ones
DE DIVINA REVELATIONE and DE ECCLESIA.

1) DE DIVINA REVELATIONE

The first great reef against which the ship of conciliar discussion crashed right at the very start, was a
most delicate and controversial theological question on the
relation between Scripture and Tradition, nerve-point for
ecumenical theology.

Against a centuries-long line of thought that interpreted the decree SACROSANCTA of the Council of Trent
ON THE RELATION BETWEEN SCRIPTURE AND TRADITION in the
sense of a twofold font of revelation, Professor Geiselman
of the University of Tubingen began teaching the sufficiency of Scripture as the only font of revelation, attri-

buting the contrary opinion to a false interpretation of the Decree of the Council of Trent.(21)

This great controversy that touched the very foundations of our holy religion found its epilogue in the Second Vatican Council, when on the fourteenth of November, nineteen hundred and sixty-two, there began in the Council Hall the discussion on the schema entitled DE FONTIBUS REVELATIONIS.

Sent back for a new and more profound study to the Doctrinal Commission and after very long discussions on it within the Mixed Commission, it was presented again under what is the present title, DE DIVINA REVELATIONE.

The solution was found in a formulation that, while conserving what had been taught by the Councils of Trent and First Vatican, at the same time keeps in mind and moves toward ecumenical demands.

In fact, in the definitive text, while for ecumenical reasons it is not said with absolute clarity that in Tradition there are QUANTITATIVELY more revealed truths than in Scripture, it is admitted that "latius patet Traditio quam Scriptura,"--Tradition is more ample than Scripture.

To convince ourselves of this it is enough to read attentively the dogmatic Constitution DE DIVINA REVELATI-ONE, with particular attention to Chapter Two which treats of the transmission of divine revelation. There not only does one read that "by means of this same Tradition the entire Canon of the sacred Books is known to the Church. . Sacred Tradition transmits integrally to their successors the Word of God consigned by the Holy Spirit and by the Lord to the Apostles"; but above all there is clearly affirmed, with an historical adjunct of the highest moment, a principle of fundamental importance, namely: "Not by means of Scripture alone does the Church reach certainty regarding all the revealed truths."(22)

The Council teaches, therefore, as is revealed in the "Relatio," that "at least in the one thing Tradition surpasses Scripture with regard to the OBJECTIVE CONTENT, namely, as a witness to the completeness of the canon and as regards the divine inspiration of the sacred books," even if it does not explicitly extend this objective content to other truths, because "up to the present time, regarding no dogma has the Magisterium declared that it is lacking every foundation in Sacred Scripture."(23)

Regarding the teaching of Duns Scotus on the relation between Sacred Scripture and Tradition--often adopted in the Doctrinal Commission of the Council and above all on February twenty-second, nineteen hundred and sixty-three(24)--there are some very recent studies brought about by the conciliar controversy. It is enough to cite the long and learned study of Father Leone Rosato, attached to the Secretariat of the Pontifical Marian International Academy, entitled IOANNES DUNS SCOTI DOCTRINA DE SCRIPTURA ET TRADITIONE, where, before his critical study of the Subtle Doctor's thought, are listed about thirty texts of Scotus relative to this problem.(25) Also, the critical study of Father Eligius Buytaert, Professor at the Antonianum.(26)

Duns Scotus treats the problem "per accidens" and so it is not easy to know exactly his teaching on it. He has not written a work DE LOCIS THEOLOGICIS, nor has he ever used the modern expressions "twofold source of revelation or unique source of revelation," a terminology that is not a very happy one, being very ambiguous and equivocal. While he asserts that "quantum ad revelationem generalem" all is transmitted through divine Scripture,(27) just as clearly he says elsewhere: "Dico quod 'Christum descendisse ad inferna,' NON DOCETUR in Evangelio, et tamen tenendum est sicut articulus fidei. . . Multa ergo docuit eos Spiritus Sanctus, quae non sunt scripta in Evangelio: et illa multa, quaedam per scripturam, quaedam per consuetudinem Ecclesiae, tradiderunt." (28)

Some, taking their cue from this text of the Gospel of Saint John, and from another text in the Apocalypse, "qui apposuerit ad haec, apponetur ei Deus plagas quae apponuntur in libro isto," both cited by the same

Scotus, resolve the apparent contradiction of the Subtle
Doctor, by having recourse to the theory of fundamental
revelation, in radice, so that all truths actually revealed are contained in Sacred Scripture, TAMQUAM IN FUNDAMENTO,
IN RADICE.(29)

To me it seems that the right solution to the
apparent contradiction of the Subtle Doctor has to be
sought in the distinction he makes between GENERAL REVEL-
ATION contained in Scripture, and some PARTICULAR truth,
as for example, the article on the descent of Jesus into
hell. GENERAL is opposed actually to PARTICULAR, while
"the explicit is opposed to the implicit."

Of everything, then, the Magisterium of the Church
is the guarantee and the authentic interpreter, as Duns
Scotus often repeats, and in this he wonderfully anticipates the last paragraph of Chapter Two of the Constitution DE DIVINA REVELATIONE where we read: "Patet igitur
Sacram Traditionem, Sacram Scripturam et Ecclesiae Magisterium, iuxta sapientissimum Dei consilium, ita inter se
connecti et consociari, ut unum sine aliis non consistat."
(30) "Ecclesiam certitudinem suam de omnibus revelatis
non per solam Sacram Scripturam haurit."(31)

2) DE ECCLESIA

Undoubtedly the principal theme of the Second Vatican Council was the Church. This Council was characterized by its preoccupation of studying the mystery of the
Church in relation to Christ, and its organization in relation to the power of the bishops.

The consideration of the mystery of the Church in
her intimate nature of Mystical Body of Christ rather than
in her juridical aspect, is the starting point of the Constitution LUMEN GENTIUM, with which the Second Vatican
Council offers a new Christocentric vision of the Church.

Whether explicitly or implicitly, this Christocentrism also pervades other conciliar documents, and
especially the first part of the Pastoral Constitution ON
THE PRESENCE OF THE CHURCH IN THE WORLD. Allow us to

quote, for its beauty, the conclusion of the paragraph "De Christo, Alpha et Omega" that carries the words of Pope Paul Sixth: "The Word of God, through which all things have been made, He Himself was made flesh so that in His quality of perfect man He might save all and restore all things in Himself. The Lord is the end of human history, the point of convergence of the aspirations of history and of civilization, THE CENTER OF THE HUMAN RACE, the joy of all hearts and the fulfillment of their desires. The Lord Himself affirms: 'I am the Alpha and the Omega, the first and the last, the beginning and the end.'"(32)

In the elaboration of the Constitutions ON THE CHURCH and ON THE PRESENCE OF THE CHURCH IN THE WORLD, the redactors certainly had in mind the teaching of Scotus, Doctor of the Primacy of Christ.(33) However, it has to be said that in teaching this Christocentrism the Council is using rather biblico-patristic language; and certainly it was not its intention to propose and approve the teaching of a particular theologico-scholastic system, as it was rather to expound the common teaching of the Church.

This is said also regarding the question that aroused long discussions and impassioned debates in the Council, namely, the function and the power of the episcopacy in the Church, with the related questions of its sacramentality and collegiality, although in this Duns Scotus was a pioneer.

As is well known, on the problem of the sacramentality of the episcopacy there were serious and long discussions before the Council and during it. And we should not marvel at this if we keep in mind that after Peter Lombard the classic masters of scholasticism commonly denied the sacramentality of the episcopacy. It is enough to recall the two leaders of scholasticism: the Seraphic Doctor and the Angelic Doctor.

Saint Bonaventure, starting with the principle that "every distinction of degree in Holy Orders is relative to the minister of the altar, relative, that is, to the Sacrifice. . . ."(34) or is relative to the administration principally of that noblest sacrament which is the

Body of the Lord,"(35) and that this fulfillment is "reached with the priesthood,"(36) affirms categorically that
"there is no other degree of Orders beyond the priesthood."
(37) He grants that the episcopacy is distinguished from
the priesthood by a certain dignity connected with the
office, but he immediately adds that to this dignity "does
not belong the name of Order, a new character is not impressed, nor is a new power given, but only is the power
already granted in the priesthood amplified."(38) And
after having invoked the testimony of Hugo and of the Master of the Sentences himself, he says" "Hoc etiam tenet
COMMUNIS OPINIO, quod in episcopatu character novus non
imprimitur, sed illi aliqua eminentia confertur."(39)

As a matter of fact, Saint Thomas does not speak
differently in commenting on the Books of the Sentences.
Starting with the fact that no one can receive the episcopal power unless he has received that of the priesthood,
he arrives at the conclusion that the episcopacy is not an
Order: "Episcopalis potestas dependet a sacerdotali,
quia nullus potest recipere Episcopalem, nisi prius habeat
Sacerdotalem. Ergo Episcopatus non est Ordo."(40) "Although," says Saint Thomas again, "there is given a certain spiritual power to the bishop in his promotion concerning some of the Sacraments, nevertheless that power
does not bring with it a character and therefore, the
episcopacy is not an Order in the sense that Holy Orders
is a Sacrament."(41)

But, as we know, there are those who seek an evolution in the teaching of Aquinas; what the young Thomas
denies, the older Thomas modifies, even affirms.

The well-known liturgist and theologian, the Dominican Father Gy, examining on this point what Fathers
Lecuyer(42) and Bouesse(43) have written, says: "Les
textes de S. Thomas ne permettent guére, croyon-nous, de
lui preter une evolution aussi nette."(44) This distinguished author thinks that Saint Thomas: "innove
lorsqu'il reconnait a l'éveque un pouvoir propre dans la
ligne de l'Ordre."(45) The matter is certain, although
it is not certain that there one finds an innovation!
However, it may be, to admit that the Angelic Doctor was

in this question, as in that of the Immaculate Conception, a man of his time, does not cause any shadow to fall on his undeniable authority as COMMON DOCTOR and Leader of the Scholastics.

At the same time, however, allow me to say that, as in the matter of the Immaculate Conception, so also in this question, there appears the accomplishment, the position, and the merit of Scotus, not without reason called the SUBTLE Doctor.

In fact, as is commonly admitted, Duns Scotus was the first among the theologians of the end of the thirteenth century and the beginning of the fourteenth, to render doubtful the common contrary opinion, and to teach with his usual respect for his predecessors, that the episcopacy is a true sacramental Order, with its own special character distinct from that of the priesthood. He well knows the famous sentence of Saint Jerome on the equality of the bishop with the priest; he knows the contrary doctrine taught by the Franciscan and the Dominican schools; but starting with the principle that "auctoritas habet nasum cereum,"--in other words, authority holds for only as much as it proves,--with his critical method he destroys one by one the arguments of his predecessors against the sacramentality of the Order.

Thus the argument deduced from the fact that the episcopacy requires the priesthood, with which the episcopal consecration would be null, he transforms into an argument in his own favor: "Argumentum cuiusdam Doctoris," he says, "'si non Presbyter ordinaretur in Episcopum, nihil esset factum,' concludit magis oppositum: nam quanto Ordo Episcopatus intimius includit Sacerdotium et alios gradus inferiores, tanto est simpliciter perfectior, quia essentialius respicit actus istorum inclusorum."(46) "It does not seem to me," he repeats in the REPORTATIO, "that the Episcopacy is not an Order because it presupposes the Priesthood; actually it pertains only to the bishop to perform certain acts, and not to the simple priest."(47)

Duns Scotus further advises that those who deny the sacramentality of the episcopacy and say that a character is not imprinted by it, discuss in vain whether this

37

episcopacy can be cancelled or not: "Vana videtur alter-catio."(48) In reality, it is openly clear that every jurisdiction in the Church can be either suspended or taken away entirely by the superior.(49)

To the bishop, as bishop, belongs a certain special power, the "Potestas Ordinis," so that if suspended and irregular he can confirm, and also confer Orders validly. Precisely from this fact Duns Scotus draws a valid argument to demonstrate that "praeeminentia gradus Episcopatus est Ordinis."(50)

However, as in almost all such questions, where he has to take a position against the common opinion, Scotus makes no categorical statement, but lets his readers draw the conclusion, so also in this matter.

In the REPORTATIO, on the other hand, not written by him but by his students from what was said in his lectures, he explicitly affirms: "Episcopatus est Ordo, quia Episcopus habet gradum eminentiorem in Ecclesia, cui coniungitur omnis alius gradus inferior, et per consequens auctoritas et potestas exsequendi omnem actum pertinentem ad quemcumque gradum in Ecclesia."(51) "Episcopatus maxime est Ordo."(52)

This was the doctrine taught before Scotus. Then, for various reasons, it became obscured and was denied by the great Master of the second half of the thirteenth century. It was suddenly taken up again by the followers of Scotus, by Durandus of Saint Porciano himself, and so, little by little it became the most common doctrine, justly and fittingly sanctioned by the Second Vatican Council.

From this truth of the sacramentality of the episcopacy the Council Fathers are not wanting in gathering other truths of fundamental importance for an exact knowledge of the organization and the constitution of the Church. Among these the main one is the theory of the universal jurisdiction of the bishops when united with the Pope. We call it COLLEGIALITY.

Undoubtedly, this conquest of the Second Vatican Council shows in a new light the constitution of the

Church. Still, like every conquest, it was arduous because many obstacles had to be overcome before it could be reached, affirmed, and above all harmonized with the doctrine of the primacy of the Roman Pontiff.

It is well known how the discussion around collegiality was conducted with different accents and shadings, and there were moments in which some saw endangered the primacy of the Roman Pontiff as defined in the First Vatican Council.(53)

The origin of the danger, in my humble opinion, is found in the insistence with which some held that the Pope is such insofar as he is head of the college; that the primacy would be INTRINSICALLY united with the college, even to the point of invalidating acts of greater moment, as for example, a dogmatic definition, if the opinion of the episcopal college is not sought first.

There is no one who does not see in this view of the doctrine of collegiality an under-estimation of the traditional doctrine that acknowledges the Pope as the Primate, the supreme universal power over the Church.

The Pope is the VICAR of Christ in the entirely SPECIFIC sense.

A long tradition allows the title of Vicars of Christ to the bishops, but the Pope is Vicar of Christ by particular, personal, and unique delegation, insofar as Jesus Christ before His Ascension gave to Peter and to HIM ALONE, and to his successors, the power that He had over His Apostles.

This is exactly the reason why Scotus, assertor of the sacramentality of the episcopacy, exalts on the other hand the authority of the Roman Church so much; and his teaching was not without influence in resolving the delicate problem.

Thus, in the ORDINATIO, Book Four, Distinction Eleven, question three, number thirteen, speaking of the sacraments, he states: "De Sacramentis tenendum est, sicut tenet Sancta Romana Ecclesia,"(54) and on this very matter he writes in the REPORTATIO: "I hold this above all for the authority of the Church which does not make mistakes in matters of faith and morals, for Christ said to His first Vicar: 'Ego rogavi pro te, Petre, ut non deficiat fides tua, et tu aliquando conversus, confirma fratres tuos.'"(55)

The cause, therefore, of the infallibility of the Pope is the special assistance of the Holy Spirit that Christ obtained with His prayer for Peter and his successors, so that in its turn the solid faith of Peter is the reason of the solidity of the faith in the other Apostles.

Scotus teaches further that the Pope has universal jurisdiction over all Christians, even over the Greeks, that is, the Orthodox. He calls the Catholic Church the "Ecclesia Petri," and the Pope "Christi Vicarius, Petrus.'" (56)

This idea of being the Vicar of Christ on the part of Peter and of his successors has entered the Constitution LUMEN GENTIUM.(57) It was the key to the solution of the delicate problem of the relation between the primacy of the Roman Pontiff and the collegiate power of the bishops. (58) Collegiality is not considered, as some have thought it, like to a certain Commonwealth,(59) so that the Pope would be the symbol of unity as is the royal crown of England; but rather according to the traditional Catholic doctrine that sees in Peter and his successors not only the head of the College of Bishops, but above all the true Vicar of Christ "gerens ipsam personam Christi."

The bond, therefore, between the collegiate power of the bishops and the power of the Roman Pontiff is looked for not in the horizontal line but in the vertical.

III. THE CHURCH OF DIALOGUE

To outsiders the profound analysis the Church has wished to make of herself, with the Second Vatican Council, could seem perfectly useless.

In reality, the knowledge of herself, the awareness of her nature and of her mission, appears more than ever necessary for the realization of that dialogue the Church wishes to establish with the world and with all men of good will.

The Church of this recent Council is the Church of dialogue, as Pope Paul Sixth beautifully presented her in his encyclical ECCLESIAM SUAM.

From this derives the significance and the importance of the two great documents of the Council, the Decree ON ECUMENISM and the Pastoral Constitution ON THE PRESENCE OF THE CHURCH IN THE WORLD. They develop the theme of dialogue of the Church with the separated brethren and with the modern world.

In this dialogue, whether it is a question of horizontal or vertical dialogue inside the Church itself, or a matter of dialogue with the separated brethren and with the world in its different expressions in science, culture, and progress, we hold that Scotus can have a positive influence.

Dialogue does not necessarily and of itself mean the search of an agreement, or of elements that allow an agreement between different persons; rather it signifies a serene study and the mutual knowledge that imply understanding of, and respect for, different opinions. Methodologically dialogue stands before agreement.

Toward this highest of ends we wish first to mention some theories of Scotus, above all in the philosophical field, that could offer a starting motive for a dialogue with modern philosophy. Then we will indicate some principles that were like the basis and the soul of the dialogue Scotus carried on with his contemporaries and predecessors.

In the second half of the last century and at the beginning of this one, it was almost the style to present

Duns Scotus as the precursor of modern philosophy. Blanc Elie calls Scotus "le precurseur de Kant,"(60) and Cardinal Gonzales echoes him in writing: "En suma: Escoto es el Kant de siglo XIII."(61) Bayle and Rousselot have said that Scotism would be "Le Spinosisme avant Spinose."(62) Vacant is in agreement with them.(63) Fox writes a dissertation with the sensational title SCOTUS REDIVIVUS, (64) to show that with the modernistic theories Scotus had reappeared, etc.

It was easy to combat and refute such affirmations which today no one repeats any longer, simply because Scotus is distinct from modern philosophy for the same reasons common to all the Scholastics. When the Subtle Doctor teaches that theology is a practical science, this has nothing to do with pragmatism or with modernism, because in Scotus practical theology is opposed to a theology purely speculative for its own sake, and not to an intellective theology, or a theology that uses speculation so as to act.

In the field of ethics, Scotus has never taught that the goodness or the malice of an action depends only on the absolute will of God, because he clearly teaches that the morality of our acts depends on the object, the circumstances, and the end in view.

His criticism, observes Gilson, and one can believe Gilson, "s'explique tout autrement que celui de Kant, avec leguel il n'a autrement rien de commun."(65)

However, already in the eighteenth century Charles of San Floriano in a work of seven volumes with the title IOANNIS DUNS SCOTI PHILOSOPHIA NUNC PRIMUM RECENTIORUM PLACITIS ACCOMMODATA, Milan, seventeen hundred and seventy one, tried to harmonize the philosophy of the Subtle Doctor with that of his time. And, not to speak of the many who have worked in this field, it is enough to recall the ponderous study of our days by Father Longpre entitled PSYCHOLOGIE SCOTISTE ET PSYCHOLOGIE MODERNE,(66) as also the work of Sister Ursuline, a Canadian, DUNS SCOTUS DOCTEUR DE TEMPS NOUVEUX.(67)

In these and other works it is underscored that

the metaphysics of Scotus has as object BEING AS BEING, and this Being par excellence is God, Infinite, God-Charity-Love, the idea that pervades the entire scotistic system. Especially the scotistic opinions in the psychological field are put in evidence: the theory of ideas without images; his little esteem of the Aristotelian theory on phantasms; psychological intuition and intuitive intellectual knowledge; the influence of obscure, hidden ideas on the determination of the will; the idea of activity and spontaneity; the exaltation of the individual, of the singular, and many other particular points of the scotistic doctrine.

We will limit ourselves to a few examples.

The Spirit is an activity: abstraction, synthesis, comparison, judgment cannot be reduced to the mechanism of phantasms and of sensation. Above all the most noble powers are active: intellect and will. In fact, the will is intrinsically active: "De appetitu intellectivo tenetur quod simpliciter est activus."

Experience reveals that we are free: whoever wills, also experiences that he is able not to will.(68) Further, experience reveals to us the synergy between will and intellect.(69)

Obscure perceptions, hidden ideas have an influence on the decision of the will. Besides, experience gives the certainty of many other things: that I understand, that I feel, etc. Scotus enumerates an entire litany of things we know through experience, that no sensitive faculty can manifest to us. He concludes that he who would deny all this is blind, and that it is not worthwhile disputing with him. "If someone denies this," he writes, "it has to be said that he is not a man, since he does not have that interior vision that others experience as having."(70) As we see, the Subtle Doctor gives much importance to introspection and psychological experience. He further gives particular importance to ideas without image, and to intuition. He does not hesitate to state that whoever denies the intuition of his own EGO simply is not a man: "Man is formally intelligence; this is so manifest that who denies it is not a man; everyone in fact experiences understanding in himself."(71)

One could continue with other examples endlessly. But I think what has been said is sufficient for understanding why it is that authors of every age, and even our contemporaries, have found in Scotus certain statements that are a prelude to modern philosophy; in his system they have found elements that could at least serve to facilitate the beginning of a dialogue with modern philosophy.

On the other hand, however, one must not forget that between scholasticism, of which Scotus forms an integral part, and modern philosophy, there is an abyss. It is not enough, then, to report some phrase of Scotus and put it alongside a similar expression, whether of Catholic philosophers (Gemelli, Morin, Baudin, Frobes), or of non-Catholic philosophers, so as to find there an identity of thought. From the surface one has to penetrate into the context and into the essence of scotistic thought, and then many times the difference that appears is greater than the likeness.

It still remains valid that Scotus could constitute a bridge between modern and scholastic philosophy. This is the scope of the Second International Scholastic Congress which will be held at Oxford, Edinburgh, from September eleventh to seventeenth of this year; it will have as its theme: THE INTELLECTUAL FIGURE OF SCOTUS.

With this we propose to highlight his personality and his doctrine in view of the dialogue to be started with modern philosophy, in the light of the principles that Scotus himself followed in his teaching and life, principles that were the soul of his critical method.

Let us look at the principles of dialogue in Scotus:
1) One of the first principles on which the critical method of Scotus is founded in his dialogue with the philosophers, theologians, and Fathers of the Church, is expressed in the following words: "As humanity pro-

gressed, the knowledge of the truth has always increased."(72)

Truth is always the same, immutable; but the knowledge of it is another thing. And Scotus underlines the
word KNOWLEDGE of the truth, its dynamism.

We will be better able to understand this scotistic concept of the dynamism of the truth if we keep present his attitude both with regard to pagan philosophers
and the Fathers, Doctors, and theologians.

Saint Augustine himself has said, Scotus tells us,
that the philosophers have said false things;(73) in fact,
they have taught very absurd things,(74) not excepting
Aristotle himself.(75) Authority, therefore, has only as
much value as the arguments it advances.

According to Duns Scotus, various are the motives
why man does not always arrive at the truth.

First of all, it often happens that while desiring
to reach an objective, whether in defense of the truth or
to know the truth, one falls into the opposite extreme.
In this regard Scotus gives an example, the Fathers of the
Church, who "FREQUENTLY have gone to EXCESS in their mode
of speaking to combat heresies, wishing to combat the opposite extreme."(76) Therefore, warns Scotus, we always
have to see against whom the Fathers have spoken and how:
"Multum ponderandum est contra quos haereticos sancti lo-
cuti sunt."(77)

Another reason why man does not arrive at the truth
is laziness, or "fuga quaestionis,"(78) or lack of skill
so that one is not well up on the question; because a person cannot be a "peritus" in everything. "Et si dicunt
hoc doctores PERITI," says the Subtle Doctor, "non tamen
IN HOC sunt periti."(79)

2) The second principle that illustrates the
foundations and nature of the Subtle Doctor's dialogue is:
"to no author are we to posit or attribute a false opinion,
or an absurd one, except in the case where this is EXPRESS-
LY clear from what he says, or openly follows from it."(80)

45

Duns Scotus, in fact, always interprets the ancient philosophers with sympathy, seeking to extract the most rational meaning from their writings.(81) That is why he prefers to examine the author's text directly. He has no confidence in commentators.(82)

The same method and the same criteria Scotus follows in speaking of contemporary theologians or of Doctors who preceded him.(83)

3) The third principle one can take from his following words:

"To adduce sophisms (so as to defend the faith) is dangerous, because one exposes the faith to derision. . . It is better, actually, not to know something, and to acknowledge one's ignorance, than to pretend to be wise through the sophisms that are adduced."(84)

In enunciating this principle the Subtle Doctor has in mind those who think they are able to know and prove all revealed truths with the intellect alone.

Speaking of the method in teaching philosophy the Second Vatican Council warns that this teaching must lead to a perception of the limits of human knowledge: "simul cum honesta agnitione limitum cognitionis humanae."

Precisely by reason of the weakness and limitation of human reason concerning certain truths, Duns Scotus has taught that one cannot give a STRICTLY SCIENTIFIC DEMONSTRATION of the immortality of the soul.(85)

To understand him well on this point you must remember that the Subtle Doctor was educated at Oxford where the mathematical method was in force. He generally considers things with a metaphysical, rather than physical, view, and builds his demonstration on internal reasons. At the same time, he examines and evaluates the arguments of others, according to their demands for a scientific demonstration.(86) This is the source of his proverbial subtleness and the critique to which he submits the arguments of different opinions.

4) Briefly we enumerate some other principles and norms of Scotus in his dialogue which have not lost their relevance.

a) Scotus desires that, as far as possible, dogmas be explained by natural reason, while limiting and removing, as far as possible, whatever of the wonderful and supernatural is added there: "Even in matter of faith," he says, "neither unnecessary proofs nor many miracles should be multiplied."(87)

b) Likewise he asks that Sacred Scripture, as much as possible, be explained literally and naturally, using the profane sciences also, in order to reach a clearer meaning.(88)

c) He requests further that dogmas be not unnecessarily restricted to a particular sense, but that a certain liberty be enjoyed in explaining them.(89)

d) From the way one or the other Father of the Church has argued, it does not follow that a proposition has to be considered DE FIDE, but only that the Father thinks of it in that way. Finally Scotus holds that "although everything authority teaches is to be held as true, it is not to be denied that that may be true, which it does not teach."(90)

5) The last and fundamental principle of all scientific investigation by the critical method in dialogue is expressed in the following words of Scotus: "If something new is proposed by someone who is a Doctor, no one is held to consent to it, but first HE IS BOUND 'consulere Ecclesiam' and thus avoid error."(91) The Church, in fact, is the true community above everything. . .in whose testimony one can believe most certainly; in fact, the authority of the Church "is perhaps greater than Scripture." As Saint Augustine says, "Evangelio non crederem nisi Ecclesiae credidissem."(92)

This rule of Scotus is of pulsating actuality in this our post-conciliar epoch.

After the Council of Trent Paul Fourth said: "If
to anyone it seems that, in what has been decreed or said,
there is something obscure, and which therefore needs an
interpretation or a decision, let him ascend to the place
chosen by God, to the Apostolic See, the Teacher of all
the faithful."(93) These same words Paul the Sixth, on
the first of February, nineteen hundred and sixty-six, spoke
to the Central Commission for the coordination of the post-
conciliar work, and for the interpretation of the Decrees
of the Council.(94)

In these words of the two Pontiffs, it seems to
us there is heard an echo of the words spoken by Scotus.

Before concluding I would like to give at least
one example of dialogue that Scotus developed on one point
that divides the Catholic Church from the brethren of the
Orient: the question of the FILIOQUE.

Scotus speaks of it in the eleventh Distinction of
the first Book of the ORDINATIO. At first he gives the
STATUS QUAESTIONIS by indicating the point of distinction
according to the different expressions: Oriental--"The
Holy Spirit proceeds from the Father through the Son";
Latin--"The Holy Spirit proceeds from the Father and the
Son,"(95) and he shows that the difference is simply verbal.(96) Besides, it seems impossible to him that outstanding Doctors and Saints of the Church on both sides
should have upheld a heretical belief.(97)

After this he demonstrates that the addition of
the term FILIOQUE in the Symbol is formally and materially
licit,(98) in as far as it does not treat of a corruption
of the faith, but only of an explanation.(99)

CONCLUSION

In these last decades, thanks to the application
of literary criticism to the works of Duns Scotus, the
judgment of Doctors, medievalists, theologians, and phil-

osophers on Scotus has changed radically, in comparison to what was said of him at the beginning of this century.

So for example, Gilson, Carrera Y Artau, Harris, DeWulf, Geyer, Grabmann, and many others recognize in John Duns Scotus the last great figure of the Golden Age of Scholasticism and they define him THE MOST SUBTLE THINKER (der schafsinnigste Denker) of the entire Middle Ages. Scotus' system--they say--represents the most significant attempt at conserving in its integrity and demonstrating the philosophical patrimony that in the Middle Ages was considered the foundation of the Christian conception of life and the world.

Monnet writes: "Le scotisme bien que parfois vilipendé par des catholiques mal informés, reste en philosophie comme en théologie une des formes reconnues de la pensée chrétienne."(100)

This positive judgment on Scotus finds greater confirmation from the comparison we have made of certain of his doctrinal positions with the teaching of the Second Vatican Council.

That which counts above all for his relevance seems to be that sense of modesty, of equilibrium, and of understanding of every other opinion. This is why his ORDINATIO is rightly considered a work constructed of dialogue with his questioners. We can, then, point to him as a theoretician and exemplar of the dialogue the Church wants to carry on in this post-conciliar period. Right when speaking of the question between the Orthodox and the Latins over the FILIOQUE, Scotus uses words that to us seem indicative of a concrete will to dialogue: "If two wise men--one Greek and the other Latin--both lovers of the truth and not of their own way of speaking simply because it is theirs, discussed this difference, it would finally appear that the difference is not truly real, but verbal."(101) And he adds: "Multipliciter enim dicitur (sicut hoc 'huius,' ita hoc 'ex hoc' vel 'illo,'vel 'ab illo'), qua multiplicitate forte subtilius intellecta et distincta, pateret contrariorum verborum non discors sententia."(102)

Too often the static possession of a mode of expressing oneself, accepted passively and uncritically, too often a different mentality and different way of speaking, are the cause of a mutual incomprehension, when a sincere and mutual search of the truth in charity could lead to understanding.

(1)   Canon 1366, section 2.

(2)   DE TOTH P., Della preminenza in se secondo le di-
      chiarazioni dei Sommi Pontefici Leone XIII, Pio X,
      Benedetto XV, e Pio XI, della filosofia e teologia
      tomistica, a proposito di un opuscolo su "La aco-
      lastica e i suoi compiti odierni,". Acquapendente
      1936, 59.

(3)   PEGUES Th. M., O.P., L'autorite pontificale et la
      philosophie de Saint Thomas, Toulouse 1930, 6,
      IDEM, Autour de Saint Thomas, Toulouse-Paris 1918,
      28: "S. Thomas, comme Docteur unique de l'Eglise
      catholique, est literalement canonise."

(4)   Cf. PEGUES TH., Autour de Saint Thomas, 13-29;
      HORVATH A., O.P., Campf um dem hl. Thomas, in Divus
      Thomas (Fr.) 4(1917) 186-243; SCHULTES R., O.P., De
      doctrina S. Thomae magis magisque fovenda, in Der
      Katolik 22 (1918) 21-26.

(5)   FESTUGIERE M., Quelle sera la philosophie de l'Eg-
      lise? L'Eglise, la philosophie traditionelle, les
      philosophies modernes, in Revue Benedictine 23(1906)
      394, 416.

(6)   DE TOTH, op. cit., 73: "Suarez sta a San Tommaso
      come il si al no, come il giorno alla notte: fra i
      due vi e opposizione di Contrarieta: dunque bi-
      sogna decidersi: o con San Tommaso e la Chiesa o
      con Suarez contro San Tommaso e contro la volonta
      della Chiesa. Non datur medium"!

(7)   GASPARRI P., Codicis Iuris Canonici fontes, III,
      Romae 1933, 146. Cf. BALIC K., O.F.M., Die Bed-
      eutung der historisch-kritischen Metode fur die
      Erneurung der skotistischen Schule in der Gegen-
      wart, in Wissenschaft und Weisheit 4(1957) 188-197.

(8)   Cf. D'ALENCON U., Innocent VI a-t-il declare suspect

d'erreur les adversaires de St. Thomas?, in Revue Duns Scot 9(1917) 138-40; BALIC, art. cit., 191ss.

(9)   Cf. VAGAGGINI C., O.S.B., San Tommaso e il Concilio, in L'Avvenire d'Italia, 8 marzo 1966: "Nello schema sugli studi ecclesiastici, presentato dalla Commissione preparatori, all'esame della Commissione centrale c'er tutto un capitolo "De doctrina S. Thomae servanda . . ." quel capitolo e lo spirito che lo animava furono silurati sin d'allora e non si salvarono piu, . . . il risultato e stato che di tutto il capitolo "De doctrina S. Thomae servanda," nei testi finali promulgati dal Concilio sono state salvate solo sette parole. . . ."

(10) Cf. Sacr. Conc. Vat. II, Schema decreti De institutione sacerdotali. Textus emendatus et modi, . . . Typis polyglottis Vaticanis 1965, 88.

(11) Sacr. Conc. Vat. II, Declaratio De educatione christiana.

(12) Sacr. Conc. Vat. II, Schema decreti De institutione sacerdotali, 35.

(13) Ibid., 104.

(14) Ibid., 101-102.

(15) Ibid., 100.

(16) Sacr. Conc. Vat. II, Decretum De institutione sacerdotali, n. 16. Cf. PIUS XII, Sermo ad Alumnos Seminariorum, 24 iunii 1939, in AAS 31 (1939) 247.

(17) Sacr. Conc. Vat. II, Decretum De institutione sacerdotali, n. 16. Cf. PAULUS VI, Allocutio coram VI Congressu International thomistico, 10 sept. 1965.

(18) Cf. Sacr. Conc. Vat. II, Schema decreti De institutione sacerdotali, 588-97.

(19) Ibid., 103.

(20) SEPER Fr., La Scolastica nella luce del Concilio Vat. II. in Acta Ordinis Fratrum Minorum 85 (1966) 53.

(21) GEISELMANN, J.R., Das Missverstandis uber das Verhaltnis von Schrift und Tradition und seine Ueberwindung in der katholischen Theologie, in Una Sancta 11 (1956) 131-150; IDEM, Die Heilige Schrift und die Tradition (Quaestiones disputatae, 18), Freiburg-Basel-Wian 1962. Cf. BEUMER I., S.J., De statu actuali controversiae circa relationem inter Traditionem et Scripturam, in De Scriptura et Traditione (Pontificia Academia Mariana Internationalis), Romae 1963, 17-43.

(22) Sacr. Conc. Vat. II, De divina Revelatione, nn. 8.9.

(23) Sacr. Conc. Vat. II, Relationes super schema De divina Revelatione, Typis polyglottis Vaticanis 1964, 11.

(24) IOANNIS DUNS SCOTI, Opera omnia, VI, "Praefatio" (ed. Vat. VI, p. IX-X).--This text of Scotus was read in the meeting of the Pontifical Theological Commission , on the 22 of February 1962.

(25) ROSATO L., O.F.M., Ioannis Duns Scoti doctrina de Scriptura et Traditione, in De Scriptura et Traditione, 233-252.

(26) BUYTAERT El., O.F.M., Circa doctrinam Duns Scoti de Traditione et de Scripturae sufficientia, in Antonianum 40 (1965) 346-362.

(27) Ord., Prol. n. 204 (ed. Vat. II, 137-138).

(28) Ord., I d. 11 n. 20 (ed. Vat. V, 7-8).

(29) BUYTAERT, Art. cit., 358-359.

(30) Sacr. Conc. Vat. II, De divina Revelatione, n. 10.

(31) Ibid., nn. 8.9.

(32) Sacr. Conc. Vat. II, <u>Const. De Ecclesia in mundo</u>
      <u>huius temporis</u>, n.45.

(33) Since the preparatory redaction of the first part of
      Schema XIII spoke repeatedly, in chapters one, two,
      and three, of the primacy of Christ, the suggestion
      was made to indicate the Christocentric basis in the
      following way:

      "Secundum credentium et non credentium fere concor-
      dem sententiam, tota socialis vitae ordination homi-
      nem respicere debet, si intimiori eius cordis desi-
      derio respondere velit.
      Ut autem dignitas et significatio hominis intelligi
      valeat, iugiter prae oculis habendum est hominem cre-
      atum esse ad imaginem Dei, videlicet ad perfectam
      imaginem Dei, perfectum Deum et perfectum hominem,
      qui est imago Dei invisibilis, splendor Patris aeter-
      ni, primogenitum omnis creaturas, summum opus Dei,
      in quo condita sunt universa in caelis et in terra,
      visibilia et invisibilia; omnia per Ipsum et in Ipso
      creata sunt (Ioan. 1,3); et Ipse est ante omnes et
      in Ipso omnia constant (Col. 1, 15-17), cuius adven-
      tum pollicebatur "Omnis dispensatio, quae et ante
      mundum et postea esse coepit in mundo, tam invisi-
      bilium quam visibilium creaturarum," "Iesus Chris-
      tus, per quem omnia et nos per Ipsum"(1Cor. 8,6).
      "Nam propter Christum sive Christi mysterium, omnia
      saecula, et quae in ipsis saeculis sunt, principium
      et finem ut essent in Christo nata sunt. Prior enim
      saeculis concepta unio: ipsa finis. . . .
      Primus homo Adam, figura alterius secundum quem crea-
      tus est, in saturali sua constitutione participat
      dona Christi, hominis perfecti, et ut talis super
      cunctas creaturas visibiles dominus est constitutus
      atque ad Deum ut ad finem suum dirigitur et quidem
      per Dominum Nostrum Iesum Christum unicum Mediatorem
      Dei et Hominum."

      This redaction did not give satisfaction, since it
      did not correspond to the eminently pastoral nature
      of the Constitution, but the elements of it can be
      read here and there, and are summarized in the last
      paragraph of the first part. Already in Chapter I

under the title De Christo Novo homine, we read that Adam, the first man, was a figure of the future man, namely Christ our Lord, and footnotes refer to the well-known text of Tertullian, De carnis resurrectione, Chapter 6: "Quodcumque limus exprimebatur, Christus cogitabatur homo futurus." This text of Tertullian if frequently quoted by the Scotists when they explain the doctrine of the Primacy of Christ. Cf. BONNEFOY J. Fr., O.F.M., La Primaute du Christ selon l'Ecriture et la Tradition, Roma 1959, 165. 302.

(34) S. BONAVENTURA, Sent. IV d. 24 p.2 a.2 q.3 arg.2 in opp. (ed. Ad Claras Aquas, IV, 633a).

(35) Ibid. in corp. (IV, 633a).

(36) Ibid., arg. 2 in opp. (IV, 633a).

(37) Ibid., in corp. (IV, 633a).

(38) Ibid., (IV, 633b).

(39) Ibid.

(40) S. THOMAS AQ., Sent. IV d.24 q.3 a.2 arg.1 in opp. (ed. Parm., VII, 901a).

(41) Ibid., ad arg.2 (VII, 901b-902a).

(42) LECUYER J., C.S.P., Aux origines de la theologie thomiste de l' episcopat, in Gregorianum 35 (1954) 56-89.

(43) BOUESSE' H., O.P., Episcopat et sacerdoce, in Revue des sciences religieuses 28(1954) 240-257, 368-391. (f. JOURNET Ch., Vues recentes sur le sacrament de l'Ordre, in Revue thomiste, 53(1953) 81-108.

(44) GY P.M., O.P., Ordre, in Bulletin thomiste 9(1954-1956) 882.

(45) Ibid.

(46) DUNS SCOTUS, Ord. IV d.24 q.un. n.5 (ed. VIVES, XIX, 49b).

(47) Rep. IV d.24 q.un. n.7 (ed. VIVES, XXIV, 352b-353a).

(48) Ord. IV d.24 q.un. n.6 (ed. VIVES, XIX, 50a).

(49) Ibid.

(50) Rep. IV d.24 q.un. n.8 (ed. VIVES, XXIV, 353a).

(51) Ibid., n.7 (XXIV, 352b).

(52) Ibid. (353a).

(53) When for example, in October 1963, Bishop Rusch of
Innsbruck, speaking in the name of the German episcopate, said that the concept of collegiality, in itself, besides containing a moral element, includes
also a juridical aspect: "in eo consistens, quod
in causis majoribus requiritur Collegium," it was
easy to understand a limitation of the universal
jurisdiction of the Pope. Likewise, it was easy to
see in his exposition the influence of the doctrine
of Karl Rahner, who, in his book The Episcopacy and
the Primacy (RAHNER K.--RATZINGER J., Episcopat und
Primat, Freiburg 1961), does not once say that the
Pope is the vicar of Christ, but always calls him,
either the head or the apex of the episcopal College.
He governs the Church not durch,- through, by means
of, -but mit, -with, -the episcopate. Consequently,
the primacy would be tied intrinsically to the College of Bishops, so that the Pope would be the head
of the Church insofar as he presides over the College of Bishops. The logical consequence of this
doctrine is that the Pope, not only for the sake of
acting prudently, but also for validity's sake, must
at least ask the opinion of the Episcopal College
before coming to any act of major importance, and
especially that of a dogmatic definition.

In my modest opinion this doctrine comes very

close to the opinion which Bishop Maret held in the
first Vatican Council, but with this difference, that
Bishop Maret proposed the papacy as the principal
element, whereas Father Rahner places the papacy
within the College which latter would be the primary
and preordained reality.

Wherefore, the First Vaticam Council rejected
the opinion of Maret, declaring: "Uni Simoni Petro
contulit Jesus post resurrectionem summi Pastoris et
rectoris jurisdictionem in totum suum ovile . . .",
and then says: "veram plenam et supremam potestatem
traditam esse Petro et suis successoribus etiam in-
dependenter ab actione cum aliis Episcopis" (Denz-
Schon.,n,3053); in the discussion of this theological problem the doctrine of John Duns Scotus was
also present.

(54) Ord., IV d.11 a.3 n.13 (ed. VIVES, XVII, 372b).

(55) Rep., IV d.11 q.3 n.13 (ed. VIVES, XXIV, 120b).

(56) Ord., IV d.11 q.6 n.6 (ed. VIVES, XVII, 484b-485a).
Cf. De perfectione Statuum, n.46 (ed. VIVES, XXVI,
531b); n.92 (558b): "Dominus Papa. . . Christi
Vicarius est. . ., unusest et singularis." - "beat-
us Petrus, tamquam Christi perfectus et universalis
vicarius. . ., cui succedit in potestate et digni-
tate Papa, Christi Vicarius".

(57) Cf. Gacr. Conc. Vat. II, Const. Lumen Gentium, where
among other things one reads: "The Roman Pontiff,
in virtue of his office, that is as Vicar of Christ
and Pastor of the whole Church, has over the Church
a full, supreme and universal power, which he can
always freely use"(n.22). Then it says that also
the College of the Bishops "together with their head,
the Roman Pontiff, and never without this head, is
indeed the subject of supreme and full power over the
whole Church, although this power cannot be exercised
if the Roman Pontiff does not consent." A little
farther on, it affirms that this collegial power can
be exercised not only in an Ecumenical Council, but

"it can be exercised, together with the Pope, by the
Bishops spread throughout the world, provided that
the Head of the College calls them to a collegial
action, or at least approves or freely accepts the
united action of the dispersed Bishops so that there
comes about thereby a true collegial act"(n.22).

Precisely in these last words, some suspect and
discern a danger for the Primacy of the Roman Pontiff. If, in fact, it were not the Pope who would
call the Bishops to that meeting whose decisions
would hold for the whole Church, who would be obliged to call them together? The Secretary of the
Episcopate? And if decisions were presented to the
Pope, he would be constrained to approve them, at
least tacitly, and in the opposite case would be
obliged to place himself in opposition to the majority. It is evident that in approving a text similar
to this which could imply such consequences, a certain shadow was cast over the Primacy. And, therefore, the Pope has heddet, in a motu proprio, the
famous explanation of the nota praevia, without
which the Constitution Lumen Gentium would not have
been signed. In this it is rendered precise that
the Pope determines when and how the supreme power
is exercised, whether personally or in collegiality,
and determines it according as the good of the
Church requires it; and finally it is said that only
the Pope is judge of all this.

(58) Sacr. Conc. Vat. II, Nota explicativa praevia, n.3:
"Ad iudicium Summi Pontificis cui haec cura totius
gregis Christi commissa est spectat, secundum ne-
cessitates Ecclesiae, decursu temporum variantes
determinare modum quo haec cura actuari conveniat,
sive modo personali, sive modo collegiali. Roma-
nus Pontifex ad collegiale exercitium ordinanum,
promovendum, approbandum, intuitu boni Ecclesiae,
secundum propriam discretionem procedit". Ccf.
BROWNE M., II Collegio episcopale soggetto di po-
teste suprema di governo della Chiesa cattolica e
la "Nota explicativa praevia", in Divinitas 9 (1965)
379-384.

(59) KUNG H., Kanzil-Ende oder Anfang?, in Civitas (Monqt-
schrift des schweizerischen Studtenvereins), January
1965, 198: "Wird
es Moglich sein, diesen traditions-und listenreichen
burokratischen Apparat (id est Curia Romana) auf die
ihm im Dienste an der Kirche zustehenden Funktionen
zu beschranken, so dass eines Tages die katholische
Kirche doch aus einem romischen Empire zu einem katholische Commonwealth werden kann? Cf. WIEDERKEHR
K., War der Primat in Gefahr?(Separat druch aus DAS
Neue Volk", Goldach (Schwezi) 1965, Nr. 36-38) 15.

(60) BLANC ELIE, Histoire de la philosophie, I, Paris
1896, 501.

(61) GONZALES Z., OP., Historia de la filosofia, II,
Madrid 1878, 266.

(62) Cf. DE MARTIGNE' Pr., La scolastice et les traditions franciscaines, Paris 1888, 310.

(63) VACANTA., Etudes comparees sur la philosophie de
Saint Thomas et celle de Duns Scot, Paris 1891, 25.

(64) Cf. The New-York Review 1905, 34-6.

(65) GILSON E., Jean Duns Scot. Introduction a ses positions fondamen-TALES, Paris 1952, 641.

(66) LONGPRE' E., O.F.M., Psychologie scotiste et psychologie moderne, in Etudes Franciscaines 44 (1922)
247-284; IDEM, The psychology of Duns Scotus and its
modernity, In the Franciscan Educational Conference,
13 (1931) 19-77.

(67) BERAUD DE SAINT-MAURICE, Jean Duns Scot. Un Docteur
des temps nouveaux, ed. 2, Rennes-Paris 1953; IDEM,
in John Duns Scot, 1265-1965, ed. Ryan K. Monansea
B.M., Washington 1965, 345-367. Cf. GUINET F., Act-
ualite de Duns Scot, in Recherches de Philosophie II,
Paris 1965, 315.

(68) DUNS SCOTUS, Quaestiones in Metaph. Aristot..IX q.15

n.5 (ed VIVES, VII, 609b-610a).

(69) Rep., II d.42 q.4 n.14 (ed. VIVES, XXIII, 221a);
cf. Ibid., III d.14 =.3 n.5 (ed. VIVES, XXIII,
356b).

(70) Ord., IV d.43 q.1 nn.10-11 (ed. VIVES, XX, 40).

(71) Rep., IV d.43 q.2 (ed. VIVES, XXIV, 491).

(72) Ord., IV d.1 q.3 n.8 (ed. VIVES, XVI, 146a).

(73) Ord., Prol. n.66 (ed. Vat., I, 41).

(74) Ibid, n.41 (I, 25).

(75) Ibid., n.67 (I, 41). Cf. Ord. IV d.43 q.2 n.16
(ed. VIVES, XX, 46a); Rep., II d.1 q.3 n.11 (ed.
VIVES, XXII, 536a); Quaestiones in Metaph. Aristot.,
prol. n.1 (ed. VIVES, VII, 2a); Ibid., I q.2 n.5
(VII, 42a).

(76) Ord., II d.33 q.un. n.4 (ed. VIVES, XIII, 331a).

(77) Ibid.

(78) Ord., I d.11 n.28 (ed. Vat., V, 11.).

(79) Ord., II d.12 q.2 n.8 (ed. VIVES, XII, 603b). In few
words, it seems to us that our Doctor would willingly
subscribe to the declaration of his confrere and predecessor in the Chair of Paris, Gilbert of Tounay:
"Nec, unquam veritas invenietur si contenti fuerimus
inventis. Qui ante nos scripserunt non domini nos-
tri, sed duces fuerunt; veritas patens est omnibus;
nondum est occupata. Multum etiam ex illa nostris
est posteris relictum" (cf. BALIC, C., O.F.M.,
Ioannis Duns Scoti, Mariologiae Marianae elementa,
Sibenici 1933, CXLV).
In unravelling these affirmations of Duns Scotus, it
seems to us that the long and at times heated discussions that took place in the Second Vatican Council about the most sublime truths are fully legiti-

mate; we fully consent to the fact that the Council
did not want to sanction either the term "philosophia perennis," or the term "philosophia aristotel-
ico-thomistica," and rather insisted on the dynamism of the knowledge of the truth. "Recte iudicat
homo--one reads in Schema XIII--divinae mentis lumen participans, se intellectu suo universitatem
rerum superare. . . ."
Man has progressed in science, obtaining very great
success. Yet he sought and found truth ever more
profound (p.15, n.15). Already in the introduction
to the Schema XIII it is already underlined as: "Ho-
die genus humanum in nova historiae suae aetate ver-
satur, in qua produndae et celeres mutationes ad uni-
versum orbem gradatim extenduntur" (n.4); the progress of technology, biology, psychology is praised:
"Technicae artes eo progrediuntur ut faciem terrae
transforment et iam spatium ultraterrestre subigere
conentur" (n.5).

(80) Quodl., q.7 n.38 (ed. VIVES, XXV, 313b-314a).

(81) Ord., I d.8 n.250 (ed. Vat., IV, 294).

(82) Quodl., q.7 n.24-25 (ed. VIVES, XXV, 303ab); Ibid.,
n.38 (XXV, 314a); similiter cf. Ord., IV d.12 q.1
n.15 (ed. VIVES, XVII, 549ab); Ord., I d.3 n.373
(ed. Vat., III, 226).

(83) Ord., I d.12 n.37-40 (ed. Vat., V, 44-47).

(84) Ord., II d.1 q.3 n.10 (ed. VIVES, XI, 76b-77a).

(85) Ibid., IV d.43 q.2 n.33 (XX, 59b); Rep., IV d.43
q.2 n.19 (ed. VIVES, XXIV, 498a).

(86) Ibid., prol. n.4 (XXII, 7b-8a); cf. etiam Ord.,
prol. n208 (ed. Vat., I, 141); Rep., prol. n.4 (ed.
VIVES, XXII, 8a); Ibid., (XXII, 8ab); Ord., I d.2
n.15-17 (ed. Vat., II, 131-132).

(87) Ord., IV d.11 q.3 n.3 (ed. VIVES, XVII, 352a); Ibid.,
n.14 (XVII, 375b).

(88) <u>Ord.</u>, III d.14 q.3 n.8 (ed. VIVES, XIV, 528b); d.38 q.un. n.12-15 (XV, 955a-956b, and 965b-966b).

(89) <u>Ibid.</u>, IV d.11 q.3 n.15 (XVII, 376a); I d.26 n.71 (ed. Vat., VI, 28).

(90) <u>Ibid.</u>, I d.26 n.68 (ed. Vat., VI, 27).

(91) <u>Rep.</u>, III d.25 q.un. n.6 (ed. VIVES, XXIII, 462a).

(92) <u>Lectura Examinata</u>, I d.5 n.24.

(93) <u>Concilii Trident. Acta</u>, VI, ed. St. EHSES, 1926, 1154.

(94) <u>L'Osservatore Romano</u>, 2 Febr. 1966.

(95) <u>Ord.</u>, I d.11 n.9 (ed. Vat., V, 2-3).

(96) <u>Ibid.</u>, (V, 3).

(97) <u>Ibid.</u>

(98) <u>Ibid.</u>, n.10-18 (V, 4-7).

(99) <u>Ibid.</u>, n.20-21 (V, 7-8).

(100) MONNET, <u>Scot</u>, in Dictionnaire des connaissances re<u>liqieuses</u>, VI, 268.

(101) <u>Ord.</u>, I d.11 n.9 (V, 3).

(102) <u>Ibid.</u>

Discussion

JUNIPER CUMMINGS, O.F.M. CONV., S.T.D.

Assistant to the Minister General
Rome, Italy

Father Balic, an eminent Scotist and member of the former Holy Office, speaks at times with the accent of the Holy Office, but with the vocabulary and heart of the renewing Congregation of Sacred Doctrine and the spirit of the Vatican II.

The first part of his paper is pro-Scotus, yet not anti-Thomas nor even anti-Thomistic. For the richness of Catholicism and the deepening of Christianity, someone--preferably the Franciscan family--needs to keep Scotus in the refreshing, purifying, enlarged stream of Catholic thought. Scotus is an important element in that "dynamic patrimony" referred to by Vatican II. (1) The commission that is producing the excellent critical edition of the works of Scotus, headed by Father Balic, is giving us the necessary tool for this work.

In the tradition of his spiritual father, Saint Francis, Scotus stressed the importance of the Bible. J. L. Nevs has written that Scotus' contribution was "his stress of the authority of Scripture and the Church" and that he "marks a milestone toward the rediscovery of the personal God of the Bible". (2) In trying to give us Scotus' position, Father Balic presents the fine distinction between all things which are particularly in Scripture and those which are generally in Scripture but not in particular. It is true that the Scriptures are an expression of the faith of the community and are then to be interpreted in the light of the community. While the Roman Church is more explicitly claiming that nothing can be taught that is not according to Scripture, we are becoming more and more aware of the teaching of the separated brethren that the Church has a role in interpreting them. (3) In this matter as in many others, a sincere dialogue keeps us from mininterpreting each other's teaching and helps us to understand better our own. Together we seek the will and truth of Christ. As Father Balic remarked, it is only the gift of faith that enables us to accept Christ and revelation in and unto Him.

In regard to Father Balic's analysis of the Scotistic and now-again common doctrine of the episcopacy as an Order, I would venture a clarification concerning the power of the bishops and the unique role of the Pope. Our doctrine of infallibility says that we believe that God would protect his Church by keeping the Pope from declaring something as divinely revealed which "de facto" the bishops do not teach and the faithful do not believe. This is not a question of what the Pope may not do; it is a question of what the Pope cannot do. Infallibility is a gift to the Church as the Mystical Christ, and the Pope can be a spokesman for the Church. We believe that the Church has a charism that prevents the Pope from declaring "ex cathedra" something as divinely revealed which is not actually divinely revealed.

The Pope has universal jurisdiction, and so have the bishops "collegialiter," therefore, together with the Pope. The use of this jurisdiction or authority is a prudential matter. Many, including Pope Paul, think that in our day and age the Pope should consult with and share responsibility with a representative body of bishops. The Pope is no mere symbol, but he is in some way a sacrament signifying and causing visible unity. The collegiality and papacy are of divine institution, as is the unity of all Christians in the Holy Spirit. Universal jurisdiction of the Pope, of the College of Bishops, and real God-given authority on the local level, as well as individual charisms of the people of God, are of divine institution. There is no contradiction in this authority, anymore than there is a contradiction in the special supernatural actual presence of Christ in the Eucharist and in the Church and in the poor and neglected. Government in the Church does not fall into natural human categories of monarchy, oligarchy, and democracy. It is something akin but beyond these forms.

Christocentrism, the Primacy of Christ, is a revealed truth that shines on and through the documents and spirit of Vatican II. Father Balic in his remarks has humbly minimized his and the Franciscan contribution to this doctrine. But as Christians, Franciscans, and theologians we seek Christ and His truth, no matter by whom it is proposed. It seems a thesis once considered Scotistic is acknowledged by all. Here are a few Christocentric quotations of non-Scotistic theologians:

"Man becomes man because God became man."

"It is the ultimate which determines the penulti-
mate."

"To speak of the world without speaking of Christ
is empty and abstract."

The above are a few passages from Ethics by Dietrich Bonhoeffer.(4)

Schoonenberg writes: if sinning man continues to
exist and to remain a human being on account of his finality towards the future Redeemer, the reason is that
this finality coincides with (natural) creation itself,"
and in the same place, "the mere subsisting exists actually because God intended that self-communication."(5)

Examples could be multiplied. I will conclude
with a reference to First Colossians. When I went to
school, the first part of Colossians was taught as referring to the Eternal Word; only the Scotists maintained
that it pertained to the humanity of Christ. Father
Yarnold, a Scripture scholar, writes: "Jesus is the
Father's eternal Word translated into human language. So
too, St. Paul's description of the Son as the "image of
the unseen God" (I Col., 15) applies not only to the inner
life of the Trinity...but also to the Son's incarnate existence: for the point of the description is that the image
is visible."(6) We need not add how most "new theologians"
stress the role of will, person, love.

Father Balic mentioned in one of his erudite and de-
lightful Latin digressions that he did not think that one
could say that Scotus taught two decrees--one before sin
and one after (this is priority of intention, of course, and
not a temporal "before"). It seems to me that we can say
that God wills Christ first and together with Him, Mary and
us all, and all things including the permission to sin.

We do not want to be guilty of triumphalism or
theological "me too-ism." Since our symposium is Scotus
today, might we ask, is the absolute primacy of Christ,
the sound theological element in the theories of Teilhard
de Chardin and Incarnational theology, including the Sec-
ular City approach of Cox? I would also suggest that the

element of soundness in the "male sonans" of "God is dead"
but "Christ lives" theology is the absolute primacy according to the principle of finality. An intelligent willer
wills first and foremost the end; then all other things
are willed in an order of dependence in their relation to
that which best fulfills the end. In the present order,
God is most loving and loved in the humanity of Christ.
All else is "de facto" for and unto Him. The true and
existing God is inseparably united to creation in Christ.
Through Christ the transcendental triune God is immanent
in nature.

Father Balic has pointed out that the conception
that God is love is central to Scotus' theology. In this
point we have a confrontation with the psychology that
maintains that it is only through love that man can find
meaning to existence.(7) Since nature is for supernature
and Christ is existent divine-human love, we can say
wherever there is integral human love, there is Christ and
his Grace.(8)

Father Balic has given us some excellent principles of dialogue from Scotus. May I add that this open-
ness of dialogue is not only to convince the other, but
to learn from him. The Declaration of the Church's to
non-Christian Religions refers to the holy and true in
non-Christian religions as a ray of that truth that is
Christ.(9) We as lovers of Christ seek Him in these
religions as well as seeking to share the light we have
from Him with them. In a sense we need them more than
they need us. Man can be saved without visible unity to
the visible Church, but the Church is not yet fully
Catholic until all these rays of Christ's light are
brought into focus. This is all the more true of other
Christian bodies. This outgoing and for-other-ness of
the Church is an indication of a maturing Church.(10)
Father Balic told us about the copy of the Vatican edition of Scotus that he presented to Archbishop Fisher
of the Anglican communion. In Scotus, Father Balic
remarked, we have a common heritage of the English and
Roman Churches.

Father Balic indicated that there should be chairs
of Scotism at universities. Scotus may be relevant to our
day, but until we have more Scotiscally-grounded men, there

will be no one to fill the chairs. The work of the Vatican edition will make it possible to be so grounded but "ab posse ad esse non valet illatio." It takes will and work to bring about the "esse."

May I close with an entry from the Theological Dictionary by K. Rahner and H. Vorgrimler: This shows the affinity if not dependence of the so-called "new theology" and Scotism; its characteristics are "that the divine essence is best envisaged as love, the consequent primacy of the will, of freedom and the individual, Christocentrism, the identification of justifying grace with love and the 'existentialist' and critical view of the function of theology ifself." This is the entry under "Scotism." (11)

FOOTNOTES

(1)   Cf. BALIC'S remarks and references to Vatican II.
        According to the 17th century Cistercian theolog-
        ian, John Caramuel, the Scotistic School was more
        numerous than all schools put together. Theologia
        Intentionalis, Lib. 2, cap. 3, disp. 10, #1264,
        p. 273.

(2)   NEVS, N.L., A History of Christian Thought, Vol. I
        Philadelphia, Pa., The Muhlenberg Press, 1964.

(3)   "the tradition of the Church is exegetical...nor
        can the Scriptures be properly understood apart
        from the Church", JAROSLAV J. PELIKAN, "Protestant
        Concept of the Church" in Proceedings of the Cath-
        olic Theological Society of America, June 1962,
        p. 137. Cf. ROBERT MCAFEE BROWN in An American
        Dialogue by ROBERT MCAFEE BROWN and GUSTAVE WEIGEL,
        S.J., New York, Anchor Books, 1961: "Protestants
        who live under the corporate discipline of the
        Word of God", p.30. Cf. also p.93.

(4)   DIETRICH BONHOEFFER (ed by E.Bethage), Ethics, The
        Macmillan Co., New York, 1965.

(5)   PIET SCHOONENBERG, S.J., (translated by J. Donceel
        S.J.), Man and Sin, Notre Dame, Indiana, University
        of Notre Dame Press, 1965, p. 67. Cf. EDWARD
        SCHILLEBEECKX, O.P., The Church and Mankind in
        Concilium, Vol. I, Dogma, New York, Paulist Press,
        1865: "An analysis of the Trinitarian character of
        grace as well as its postponed revelation in Christ
        shows that its original conferment and God's est-
        ablishment of mankind as His People were a conse-
        quence of man's creation in view of Christ.
        'Adam's' creation was implicitly directed toward
        Christ, and because of this, grace was bestowed on
        him." p. 92.

(6)   EDWARD YARNOLD, "The Trinitarian Implications of
        Luke and Acts" in The Heythrop Journal, January
        1966, Vol VII, No. 1, p.18, Oxford, England,
        Blackwell.

(7)   e.g., FROMM, LEPP.

(8)   SCHOONENBERG, op. cit., p.70.

(9)   Declaration on the Relation of the Church to Non-Christian Religions, #3.

(10)   "The Church too is beginning to realize that her Christianity is still in its childhood. The Church is passing through a crisis of growth...She too must emerge from Mediterranean civilization." LOUIS MONDEN, S.J., Sin, Liberty, and Law, New York, Sheed and Ward, 1965, pp. 181-2.

(11)   KARL RAHNER and HERRBERT VORGRIMLER (Translated by R. Stracham, edited by C. Ernst, O.P.) New York, Herder and Herder, 1965.

DR. JOHN R. CRESSWELL received the Ph. D. degree from Cornell University and at present is
Professor of Philosophy at West Virginia
University. In 1943 he received an ACLS grant
for the study of Arabic; he was assigned to
Lebanon and Syria from 1965 to 1967. In 1953
he was Invited Delegate to Colloquium on
Islamic Culture at Princeton University; in
1954 he was Delegate to Natural Resources Conference, April 12-26. He received West
Virginia Foundation Grant for study of Arabic
Philosophy, February to June, 1966. He is
author of articles on Franciscan Philosophy and
on Arabic Philosophy.

What There Is

According to

DUNS SCOTUS

JOHN R. CRESSWELL, PH.D.

Duns Scotus is concerned with, among other matters, the usage of terms like "being" (esse, ens) and "thing" (res), and of the extent of their application. The subject matter of Metaphysics, he says, is being in its generality. But in discussing these questions, he must examine two others. One is an epistemological question, whether being is the primary and adequate object of the intellect; the other is what reason is there for saying that the subject matter of Metaphysics is really being. The first Question of the Prolog to Scotus' Ordinatio (1) exhibits this interconnection.

> Every faculty that has for its primary and natural object something common is adequate to everything contained in it as its intrinsic natural object. An example of this is vision and all contained in it, and so in the case of primary objects and their corresponding faculties. This is evident since the primary object is said to be what is adequate to the faculty. . . . The natural object of our intellect is being as such, therefore our intellect is naturally adequate to the act of apprehending any being whatsoever, and hence it is adequate to anything intelligible, even to non-being because a negation is known by means of an affirmation. . . . Being (ens) and thing (res) are the first to be impressed on the mind and cannot be inferred from other things.

Several of the characteristics mentioned in this extract must be clarified in the course of this essay. We can note one thing at once. The extract takes for granted that the term being is applied in one sense only, that is, univocally. There are philosophers, for example, Aquinas, who stoutly maintain that "existence" said of physical objects and "existence" said of God or of an infinite being, are two usages of the ambiguous term "existence". That is to say, the term is applied "analogically" in the two cases, as though there were two kinds of existence. More will be said of this later in this essay; for the present I shall not enter into this controversy except to ask, What can possibly count as evidence for this view? When the question is transferred to philosophical theology, one can maintain with good reason that there is a Creator and there are creatures, statements in which the forms of the verb to be are univocal. The matter under consideration in this essay is simply to set forth Scotus' view of what fundamentally is by means of rational analysis. I suppose the presupposition of the undertaking is this: Human beings are distinct from the beasts that perish by the possession of the faculty of reason. In order to be human, then, let us exercise that faculty in the pursuit of knowledge. Duns Scotus is one who is continually aware of the difference between supernatural and natural knowledge, and of the kind of evidence necessary for the latter. For such reasons, Scotus has much to say to philosophers of today.

Let us first ask to what things or situations is the term being applicable. The answer of our philosopher is set forth in one of his Quaestiones Quodlibetales.(2) Here Scotus says he derives answers from the views of different writers and in that way the following results are obtained:

Being is anything which is not nothing. (a) That is most truly nothing which involves a contradiction whether this be an item within the intellect or outside of the intellect.

To illustrate what is meant, one may say that the concept of a pentagon the sum of whose interior angles is 600° is a contradiction, hence not conceivable by the mind; the extra-mental existence of a cylindrical, rectangular box is also impossible. This first statement appears to lay down a criterion for existence in the most general sense, namely, to exist is, at least, to be non-contradictory; it is clear that this is not a definition of existence in which the predicate-term is identical with the subject-term.

(b) In another way, that is called "nothing" which neither is, nor can be an extra-mental being. Being or thing (ens, res), therefore in the first

sense (a) is taken in the widest possible way to include everything non-contradictory whether it be an
"entity of reason" namely something having existence
in the intellect which considers it, or a real being
having existence beyond the intellect's consideration
of it. In the second sense (b) it is taken to include any being which has or can have reality not
dependent on the intellect's considering it. The
first way seems correctly to extend the word thing;
yet in the light of the common way of speaking, it
is sufficiently evident that we call both "logical
intentions" and "relations of reason" things (entia)
of reason, even though these cannot exist outside of
the intellect. The word "thing", according to this
way of speaking (b), is not directed towards an extra-mental thing; hence it is said to be anything
conceivable, which does not involve a contradiction.
Whether the extent of application of this term be
one of analogy or of univocity, I care not, for it
can be posited as the primary object of the intellect.

Scotus then states briefly two other uses of the
term which contract the extent of the things referred to;
one makes reference to being as distinct from it circumstances or modes of being, that is, being as a sort of
absolute entity; the other use refers to being as per se
intelligible, or being taken as substance alone. Both of
these uses are restrictions on being in the first and widest possible sense; being as not nothing whether referring to things of reason or to extra-mental things. We
can have a concept of being with these varying ranges of
applicability. Let this suffice for an exposition of the
meaning and the references of the term being taken univocally.

In what follows, I propose to consider first, the
genesis of the concept, second, the question concerning
its basis in reality, and third, a discussion of some
question about possible being and infinite being. I proceed to give an account of the first point, briefly stated, since it is, I think quite familiar to all Scotists.

Let us follow Duns Scotus by investigating what is
the primary, natural and adequate object of the human in-

tellect in this life (<u>viatoris</u> <u>intellectus</u>). By the primary object is meant the first notion formed as the intellect passes from a state of ignorance to a state of
knowledge. By the adequate object is meant that concept
which is commensurate with the faculty as such; we call
the object of a faculty adequate when it includes all
that it can know completely. If the primary and adequate
object of the intellect is being, we can know all that
merits the term "being" in any sense of that term.

The intellect in this life is, of course, embodied and operates through the senses. But we can still
ask what its primary object is, and this we can do in a
threefold way (3): one is in the order of origin, another
is in the order of adequation, and a third is in the order
of perfection.

In the order of temporal priority, the first thing
actually known is the singular, a singular which, whether
audible, visible or tangible, efficaciously and strongly
moves the senses. I first know, for example, this or that
white thing, then whiteness, and finally conceive color.
The singular is not, however, known in its complete singularity, but only confusedly. To understand a thing confusedly is to understand it by its name (<u>per</u> <u>nomen</u>); that
is, naming an object merely signifies the thing immediately and prior to analysis; that is, it points out the particular referent, the "this" denoted by the name. The
fact that, for example, we identify an object as a man
signifies only that we know it vaguely. To understand a
thing distinctly is to know an object (conceptual or
otherwise) through its definition. Nothing is distinctly
conceived unless we know all that is included in its essential nature. But being is included in all quidditative and inferior concepts. Hence, no inferior concept
is distinctly conceived except by way of the concept of
being. Moreover, since being has only the one characteristic (<u>rationem</u>), or, perhaps better, being is its own
characteristic, it cannot be conceived otherwise than distinctly. Therefore, being is the first concept distinctly
conceived.

I take the foregoing to mean that to understand a
thing confusedly when naming it merely points out a par-

ticular thing that may be further characterized. To say "That's a man" or "There's a man" identifies a particular sense-object, but does not characterize it any further as, for example, a black man or a white man, or an intelligent man, or a stupid man. But "nothing is distinctly conceived unless we know all that is included in its essential nature." Obviously I do not know all there is to know about this man present to my senses. I do know, however, that he is and that he may be further (quidditatively characterized. I may never know the complete characterization of this singular, and hence I may never conceive it distinctly. But in any closer characterization, expressed in sentences such as "This man is an American." or "This man is a professor.", I am at least conceiving him to be. Thus "being" is not further characterizable. Even if I should utter the sentence "The existence of leprechauns is mythical," I am not asserting of them a special kind of existence; rather I am saying that those who accept certain myths or folk tales believe such beings exist.

That the concept of being is first by way of adequation can be shown by the critical examination of an alternative view, namely, that the intellect is limited to knowing the "sensible quiddity of a material thing".(4) This view is founded on the assumption that omne ens agit sibi simile, that is there is some connaturality between the agent and that acted upon. When applied to cognition, the principle reads: similia similibus cognoscuntur, a principle traceable to Empedocles. In the light of this assumption, there must be a proportionality between the knower and the object.(5) These consequences follow: the quiddity separated from matter must correspond to a separated disembodied faculty; the quiddity of the material thing must correspond to an embodied faculty, i.e., the intellect in this life. The consequences cannot, however, be true for the following reasons: 1. There is first a theological objection. If you say that the intellect will be elevated by the light of glory so as to know immaterial substances, then you must admit that the light of glory must change the nature of the intellect so that it really does have power to know what previously exceeded it. But then it would no longer be the human intellect, but another sort of intellect. Scotus thus makes it evident that he is concerned about the intrinsic power of intellect whether embodied or not. 2. There is, second, a philosophical objection. If you say that our intellect, because

of its infirmity and because of its suitability for knowing
by way of the "phantasm", is immediately ordained to know
in that way and cannot be moved by anything other than objects derived through sense, then you would have to say
that our intellect, not merely by virtue of its status but
by the very nature of its power can understand nothing but
what is abstracted from the "phantasm". But this is false
for three reasons. In the first place, the intellect, in
knowing an effect, has a natural propensity to know the
cause, and in knowing a cause in general, it has a propensity to know it in particular. A natural propensity is not,
however, for the impossible since then the propensity would
be in vain (frustra). It follows, then, that it is not
impossible for the intellect to know an immaterial substance in particular by way of its material effects. For
example, we can know our acts of will by way of their material effects. Hence, the first object of our intellect
does not necessarily exclude the immaterial. In the second place, no power can know any object under a principle
more common than the principle making intelligible its
first object. Thus, sight does not know something under a
principle more common than that of color or light. But
our intellect knows something under a principle more common
than that of the material thing, because it knows a thing
under the principle of "being" in general, otherwise Metaphysics would not be a science of our intellect. The third
reason is connected with the second. Whatever is known per
se by the cognitive power is either its primary object or
is included in that object. Being, however, as it is more
common than the sensible, is understood by our intellect,
otherwise Metaphysics would be no more of a transcendent
science than Physics. Therefore, anything more particular
than being could not be the primary object of our intellect,
for otherwise being as such would not be known to us. It
is evident, then, that to say "the sensible quiddity is
the primary object of our intellect" is false.

The assumption of congruence between the known and
the knower is also false. The faculty and its object are
not similar to each other in their mode of being; they are
related as motivum and mobile and can be dissimilar to each
other in their respective modes of being. To deny this is
to assert that the bronze is assimilated to the idea by
the figure impressed on the bronze. Or, again, to deny it
is to argue thus: an idea in the Divine mind, which is the

similitude of an object, is non-material; therefore, a
stone, of which there is such an idea, is non-material.
For the foregoing reasons, then, it is not correct to restrict the intellect in its proper power to knowledge only
of the material quiddity. For similar reasons, we cannot
say that substance is the primary and adequate object of
our intellect, for accidents also motivate the intellect.

We might add that to know without recourse to a
"phantasm" (sense-datum), that provides the basis for our
acquaintance with a sensible quiddity, is not incompatible
with the nature of the intellect, since the soul separated
from the body can do so; it is not incompatible with the
union of the soul and the body, since the intellect can
know in this manner when united to the incorruptible body
in a future life; finally, it is not even incompatible with
the state of men in this life, since, without original sin,
man would have preserved the complete domination of his
soul over his body and of his intellect over his senses,
that is, he would have remained capable of knowing intellectually with or without the phantasm, as seemed good to
him. (6) Moreover, Scotus has offered evidence to show
that, besides being capable of abstractive knowledge in
the usual sense, the intellect is capable of intuiting particulars present and existing. The difference between abstractive and intuitive cognition lies not in what is known,
but in how it is known. Abstractive cognition abstracts
entirely from the actual existence and presence of the object, whereas intuitive cognition grasps directly the particular as present and existing. Intuitive cognition is
not dependent on a "phantasm" (sense-datum) or species,
but only on the object immediately. (7) The establishment
of this kind of cognition strengthens the case against the
view that the primary and adequate object of the intellect
must be the material quiddity, because there is a connaturality between knower and known. Instead of adjusting
the theory of knowledge to fit a preconceived philosophical
scheme, Duns Scotus' custom is to refer the reader to experience. The entire inference from the fact that in our
present state the intellect often operates by way of sense
material to the conclusion that its peculiar nature is
such as only to operate in that way is a gigantic fallacy
of accident. To make it worse, the further inference is
drawn that the intellect, since it is embodied, can know
only something proportionate or assimilated to such an
entity, namely, the quiddity of a material object.

The primary object of the intellect in the order of perfection is discussed quite briefly. The term "perfection" is by no means clear and needs clarification. I suggest that a "perfection" is a characteristic of a thing that realizes some important or essential capacity to a greater or lesser degree. Scotus distinguishes between what may be known in a simply more perfect manner, and what may be known more perfectly according to a kind of proportionality. Thus, according to the former, the eagles' vision of the sun is of a "more perfect" object than is our vision of a candle, since the sun presumably possesses the characteristic of brightness to a greater degree than other luminous objects. But, in the latter sense, our vision of a candle is proportionately more perfect insofar as our vision has more of the character of vision by means of a candle's light than the eagle has by means of the sun's light. That is, according to the suggestion, the human eye is a more perfect organ of vision than the eagle's eye, because the human eye is better (proportionately) adapted to seeing a variety of things than is the eagle's eye. In a similar way, the primary object of the intellect is more perfect according to proportion. Being thus has more of the character of an efficacious mover of the intellect than other things. I cannot say that this argument has much meaning today.

For reasons similar to those set forth in the preceding paragraphs, we cannot say that substance is the primary object of our intellect, since accidents also may motivate the intellect. Having disposed of this traditional but erroneous theory of knowledge, Duns Scotus can continue to set forth his own view of the primary and adequate object of our intellect.

A pretty clear intimation of his view has already occurred in the refutation of the Thomistic or Aristotelian doctrine. The intellect in this life knows something first confusedly, for example, the species specialissima, or the singular, whether audible, visible or tangible, which may be said to include a content that later becomes intelligible. Thus, if you ask, "What did you see?" - one might answer, "I saw something." (8) The "something" is vague, but the fact that a something exists, that there is "being," is our first distinct notion; we have a distinct concept of a being without analyzing the object apprehended into its elements (rationes). Further evidence of our acquaintance with "being" is given in another connection. We have a direct introspective grasp of my own mental acts. (9) By direct reflection on the operation of my own mind, I know myself as a thinking and willing being. "This operation is so evident that he who denies it is not a man." (10) I, then, am one instance of "being." Here, too, the knowledge of myself as a "being" enables me to obtain a clear and distinct notion of being. Scotus emphasizes that this concept of being is not vague or indistinct, for the reason already mentioned, that it has only one simple, intelligible characteristic. (11) It is so simple that I am either altogether ignorant of it or else I know it completely. (12)

Let this suffice for an exposition of how we come by the concept of being. That it is univocal applying to all that is from concrete existences to God remains to be shown. We proceed first to a definition of the univocity of being. "Now lest there be a dispute about the term univocation, I say that the univocal concept means a concept the unity of which is sufficient to involve a contradiction if one affirms and denies it of the same thing. It is also sufficient for a syllogistic middle term, so that, by means of it, the conclusion unites the extremes without the fallacy of equivocation." (13) The notion of being widest in extent is the concept of "not nothing" (non-nihil). "It is the most common insofar as it embraces everything that is not nothing. The term nothing can be understood in a two-fold manner. 1. That is 'nothing' which involves a contradiction, since that excludes all being whether outside the intellect or in it. What thus involves a contradiction cannot be outside the intellect, for then it cannot be intelligible to the mind.... 2. The other way asserts that 'nothing' is what is not, and hence cannot be anything outside the mind. "Being" therefore, or 'a thing,' regarded as not nothing....embraces everything that does not involve a contradiction whether it be ens rationis or an ens reale." (14) It is "that to which to be is not repugnant." (15) Thus the concept of being is simply the universal and completely undetermined concept of not nothing. The situation is something like this: Suppose I speak of non-zero. Zero is, in a sense, the denial or negation of number. Non-zero then is the negation of that negation; that is, it is a completely indeterminate and all-embracing expression for anyone or all of the series of whole numbers. No number is called merely non-zero. In a similar sense, no fact of being or of existing is called merely not nothing, though the expression can apply to any kind of being. (16) Moreover, being in this sense does not represent a mere essence detached from existence. In fact, Scotus denies the separability of essence and existence. (17) It would be false to ascribe being as a particular property in addition to the actual properties of the thing. He says, "I do not comprehend how any being whatsoever is found outside its causes, so that it would not have its proper existence." The concrete thing is at once a being and a particular thing. We do not need to distinguish, for example, between that which makes a horse a non-nihilum and that which makes it a horse.

If, in the light of this exposition of being, we consider the definition, given at the beginning of the preceding paragraph, we can now see why the concept of being is univocal. The first part of the definition asserts that the unity of being is sufficient to involve a contradiction, if one affirms and denies it of the same thing. If one were to say "the centaur is" (meaning thereby that the centaur can be described as if it had an intra-mental existence) and "the centaur is not" (meaning that the centaur does not exist, extra-mentally or in any other way) there would be no real contradiction. It is this unfortunate confusion (or play on words) that vitiates so much of the thought of the Pseudo-Dionysius and of the ninth century Irish philosopher John the Scot. How easy it is to assert "God is" and "God is not," when the word "is" has such a highly ambiguous meaning! "In the judgments 'God is' and 'God is not' it is sufficient for the production of a contradiction that 'is' should mean opposed to nothingness or not nothing." (18) In this respect, as already noted, being is a universal concept which is applicable to God and to creatures, so that both are opposed to nothingness.

In the second part of the definition, Scotus states that the unity of being is sufficient to serve as the middle term of a valid syllogism. Consider the following syllogism:

83

              That which is is God
              A stone is
              Therefore, a stone is God

This is either wicked nonsense or an obvious fallacy of
equivocation. Scotus will have us use the concept being in
so common and unambiguous a sense that it will be sufficient
to serve as a middle term in an argument proceeding from the
creature to God.

        In order to corroborate this view of the univocity of
being, Scotus advances three arguments. The first shows that
the most universal concept of being says nothing with regard
to the mode of being, whether finite or infinite, substantial or accidental. The second shows that the Aristotelian
doctrine of the origin of ideas does not and cannot provide
us with an analogous concept of being. The third suggests
the absurdity of the analogical method of reasoning.

        The first argument proceeds as follows. Every in-
tellect in judging that a subject is the predicate can be
certain about one concept and uncertain about other concepts
stated in the predicate. The intellect can thus be certain
that a thing is, though uncertain whether it is finite or
infinite, created or uncreated. Therefore, the concept of
being applied to a thing is different from these predicates,
and is neutral with regard to them, though included in such
predicates. Therefore, it is univocal. Thus, some ancient
philosophers were certain that the first principle was being, though one asserted it was fire, another water. They
were certain of being but uncertain of the other concepts.
Moreover, someone seeing that the philosophers disagreed,
could be certain that the first principle was being, but
could doubt whether it was this or that being. (19) Fr.
Allen B. Wolter draws attention to the same argument as
applied to substance and accident. (20) We experience in
ourselves an ability to conceive being, not, however, being
in itself or being in another, for we may be doubtful
whether the being conceived is substantial or accidental.
Thus, for example, light is a being but we may be uncertain whether it is a substance or a property.

        The second argument reads thus: In the present life,
every concept naturally caused in the intellect is caused by
the factors which naturally move our intellect. These are

the phantasms (sense-data) or objects revealed therein, and the active intellect (according to Aristotle). Now although no simple concept arises except by virtue of these factors, a concept that is not univocal, but entirely different from and analogous to the object revealed in the phantasm could not arise by virtue of the intellect and the phantasms. The reason is this: Any object revealed in the phantasm produces in the intellect its proper concept as an adequate effect, and a second concept of anything essentially or virtually included in the first concept. But a different and analogous concept is not essentially or virtually contained in the first. Therefore such a concept will never occur. (21) Hence, an analogous concept will never serve as a foundation for a natural knowledge of God. No created object provides us with a concept that we can attribute properly to something uncreated.

The third argument runs as follows. Every metaphysical inquiry about God proceeds thus: we can consider the formal characteristic of something (formalem rationem), and can remove from it the imperfections it has in creatures; then we can attribute to this objective characteristic the highest perfection and ascribe it to God. Take for example, the formal characteristics of wisdom, or of intellect, or of will. Let them be considered as lacking any imperfection or limitation which accompanies them in creatures; then let them be ascribed to God in the most perfect manner. Thus, every inquiry about God presupposes that the intellect has the same univocal concept that it obtains from creatures. If, however, you should say that this is not so, but that there is another formal character which is appropriate to God, then this inconsistency follows: nothing can be inferred concerning God from any characteristic found in creatures, since the characteristics of the former and the latter are totally different from each other. We would have no reason for concluding that God is formally wise by reason of the wisdom we apprehend in creatures than that God is a stone; for any other concept can be formed from the concept of the created stone by this analogical reasoning, a concept of a nature such that we could say "God is a stone," just as we could say "God is wise." (22) The analogical method would enable us to predicate anything and everything of God, not merely the transcendentals: being, truth and goodness.

Let me return for a moment to an examination of the
relation between essence and existence. Most of Ordinatio
I, d. 36 is devoted to an exposition of the falsity of what
is sometimes regarded as the Thomistic view that essence and
existence are distinguishable and separable. The doctrine
of Aquinas that the intellect first knows the quiddity of
the material thing seems to mean that it knows only the
essence of existence, not actual existence. This is to admit that the intellect from the start is cut off from the
order of existence as such. I think it is true to say of
Scotus that we know being even before we know our own
thought about being, in the sense that what first moves the
intellect is the intuitive grasp that something is. It
seems quite clear that existence applies to every object
thus apprehended and at the same time is common to all.
This original clarity is not obscured by the darkness we
find when we try to examine existence when ascribed to such
objects as possible beings or fictional beings (the
Chimaera) or to properties and classes. We can also ask
whether the North Pole or the Equator is an existing,
though singular and abstract, object.

In one passage, Scotus himself is not too clear, for
he enumerates a list of things that he seems to regard as
beings, or as effections or modes of being. In the Preface
to his Quaestiones Quodlibetales he writes: "Being (res)
can be divided into created and uncreated being into being
from itself and dependent being, into necessary and possible
being, or into finite and infinite being. Uncreated, necessary, infinite being, a se being is called God. Created,
possible, finite and dependent being is called by the common name creature. Questions about both of these classes of
things are raised." Questions can indeed be raised as to
whether the population of the universe is so large that includes possible beings, fictional beings (e.g. the Chimaera)
and actual beings. If we adopt the Thomistic view of the
real separability of essence and existence, we can hardly
avoid speaking as though possibilities were actual entities,
and as though there were possible worlds having some peculiar form of existence. Surely by expressions such as "a
realm of essence" or "an infinity of possible universes" we
may mean that, for example, God can "conceive" of arche-
typal plans. Even more obviously, when we say "It is
possible that there is someone in the next room" I am not
talking about a "possible man" present in the next room.

The term "possible" is what the medievals can call a syncategorematic term in the same sense that "false" is in the
sentence "It is _false_ that such and such is the case."
Against all those who say or intimate or ascribe a form of
being to an existent before it exists, Duns Scotus asserts
that creation cannot be a kind of further unfolding of a
"diminished" being (_esse diminutum_) already at hand, but it
is the whole thing produced out of nothing. Such a statement as the following "From the infinity of possible things,
the Divine Will chooses from all eternity the things that at
a certain moment will be called into existence" must not be
interpreted as though existence is a kind of accident added
to a certain selection of possibles. (23) As for the Chimaera and other mythological beasts, the idea or description
of them contains incompossible components; therefore, the
Chimaera is nonexistent. Moreover, though Scotus did not
bring this up, how would one determine the difference between two Chimaeras? In what way are we justified in saying
that this Chimaera differs from that Chimaera by such and
such characteristics? To do this, we would have to examine
perceptually the two beasts and there is nothing to examine.

The results of the preceding paragraphs can be summarized thus. For Scotus, being is the primary and adequate
object of the intellect and is univocal; there are no
"floating essences," but only existences that can be characterized; possible being can mean only that which is non-
contradictory, such as ideas or plans whether considered by
the human intellect or by the Divine intellect. In most
circumstances, the decision as to what is must be left to
perception and to the metaphysics accepted. But this leaves
two things not settled, so far as I know, by the exercise
of natural reason. The first question is this: What is the
existential status of abstract, singular objects such as the
Equator and the North Pole? These two objects can at least
be located, this being a characteristic that is ascribed to
actual things. A similar question about the status of
classes (_species_) and the universal terms that denote
classes has been answered, I think rather well, by our philosopher's doctrine of the "common nature," a view that has
been examined elsewhere. (24)

The second question is: How do we pass from a
recognition of the finite to an affirmation of the infinite?
We cannot find infinite being by arguing from a vague notion

labelled "analogical" using it as the middle term of a
syllogism; Scotus has successfully shown this cannot be done.
We can see what "finite being" stands for in the case of
particular, actual existents. But how can we demonstrate
that something called "infinite being" exists? "One cannot
demonstrate propter quid that infinite being exists, although from the nature of the terms it must be possible.
But for us the proposition is quite demonstrable from the
nature of creatures." (25) Before such a demonstration can
be made, one should know the meaning of the term "infinite
being." Does it mean, as Aristotle said in the Physics,
(26) "What is incapable of being gone through?" But if infinite being cannot be "gone through,", it cannot be comprehended by a finite intellect. Suppose we speak of an
"infinitely perfect being," meaning by perfection what
was mentioned a few paragraphs before, namely, the degree
of the realization of some essential capacity or the attainment of some purpose, then we are still in difficult circumstances. If we adopt Aristotle's definition, an infintely perfect being would mean that for any degree of perfection it had, there would exist a greater degree. Hence,
there would be no "most perfect" nature, or no last term in
the series. Evidently, terms such as "infinite," "infinitely perfect" cannot be taken in the Aristotetian sense.
Scotus is aware of the difficulties since in one passage,
namely, that found in the De Primo Principio, Ninth Conclusion, he writes thus "Thou art infinite and incomprehensible by the finite."

   Scotus has at least been able to show that the concept of being is univocal, and also that "to be" refers to
what fundamentally is and to nothing else. What remains to
be undertaken is the construction of a metaphysics of being
that will exhibit the contingency of finite beings, and
show that the existence of finite beings requires the existence of infinite and necessary being, in spite of the
difficulties mentioned in the preceding paragraph. How
well Duns Scotus succeeded in this is a story going beyond
the present exposition. But at least this much is true:
in that part of his writings considered in this essay he has
given us a well reasoned and well founded prolegomena to a
Theistic Metaphysics.

FOOTNOTES

(1) J. Duns Scoti Opera Omnia. Vol. I. Vatican City,
     1950. Pp. 1-2. The Ordinatio: Liber Primus is con-
     tained in volumes I-V of this edition, and will be
     used in this essay for all quotations and para-
     phrases. References to Books II, III and IV, not
     yet published in the Vatican City edition, will be
     given thus: Op. Ox. IV, d. 8, V. I, n. 2.

(2) Quaestiones Quodlibetales, Q. III. I use this photo-
     graphic reproduction of the Wadding 1639 edition done
     by the Franciscan Institute, St. Bonaventure, New
     York, 1950. Pp. 67-68.

(3) In what follows, I offer a paraphrase of Op. Ox. I,
     d. 3, q. 2, mn. 21-23. Vatican City edition, Vol.
     III, pp. 48-67.

(4) St. Thomas Aquinas, S. Theol. I, 84, 7c: "The proper
     object of the human intellect, which is united to a
     body, is the quiddity or nature existing in matter."

(5) The succeeding discussion follows Op. Ox. I, d. 3,
     q. 3, nn. 2-25. Vatican City edition, Vol. III, pp.
     68-115.

(6) See E. Gilson, "L'Objet de la Metaphysique selon
     Duns Scotus". Medieval Studies, Vol. X (1948). P. 61.

(7) See the whole admirable exposition in Sebastian Day,
     O.F.M. Intuitive Cognition, St. Bonaventure, New
     York, 1947.

(8) ALLEN B. WOLTER, O.F.M., Transcendentals and their
     Function in the Metaphysics of Duns Scotus, St. Bon-
     aventure, New York 1946. P. 64.

(9) This is admirably set forth in the passages from Op.
     Ox., IV, d. 45, q. 3, nn. 17-18 and d. 43, q. 2, nn.
     9-11. The texts are reprinted in Sebastian J. Day,
     O.F.M. Intuitive Cognition, St. Bonaventure, New
     York 1947, Pp. 134-7.

(10) Rep. Par. IV, d. 45, q. 2, n. 8.

(11)   Op. Ox. I, d. 3, q. 2, n 24: "Ens auten non potest concipi nisi distincte, quia habet conceptum simpliciter simplicem." Vatican City edition. Vol. III, Pp. 54-55.

(12)   Ibid. q. 3, n. 12: "Tale 'simpliciter simplex', ignotum est omnino, nisi secundum se totum concipiatur." Vatican City edition. Vol. III, p. 92.

(13)   Ibid. q. 2, n. 5. Vatican City edition, Vol. III, p. 18.

(14)   Quodl. 3, nn. 2-3.

(15)   Op. Ox. IV, d. 8, q. 1, n. 2.

(16)   This illustration is derived from Deodat de Basly, O.F.M., Scotus Docens, (Paris 1934), p. 21.

(17)   Op. Ox. IV, d. 13, q. 1, n. 38.; Ibid. II, d. 3, q. 3, n. 2.

(18)   FREDRICK J. COPLESTON, S.J., A History of Philosophy, Vol. 2. (London 1950), p. 502.

(19)   Op. Ox. d. 3, q. 2, n. 6. Vatican City edition. Vol. III, p. 19.

(20)   ALLEN B. WOLTER, The Transcendentals and their Function in the Metaphysics of Scotus, St. Bonaventure, New York 1946, Pp. 49-50.

(21)   Op. Ox. I. d. 3, q. 2, nn. 8-9. Vatican City edition. Vol. III, pp. 21-23.

(22)   Op. Ox. I, d. 3, q. 2, n. 10. Vatican City edition, Vol. III, pp. 26-27.

(23)   See the discussion of this point in Walter Hoeres, Der Wille als reine Vollkommenheit. Munchen, 1962. Pp. 30-34. Ordinatio, d. 36, p. unica. Vatican City edition. Vol. VI. Pp. 290 et seq.

(24)   J. R. CRESSWELL, "Duns Scotus on the Common Nature". John Duns Scotus: 1265-1965. Catholic University of

America, Washington, D.C. 1965.

(25)   <u>Ordinatio</u> I, d. 2, q. 2, n. 10.   Vatican City edi-
         tion, Vol. II, p. 148.

(26)   Aristotle, Physics III, 4, 204 et seq.   See also
         Martin Tweedale, "Scotus and Ockham on the Infinity
         of the Most Eminent Being." <u>Franciscan</u> <u>Studies</u>.
         Vol. 23 (1963). Pp. 257-267.

Discussion

JOHN JOSEPH LAKERS, O.F.M.. PH.D.

Professor of Philosophy
Our Lady of Angels Seminary
Quincy, Illinois

In structure Dr. Cresswell's paper is expressly an imitation of Quine's essay, "On What Is There." As such, it sets forth Scotus' views on the ontological problem in general and on the particular problems of existence, distinction, possibility, and contradiction. Nonetheless, the terminology and the very formulation of the problems in the two papers are so different as to obscure the fact that Scotus and Quine are discussing the same perennial problems. Therefore, it may be useful for a discussant to compare and contrast the papers explicitly, in the hope of clarifying Scotus' import across the span of centuries.

Quine's essay begins by noting the curious simplicity of the ontological problem. The fundamental question asks "What is there?" This question can be answered with a single word, "Everything." The answer, of course, is tautologous: there is what there is. But in philosophical contexts it is an important tautology, to remind the philosopher of the absurdity of prescriptive ontologies and theories of knowledge. Philosophers too often fall victim to the temptation to adopt a theory of knowledge which will canonize their metaphysical beliefs or to insist on a metaphysics which follows from a pet theory of knowledge. In these cases, the apparent simplicity must be challenged. That further problems can arise is manifest in the fact of disagreement among human knowers, who differ radically in their specification of the entities which are there.

The difficulties in specification derive primarily from epistemological problems, problems which have become particularly critical since the discoveries of the scientific revolution. The scholastics tended to have recourse to 'hypothetical' knowers, knowers whose means of acquiring knowledge can only be a matter of speculation for us, such as disembodied spirits and God himself. Drawing on their theological beliefs, they spelled out an ideal of knowledge without sufficient awareness of and regard for the actual and practical problems of knowledge by humans. Contemporary philosophers, in contrast, are forced to begin more positivistically, for the discoveries of modern science have uncovered a host of problems of knowledge as well as many critical questions about our conception of the world.

In particular, the scientific revolution arose when Copernicus and Galileo insisted that their theories were not simply mathematical or speculative 'fictions' which 'save the appearances' but must rather be accepted as objective descriptions of the world. Theory, they argued, is needed for the criticism of the objective significance of the facts. But theorizing is obviously a human activity, an activity, moreover, which ends in empty speculation more often than in successful objective description. For any set of facts, whether these facts be a question of how we know or a problem of the relation between entities a variety of hypothetical explanation can be offered. But only one explanation is the correct explanation, and this explanation must be a factual description. Consequently, theory too must be criticized. Today this criticism centers on the meaning of concepts.

Most contemporary discussions of meaning, Quine's included, begin with the critical and analytic movement which culminated in the program of Logical Positivism. Positivists reacted to rationalistic theorizing as the critique of objective knowledge. They noted an ambiguity in the notion of theory if theory is used indiscriminately to designate both speculative hypothesizing and mathematical correlation. Mathematics, as a formal discipline, does not involve interpretation, nor does strictly formal logic, as the 'linguistic' correlate of mathematics. These 'forms of language' could supposedly be used to report the facts without interpretation. The facts would then be reported as bare, primitive data. For the positivists, such bare facts became the criterion of objective knowledge. Theory and interpretation, as human devices, became equated with subjectivism. For objective knowledge, all theory should then be eliminated, as meaningless metaphysics. The meaning of concepts is reduced to their bare empirical reference. The facts as we apprehend them may be subject to our interpretation, but this interpretation must be eliminated by reconstructing the statements reporting the facts in a formal logical framework devoid of theoretical content. Then the facts should 'show themselves.' Such a 'showing' alone constitutes objective evidence.

With the elimination of theory, positivists also believed they had dissolved the ontological problem. The simple analysis of significant existential assertions reveals a two-fold distinction in the assertions. Ask the ordinary person what he means by a statement that crows exist, and he will likely reply, after his initial puzzlement, that he means that the crows are there. Ask a scientist what he means by the statement that electrons exist, and the reply will not be so straightforward. Obviously, the concept 'electron' is devised to account for certain data given at particular places at particular times. The concept, therefore, purports to specify further what is there. Hence, the assertion claims that entities of the sort described in the concept are there. If what is there is not objectively described by the concept, the assertion is either false or empty. For example, the atoms studied by Newton exist, but Newtonian atoms, i.e., inert, impenetrable, property-less particles, do not exist. Newton may have correctly located and discriminated these atoms, but he misdescribed them. The misdescription invalidated his existential assertion, taken strictly. The location of an entity and its discrimination from other known entities is a pre-requisite for a significant existential assertion, but the assertion must also include some descriptive claim.

Therefore, when positivists eliminated all theoretical content from concepts, they also made all significant existential assertions impossible, in favor of bare empirical reports. In their program, what is there is exhaustively reported as the bare datum. Nothing exists, though data are given.

In fact, their program did not succeed in dissolving the ontological problem. The fundamental obstacle was the problem of reusable terms. Positivists required an exact and explicit meaning for each term. The term could be correctly used only if it had precisely the same reference in each use. What, then, of the terms in ordinary language, terms which we do in fact reuse in a variety of contexts?

To preserve a precise and exact meaning for such reusable terms, positivists were forced to reintroduce an ontology. The same reference in different situations could be preserved only if the referent were somehow enduring. Those logical positivists who inclined more to the empirical strain posited sense-data, as 'permanent possibilities of sensation' which endured as 'body-less' possibilities and could be given again and again. They were supposed to be there, but only as possibilities, not as existents. (1) Those who favored the logical and linguistic strain of analysis posited a variety of quasi-existents, ranging from a realm of 'unactualized possibles' such as Pegasus to a realm of negative facts such as the fact that Pegasus does not exist, on the grounds that what is named by a term or proposition must be, because it would otherwise be nonsense to say even that it is not.

The notion of 'permanent possibilities' as quasi-existents or subsistents is incomprehensible, if not incoherent. At the same time, Quine, as an empiricist, is unhappy with the logical or linguistic 'solutions' positing subsistent possibles, classes, propositions, or negative facts. He therefore relies on Russell's theory of description to reformulate the inquiry into the problems of theory of knowledge and ontological commitment. To eliminate the realm of universals, e.g., redness, he is content to say that predicates have no meaning. The explication of this view devolves basically into the thesis that a term has significance only in a proposition and that propositions have significance only in cases of actual use. Then the meaningfulness of linguistic utterances, taken as units, can become an ultimate and irreducible matter of fact. That is, objective reference is taken over by the variables of quantification. The quantification ties the terms in the proposition down to an actual case in the state of affairs. The quantified variable, rather than the bare empirical 'predicate' of strict positivism, expresses the reference of the proposition. There is then no need to say that 'red,' to be meaningful, must be regarded as the name of a single universal entity. In speaking of a red house, we speak of the individual thing. The truth or falsity of the statement depends on the correctness of both the unique reference and the factual description. Until the reference is established, the descriptive proposition remains an 'incomplete symbol.' Ontological commitment enters only in terms of bound variables, not by the use of alleged names. "To be assumed as an entity is, purely and simply, to be reckoned as the value of a variable." (2) These variables, in translation into ordinary English, are the pronouns, 'everything,' 'something,' 'one and only one thing,' and 'nothing.'

By so formulating the problem, Quine distinguishes
sharply between questions of reference and questions of
description. Nonetheless, he accepts Russell's insistence
that it is impossible to speak of an entity named, but not
described. In practice, both questions must be answered
together. The distinction in a matter of emphasis, on
what is there and on what is there.

Possibilities can be neatly disposed of. Apart
from actual use in particular cases where quantification is
justified, we can also form descriptive phrases, as candidates for existential assertion. These phrases, analysed
in terms of the theory of descriptions, lead to the doctrine
of modalities, which, in one form or other, has come to be
accepted as dogma, i.e., the doctrine that modalities must
be reduced to properties of propositions. The 'hypothetical
entity' described in a proposition is not eo ipso a possible
entity, but the sentence is a well-formed formula in a
language. If the language does not correctly refer to and
describe the state of affairs, the logical correctness of
the sentence has no ontological implications.

This doctrine receives broad application. Though we
recognize the presence of entities in experience, because
it is impossible to speak of the existence of an entity
which is not somehow described, one's ontology cannot be
determined apart from one's conceptual scheme. Of course,
one's conceptual scheme may in fact be empty, if it does
not correctly refer to and describe the entities in the state
of affair as they are. Ordinarily, however, the situation
is not a clear-cut alternative between complete success and
absolute emptiness. Generally the reference to a relatively
distinct and enduring entity can be approximately accredited on minimally descriptive grounds. But particular problems arise with regard to the existence of entities which
are not directly, i.e., physically, observable in a way in
which the interference of the means of detection is negligi-
ble. Then the fact of identification must rely on a host
of concepts interpreting experience. Quine makes the implications of this problem more explicit in his later work,
Word and Object, when he insists that, in fact, we approach
all significant inquiry from within ordinary language. We
discover new (sorts of) entities by discriminating them
from entities already known to be present. The entities
known to be present are those to which reference is made in

ordinary language. We must so 'begin in the middle' because this language of physical object concepts is about as basic as language gets. (3) It thus provides the best-established standards for objective evidence.

Nonetheless, various conceptions of the world can be formulated in ordinary language, and any conception can receive various interpretations. Various theories can account for the same facts, while having different ontological commitments. Here Quine fixes the ontological problem. One's ontology is basic to the conceptual scheme by which he interprets all experience, whether it be peculiarly personal experiences or contact with objects in the world. Judged within some conceptual scheme, an ontological statement goes without saying. But judged in another conceptual scheme, an ontological statement which is basic in the first may, with equal immediacy and triviality, be judged false. The problem of interpretation and criticism which fostered positivism is still critical.

The ontological presuppositions of a conceptual scheme serve as the standards of objective interpretation. Ideally, the object or entity in question must be allowed to 'show itself' or 'speak for itself,' in Wittgensteinian terms. But it could 'show itself' only if we had a concept which correctly, exhaustively, and objectively describes what the entity is, without distortion. How are we to decide on a conceptual scheme which will give objective knowledge of what is there? The epistemological problems are such that no simple, clear, and automatic criteria can be given. In Quine's view philosophers can and must shift the discussion to the semantical plane, so that immediate judgments on the triviality of the ontological claims of opponents are avoided. The semantical plane, as the area concerning the implications of a conceptual scheme which guide the application of the scheme to the state of affairs, can be made into an intermediary between the conceptual scheme and one's ontological commitment. Because the implications are more explicit, better articulated, and closer to the concrete than are general metaphysical conceptions, discussion can be more fruitful, both in the consideration of alternative interpretations and in the criticism of objective significance. The question what ontology to adopt is left open. For the present, no priority can be given either to the ontological over the epistemological inquiry or vice versa.

Consequently, for Quine as for most contemporary analysts, philosophy is a criticism of the implications of our present knowledge, not an independent inquiry aimed at constructing or justifying a peculiarly philosophical body of doctrine, ontological or ideological. The criticism cannot be accredited relative to any a priori theory of knowledge, for such a prescription makes a metaphysics out of a theory of knowledge. At the same time, the ontological commitments of any conceptual scheme cannot be accepted straightforwardly. What is there is there. But our discovery of what is there is problematic. Metaphysics, then, must consider a variety of alternatives.

Scotus, of course, was a metaphysician. As such, he was concerned to show what is there, and to do so while clearly distinguishing between theology and philosophy. He was also a penetrating critic. Understandably, he lacked an awareness of all the problems of objective knowledge which now confront us. But his notion of intuitive cognition was truly revolutionary, especially in the role it played in Ockham's radical reformulation of the problem of knowledge, but also in its implications for the interpretation of the notion of being. An explicit treatment of the notion of being and of the doctrine of intuitive cognition can, I believe, highlight certain important features of Scotus' metaphysics while at the same time bringing this metaphysics into contact with Quine's approach.

As a convinced believer and a theologian seeking a more objective understanding of his beliefs, Scotus undoubtedly began in the middle. This beginning surely influenced his notion of metaphysics. He accepted Avicenna's interpretation of the subject of metaphysics as 'being qua being.' 'Being,' as the most general name one can apply to what exists or can exist apart from the mind, roughly denotes an individual subject and connotes that it is of such a nature that it could exist in the extra-mental world. In this generality, metaphysics is contrasted with physics, which deals only with the class of things which are capable of change or movement. This distinction, in itself, builds on the commonplace fact that there are more things in the state of affairs than we at present know, that not all possibles are presently realized, and that physics need not be the only possible means of discovering things in the state of affairs. At the same time, the contrast sets one of the specific tasks of metaphysics, namely, to reveal God as that unique type of being to which all else ultimately owes its existence.

Scotus insists that the discovery of God cannot be accredited by rational analysis alone or by a vague and general appeal to experience. The inquiry must be set in a well-established framework for accrediting objective knowledge. His formulation of the framework recognizes the problems of both description and reference.

The question of description receives a two-fold treatment. First, in the analysis of the ontological argument, Scotus shows that the sentence, "A necessary being exists," is not self-evident, because it is not self-evident that the notions presumed to be present in the subject can go together. He concludes that, though "God exists" has terms which are purely necessary, the necessity and evidence stem from reality. (4) Consequently, to show the reference of the conception and its meaningfulness, the conjunction must be traced back to the grounds in reality.

Secondly, Scotus develops the notion of the transcendentals in a context explicitly devoted to determining the meaning and interpretation of descriptive predicates such as 'wise' and 'good' when applied to God. Applied to creatures, these terms describe entities which fall under the categories or ultimate genera. For the application to God, there must be a framework for transcending these categories without losing existential import. The framework must point to God in a way which will preserve the predicates from ambiguity without reducing God to the image of man. For this purpose, Scotus develops the transcendentals as real concepts which do not have any category above them except being. The transcendentals stand for and signify existing beings directly.

This notion of terms which 'stand for' or 'point to' beings directly is strongly analogous to the strict positivistic equation of meaning and empirical reference, where terms should simply report bare data. If there is no further specification of referential criteria, pointing to individual existents is high problematic. The failure of the positivistic effort led to the contemporary recognition

of the need for criteria of both description and reference,
criteria which, though distinguishable, function inseparably in the justification of any existential assertion. In
light of this contemporary clarification the question must
arise concerning any of the scholastics what criteria of
reference they rely on in their specification of what is
there.

In seeking an answer to this question, a consideration of the scholastic views on possibility is not particularly helpful. The scholastics were surely influenced by
their belief in an omnipotent and omniscient God. (5)
Scotus is no exception. In his framework the meaning of all
concepts, all entia rationis, must be decided relative to
'being.' As such, descriptive conceivability can be discriminated from wild speculation by the limitation to a
referential framework which points the concept directly to
an actual entity or which includes something which can
eventually produce the hypothetical entity. The determination of possibles is then related to conceivability in a
manner similar to that implicit in the theory of descriptions and yet, by reference to the omnipotent God, need not
find this theory as a means to escape from a realm of 'unactualized possibles.' Any theorizing governed by the law
of contradiction can have existential import, even though
this law is primarily a criterion for theories and concepts, for the virtual possibility can be explained by
reference to the omnipotent God.

Of course, this explication is possible only when
the existence of God has been established. In this inquiry,
the program is set in a schematic framework of reference
which requires a direct application of the criteria of reference. Basic to this program is the fact that some properties
of the infinite being must have reference to creatures, if
God is the creator. From the existence of their referents,
the creatures, we can trace the properties back to the
Creator. Therefore, the proper way to know the existence of
God and his infinity, according to Scotus, is by way of
such divine properties as have reference to creatures, in
particular, by way of causality and of goodness or eminence.

As Dr. Cresswell notes, Scotus, in this context,
desires a notion of being which will serve as the middle term
of a valid syllogism, where the syllogism expresses an argu-

ment proceeding from the creature to God. Because the middle terms of arguments are ordinarily descriptive concepts, this formulation seems to suggest a positive content to 'being,' as though the concept somehow characterized existence. But Scotus stresses the univocity of being and rejects the distinction between essence and existence. Consequently, the interpretation of 'being' as a referential framework, in a sense close to the contemporary understanding, suggests itself. In this interpretation, 'being' would point to God via the causal relation prevailing between essence and existence. Consequently, the interpretation of 'being' as a referential framework, in a sense close to the contemporary understanding, suggests itself. In this interpretation, 'being' would point to God via the causal relation prevailing between God and creatures, just as 'being' could include possibles because of their virtual or potential existence relative to the omnipotence of God. The reference to God would be justified when manifestations of his creative activity are discovered in his creation. The causality so discovered would show the presence of God and therefore his existence, and it would also function as a referential criterion for determining the objective significance of the descriptive notions, such as 'wise' and 'good.'

That this interpretation of 'being' can be given a good run becomes apparent by a consideration of the doctrines of the formal distinction and of intuitive cognition, in which reference to creatures is also in question. As Fr. Wolter points out, Scotus elaborated the formal distinction as an answer to a theological problem, in connection with the Trinity, but it was not long before he extended it to his metaphysics and psychology. (6) Fundamentally, the justification for the extension lay in the recognition that predication is an intellectual operation concerned primarily with notions and concepts. A real concept is predicated directly of things, whether the concept be a logical subject or a descriptive predicate. Therefore, Scotus is concerned with the same problem as was Quine when he asserted that predicates have no meaning. Scotus' solution is less radical. To save the objectivity of both the transcendental notions and our concepts of creatures, Scotus believed that there must be something positive in the thing corresponding to our concepts, but something which is yet not separate or even separable, even by the absolute power of God. Consequently, the formal distinction becomes at once a standard for criti-

cizing the objective meaning of any concept which purports
to describe an individual as it is and a means for avoiding
the temptation to canonize some universal.

Ockham strongly criticized the notion of the formal
distinction in all instances except talk about God. His
criticism must be correlated with his development of the
notion of intuitive cognition. If the criticism is justified, as I believe it is, then Scotus' difficulties arise
because he himself realized only vaguely the implications
of this doctrine for his whole system. To clarify the
difficulties, we must review briefly Scotus' views on intuitive cognition, views which are well set forth in the work
by Sebastian Day to which Dr. Cresswell makes reference.

Intuitive cognition is cognition of an existing and
actually present (individual) object, as present and existing. Such cognition is contrasted with abstractive cognition,
which attains the object only in a diminished similitude.
The contrast is rooted in the fact that, in intuitive cognition, there is a real and actual relation between the intellect and the object. The intellect, therefore, is capable of both intuitive and abstractive cognition. Of course,
we do not experience intuitive cognition as certainly or as
clearly as we experience abstractive cognition, but this sort
of cognition does give immediate contact with the object.

Now, these views of Scotus are compatible with the
interpretation of existential questions previously offered.
We often know the presence of an individual on minimally
descriptive grounds. The problems of description do not
seriously jeopardize the certainty that our recognition of
the presence of an object and our discrimination of this
object from ourselves and from other known objects is
correct. At the same time, in contrast to the supposed
clarity which a concept can assume in a conceptual scheme,
the grounds for the certitude of this identification are
often difficult to specify. The more objective the evidence
for any proposed descriptive conception, the more solidly
grounded is the existential assertion that an entity of this
sort exists. But the awareness of the presence of the
individual can be somehow prior to full knowledge of what
the individual is. Moreover, even if the individual is one
of a specific sort, it is also unique and may not be known
exhaustively in a sortal concept.

This is not to say that Scotus would so have understood the questions raised by the notion of intuitive cognition. In light of contemporary developments, a variety of questions could be asked of Scotus. Does intuitive cognition somehow give us positive knowledge of the individual qua individual, as though we grasp intuitively the haecceitas? Or does intuitive cognition simply show the presence of an individual, so that the individuality is known only by the location of the individual and its distinctness from other individuals of the same and of different sorts? Or are all descriptive conceptions the elaboration of our creative hypothesizing? But these questions for the most part continue the inquiry in the traditional formulation of the fundamental problem. And it seems at least likely that Scotus was groping for a reformulation of this very problem.

Basically, whether he had the conceptual clarifications and distinctions at hand or not, Scotus must have viewed intuitive cognition as the interaction between the entity and the knower. Each contributes to the interaction. Therefore, abstractive cognition is not a mere abstraction, stripping off 'properties' of the object which the object happens to have or show at the time of single cognitions, to arrive as those 'properties' which are invariable through all possible intuitive cognitions of the object. Note well the revisions in the notion of accidents which are introduced by Scotus and Ockham. I suggest that these revisions and the whole problem of objective knowledge must be seen as the question of assessing the relative contributions of the interacting entities.

If this interpretation is correct or even tenable, then there are strong grounds for holding that the reformulation implicit in Scotus' insight receives it radical expression in Ockham's reformulation of the fundamental problem. Day states this formulation as the problem how we form universal conceptions of individual entities and how we apply these universal concepts to individuals, rather than the traditional question of how ontologically prior universals are individuated. The question of universals becomes a psychological rather than a metaphysical problem, and the grounds are laid for the contemporary transposition from psychological considerations to discussions in theory of knowledge.

If the reformulation is traced to the interaction
between knower and object to which each contribute, the way
is open to the later developments in which theory becomes
the means for sorting out the interaction by following it
back to the individuals which are interacting. In this regard, Copernicus' theory, by which he exchanged his actual
terrestrial point of view for an imaginary solar viewpoint
in order to criticize the factual knowledge about the plan-
ets, is only a beginning. It does try to assess our contribution to the experience by which we acquire factual knowledge about objects, but it describes only the relative
motion of the objects involved, even though it considers
these objects as a system. The role of theory can be
developed until it functions as a means of sorting out
individuals further as individuals of specific sorts, on the
basis of their specific interactions with the same detectors
or the same prevailing conditions.

It is surely legitimate to wonder how far Scotus
has anticipated this development in his realization that
description is an operation of the intellect. Of course, he
did not yet understand the creative nature of human theorizing, and if he had realized it, he would undoubtedly have
been worried by it, as his elaboration of the formal distinction to preserve the objectivity of our knowledge shows.
But, as Fr. Wolter argues in a passage worth quoting in detail, Scotus was aware of the impact of the doctrine of
intuitive cognition on the doctrine of the formal distinction, for he relates both to the questions of description
and reference in the context of significant existential
assertions.

Some form of intellectual intuition precedes not
only every existential judgment, but probably every
abstract concept which the mind forms.... Simple
apprehension, then, can be either an intuitive or
an abstractive cognition. The latter is concerned
with "essences" or essential features in the sense
that the concepts which are the end product of such
simple awareness represent answers to questions of
the form Quid est?, that is to say, they are questions that are answerable in terms of the categories
to which the features in question belong.... Intuitive cognition, on the other hand, while it may
include all the data or information found in a

corresponding abstractive cognition, invariably includes something more, viz. that additional knowledge or information of the fact that it exists.

The proper way of distinguishing essence from existence for Scotus then would seem to be in terms of
that objective feature of any object, situation or
thing that makes it possible not merely to identify
what it is, but to assert that it is. At the primary level at which this datum is presented, existence is not strictly speaking "conceivable";
neither is intuitive awareness properly speaking a
concept. For as we ordinarily understand this term,
a concept is always the result of abstractive cognition. By reflection upon what is common to all
instances of intellectual cognition, the mind can
form an abstract concept of existence. And it is
this concept that seems to be related to the concept of what a thing is as something formally other,
or as an additional modality. But it would be a
mistake, Scotus recognizes, to argue from the super-
ficial likeness of concepts like "rational animal"
... and "an existing person" to the same ontological
structure or distinction a parte rei.

    ...it would seem that the strict formal distinc-
tion, the formal modal distinction and that between
essence and existence have something in common and
yet, for all that, differ by reason of the objective
basis for the distinction. All three arise from the
desire to distinguish those characteristics of
reality that make it possible to have different types
of knowledge about it.

But...only at the level of abstractive cognition do
they appear as formally different objects of
intelligibility. Two of the distinctions (the formal
modal and the essence-existence distinction) evapo-
rate as it were if the reality in question is known
intuitively (7)

    This formulation of the existential question makes
room for theorizing on the level of abstractive cognition,
which concerns more exhaustive and more objective description.
The objective basis for the existential assertion lies in the

interaction recognized as the interaction between an object and the probing intellect. The initial identification derives from the recognition of the specific nature of the interaction. When a previously identified object interacts in an unexpected way, the intellect must probe further to criticize the previous conception of the object and to devise a more comprehensive replacement. In effect, the intellect then moves from the initially recognized distinction between the interacting entities to a theory as to how they interact, and from a variety of theories as to how the object interacts with different conditions to a theoretical conception describing what the object is.

In metaphysics as it regards knowledge of God, interaction does not enter directly. In fact, the concept of interaction presents serious problems for any formulation of the principle of causality. Scotus seems to have been aware of some of these problems. Therefore, it would seem that the causal principle invoked in his demonstration of God expresses a causality unique to the creative relationship between God and the world. As such, the principle would seem to be the result of an analysis of a conception of the world which was truly Franciscan in viewing the world as manifesting everywhere the vestigia Dei. The demonstration, then, would function to express the causal chain, so that from God's creative activity manifested in the world we know the agent, both as existing and as having in an infinite degree those perfections found in creatures.

Whether or not Scotus achieved a synthesis between the causal notion involved in the demonstration of God's existence and the concept of interaction required for objective knowledge of the world, the framework of interaction and that of the transcendentals show forth a fundamental presupposition of Scotus' metaphysics. What is there are individuals, and a primacy and priority, both ontological and epistemological, must be accorded to these individuals. Abstractive cognition, based on a variety of intuitive cognitions of the same entity in changed conditions, can fill in details until the knowledge of this entity commensurate with all the mind can know is achieved. However, this inquiry must begin with and return to the apprehension of something distinct from the knower, something to be known. Because the enduring individual can be known in a variety of intuitive cognitions, the possibility of acquiring more exhaustive knowledge is ever open. The strictly

referential criteria--for locating entities by means of
interactions with a known detector--show the presence, distinctness, and endurance of the entities in question. Once
we can focus on these entities, the variety of interactions
provides the material for determining the objective significance of the descriptive concepts applied to these individuals. The interaction as the referential criteria, subject
the concepts to confrontation with the individual.

In this formulation, Scotus' notion of being answers
the ontological question simply, by setting the goal of the
inquiry as no less than knowledge of everything which is
there. In light of the preceding, I would suggest the
following interpretation of being. In a logical formulation, 'being' becomes a class-concept, pointing to all the
individuals there are or can be, known or as yet unknown,
enumerating them without describing them. As a referential
framework, 'being' has existential import in its 'pointing'
and further explicitly sets the inquiry as a question of the
objective description of each of the entities which are
there. The 'pointing' is governed by the referential
criteria. Therefore, the framework provides the means by
which the objective significance of concepts can be
critically shown, by tying the concept down to the individual. 'Being," to have such import, can be used only when we,
the knower, recognize the activity of an entity distinct
from ourselves. Since this is the only way we can know the
existence of God also, 'being' is to this extent univocal.
Univocity, then, implies that we must somehow experience
the activity of an entity, directly on our detectors or indirectly on an object directly observed by our detectors,
before we can make a significant existential assertion. The
entities will act according to what they are, and from the
specific activity we can move to an objective description.

I do not suggest that the class-specification of being is precisely an understanding of the notion as Scotus
himself understood it. With all the conceptual and experimental advances which have entered our intellectual heritage
and outlook, I doubt whether anyone can discover what Scotus
did understand precisely. But if the concept of interaction
implicit in the notion of intuitive cognition is made
central to the interpretation of being, Scotus' notion does
come close to the contemporary formulation of the presupposition of significant existential inquiry which does

not smuggle in one's ontological pre-conceptions. Scotus' emphasis on individuals is preserved and even highlights. And the insistence that individuals are what they are and that they are unique and irreducible sets the stage for a framework of discovery which is open to what is there prior to any of our categorizations.

This notion of a framework of discovery provides the best means for comparing Scotus and Quine. Quine's analysis stresses an important element in the criticism of our knowledge of the irreducible individuals which are there. A variety of theories can be devised to account for how the same entities in the state of affairs are interrelated and to describe what these entities are. Too often we are content to stop with a theory or explanation which satisfies us intellectually, either because it fits with our ontological pre-conceptions or because it accounts for the known facts we regard as relevant. But such an explanation is not thereby guaranteed as the description. To achieve objectivity, one of the requirements must be a consideration of all the alternatives, especially since we have solid grounds for believing that our present knowledge is incomplete. One of the primary values of philosophical discussion is that we escape from our own limited and subjective point of view, to a sort of detachment. But Quine, falling victim to his commitment to logical and linguistic criticism and his consequent interest in the descriptive criteria, fails to specify any referential criteria. When he reduces objective reference to questions of the variables of quantification, he by-passes the factual problems we do encounter in actual uses of concepts to refer to entities. He must presume that we have a conception which is a unitary conception exhaustively and objectively describing the entity referred to or at least that we can somehow achieve such a conception by discussions in semantics. In fact, we have no such conceptions. The consideration of alternative theories and of possible syntheses between differing conceptions should aid in a growth and clarification of our knowledge, as a means to a more complete and objective description. But without explicit and realistic referential criteria, there is no decisive way to allow the object to 'speak for itself.'

Scotus, on the other hand, is understandably weak on the question of semantics and theory. Moreover, he is perhaps too much the metaphysician, too susceptible to the urge to project from concepts we have to ontological correlates. But his metaphysical tendencies have a compensating effect. For in the concept of interaction he provides the basic referential criterion for recognizing the presence of a distinct entity and for allowing the object to 'speak for itself' relative to the concepts we have devised to describe it. He argues that the fact that something exists must be our first significant notion for the possibility of realistic inquiry. His two-fold reason, that we can introspectively look at ourselves and that we can be certain there is something else there even before we know what it is, avoids the philosophical dead-ends of solipsism, idealism, and phenomenalism. The fact of intuitive cognition and the impossibility of knowing a non-existent in this manner specify the interaction in a realistic manner.

This formulation leaves many problems, particularly, as Dr. Creswell notes, with regard to the contingence of the world. But it does not lead to the scepticism which worried Scotus. The certainty that there is something there provides the basis for objective knowledge, in the primary sense of knowledge pertaining to the object. Moreover, from the specific and constant interactions of the enduring entities, we can be certain that our description of the entity is approximate, even when we also know that it is incomplete. Because all proposed revisions and extensions of our descriptive concept can be referred to the entity, we further have the means for advance in knowledge of the entity. The framework, therefore, accords well with Scotus' famous dictum:
In processu generationis humanae semper crevit notitia veritatis.

Scotus, then, must be seen as a revolutionary figure in the development of philosophical formulations of the perennial problems. The partisan must beware of finding answer in Scotus to questions which Scotus could not have asked. But Scotus can provide valuable insights into the answers to questions asked in the contemporary reformulations.

FOOTNOTES

(1)   Cf. A. J. AYER, "Phenomenalism", reprinted in Philos-
        ophical Essays (Macmillan & Co., 1963), pp. 125-166

(2)   W. V. O. QUINE, "On What Is There", in From A Logical
        Point of View (Harvard University Press, 1956), p. 13.

(3)   W. V. O. QUINE, Word and Object (Massachusetts
        Institute of Technology and John Wiley and Sons, Inc.,
        1960), pp. 1-6.

(4)   JOHN DUNS SCOTUS: A Treatise on God as First Princi-
        ple, trans. by A. B. Wolter, O.F.M., (Quincy College
        Publications, 1966), pp. 158-168.

(5)   Cf. J. BENARDETE, "Is There a Problem about Logical
        Possibility", Mind, lxxi (1962), 342-352.

(6)   A. B. WOLTER, O.F.M., The Transcendentals and Their
        Function in the Metaphysics of Duns Scotus (Catholic
        University Press, 1946), p. 17.

(7)   A. B. WOLTER, O.F.M., "The Formal Distinction", in
        Ryan and Bonansea, eds., John Duns Scotus: 1265 -
        1965 (Catholic University Press, 1965), pp. 57-59.

FATHER ROY EFFLER, O.F.M., completed graduate
studies at St. Bonaventure University, New
York. At present he is Professor of Philoso-
phy and Dean of Students at Duns Scotus
College, Southfield, Michigan. He has also
taught at colleges and universities in the
Detroit area and at St. Francis College, Fort
Wayne, Indiana. His doctoral dissertation
was entitled John Duns Scotus and the Prin-
ciple "Omne Quod Movetur Ab Alio Movetur."
In September, 1966, he delivered a paper at the
International Scotistic Congress in Oxford,
England, Duns Scotus and the Necessity of First
Principles.

112

Is SCOTUS' Proof for the Existence of God an Essentialist Proof?

ROY EFFLER, O.F.M., PH.D.

Someone has more jocosely than sagely remarked that Ockham was an existentialist, because he was always in trouble. Writing in a serious vein, Beraud De Saint-Maurice finds not a few philosophical themes in Duns Scotus which are favorites of modern existentialists, and thus Beraud speaks of the "existential import" of the Subtle Doctor's philosophy. (1)

As is well known, other thinkers prefer to see Duns Scotus as an essentialist, while Aquinas is viewed as an existentialist. Now if an essentialist is defined as a philosopher who denies the doctrine of a real distinction between essence and existence, and if an existentialist is defined as one who subscribes to the same doctrine, then with good basis it can be asserted that Duns Scotus is an essentialist and not an existentialist. (2)

But no doubt one could go on elaborating different meanings for the words 'essentialist' and 'existentialist,' according to which Scotus would be and would not be an essentialist or an existentialist. Perhaps it would be better to settle for a current meaning, according to which such philosophers as Sartre, Marcel, Heidegger, and others are to be honored with the epithet 'existentialist.' According to this meaning, vague as it may be, I do not think it appropriate to style Scotus an existentialist. For as he is known to us in his philosophical and theological works, Duns Scotus is more of a scientific thinker. He employs a technical logic and puts a high premium on clarity, precision, rigor, the method of analysis and distinction. His language has the sobriety of scientific language and is without the emotive tones so characteristic of modern existentialism.

But whatever my terminological preferences may be, the fact remains that Duns Scotus has been labeled an essentialist, and I believe that the label has been quite widely accepted. Furthermore, the essentialism attributed to him is such as to change significantly his image as a philosopher.

The essentialism attributed to Duns Scotus by Etienne Gilson is wide in scope. It bears on such Scotistic doctrines and concepts as formal distinction, common nature thought being, and so forth. (3) A thorough exposition of all

114

these matters is beyond my present competence.

A medieval scholar of rank and student of Gilson, Fr. Joseph Owens finds essentialism in Scotus' proof for the existence of God. Now this is the matter I wish to ventilate. The question before us then is this: is Scotus' proof for the existence of God an essentialist proof?

Any attempt to answer this question, of course, first requires a determination of the meaning of essentialism in this context. Initially perhaps, we can consider the meaning as already determined by Fr. Owens. According to him, Scotus' proof does not proceed "from a properly existential starting-point, but rather from a quidditative notion of being which can be the basis for reasoning to actual existence." (4) In the absence of an existential starting-point, the actual existence of God is established from the concept of supreme perfection, which is really to be equated with infinite perfection. Hence the concept of infinity is the ground for proving that God exists. (5) Because existence "does not enter the probative force of the argument, it can be disregarded," and as a matter of fact, is "eliminated from the starting-point of the proof." (6)

As is well known, the goal of Scotus' extended proof for the existence of God is to establish the actual existence of a unique infinite being. The journey to this goal is long and arduous. The first principal conclusion reached in this long journey is that a first efficient cause actually exists. This conclusion is established by first proving the possibility of such a being and then by showing its uncausability. From the possibility and uncausability of a first efficient cause, the actual existence of the first efficient is inferred. (7)

The proof for the possibility of a first efficient cause starts with the proposition: some being is effectible, or some being can be produced. (8) Obviously, this proposition is not a proposition of fact, simply asserting the existence of an effect. Rather it is a proposition asserting the possibility of an effect. What is the evidence for this proposition?

While this question is all-important, I prefer to discuss it later. For it still seems that an answer denying

115

the essentialist view would not settle the issue before us, at least entirely. For later on, in his 5th argument against infinite regress in essentially ordered causes, Scotus quite clearly reasons to the possibility of a first efficient cause in a conceptual, nonempirical manner.

Efficient causality, viewed in itself, does not bespeak imperfection. Therefore, it is possible that it exists in some being without imperfection. But if an efficient cause without imperfection is possible, then a first efficient cause is possible, namely, an efficient cause which itself is not efficiently caused and does not cause by the power of another. (9)

One who favors an empirical interpretation of this argument might contend that at least the notion of an efficient cause is derived from experience. But this contention would not hit the essential element of the matter. For the fact remains that Duns Scotus argues to the possibility of a first efficient cause from a conceptual consideration of the notions of efficient cause, perfection and imperfection.

Duns Scotus' argument here for the possibility of a first efficient cause might appear to be acceptable enough. But most disturbingly, it seems to render unnecessary all the preceding argumentation. It would also seem to render unnecessary a good deal of the subsequent argumentation. Thus there would be no need for arguing that an infinite regress in a series of accidentally ordered causes is impossible, unless an essential order is admitted in which there is a terminus. (10) Furthermore, Scotus' entire doctrine concerning the distinction between essentially and accidentally ordered causes, which he introduces into his proof, would become unnecessary baggage. This result surely strikes any student of Scotus' proof as most strange. For it is precisely in explaining and using the distinction between essentially ordered and accidentally ordered causes that the Subtle Doctor labors so painfully and conveys some of his finest metaphysical insights. (11)

Granted that this situation is puzzling enough, one's puzzlement might only be increased when he comes to the 2nd article of Scotus' Ordinatio proof. I will briefly review the contents of this article.

After showing in the first article the existence of
a nature first in the orders of efficient causality, final
causality, and eminence, and which also is essentially one,
the second article proceeds to demonstrate the infinity of
this nature. To reach this goal, four conclusions are
demonstrated: 1) the first efficient is endowed with an
intellect and will; 2) the first being's knowing and willing of itself is really identical with its essence; 3) all
the thinking and willing of the first being is really
identical with its essence; 4) the intellect of the first
efficient always and distinctly knows all intelligibles,
and this knowledge is prior to the existence of these
things. These four conclusions are introductory to the
demonstration of infinity. The proofs for infinity are
five in number: 1) from efficient causality; 2) from this
that the first being distinctly knows all intelligibles;
3) from this that the first being as ultimate end is infinite good; 4) from the eminence of the first being; 5)
from this that the first being does not have an intrinsic
cause. The last proof Scotus considers to be unaccept-
able. (12)

Worthy of special consideration here is the fourth
proof. In the Ordinatio it is given two formulations and
is then reenforced with a series of persuasive arguments.
In connection with these arguments, Scotus presents his
adaptation of the ratio Anselmi. (13)

While Fr. Owens sees an all-pervasive essentialist
character in Scotus' proof for the existence of an infinite
being, he appeals to these proofs and particularly the
adaptation of the ratio Anselmi as clearly testifying to an
essentialism. (14) To me it seems that if the essentialist
view of Scotus' proof is in some measure plausible, special
importance will have to be given to the argument for infinity from the way of eminence and the adaptation of the
Anselmian argument.

Looking at Scotus' proof as a whole, I think that
there are three parts which prima facie lend themselves to
the essentialist interpretation. These parts are: 1) the
proof of article one for the possibility of a first efficient cause, which starts with the proposition, some being
is effectible; 2) the fifth argument in article one
against infinite regress in essentially ordered causes;

3) the proof for infinity from eminence together with Scotus' adaptation of the Anselmian argument. I will now consider these three parts in reverse order.

In the effort to reach the real thought of Scotus, I will try to take the Subtle Doctor at his best. Every philosopher, of course, always reserves to himself the right to disagree with another philosopher. But as Fr. Boehner used to say, one accomplishes little in disagreement in critique, if he takes his opponent at his worst. Straw men are easily constructed and knocked down. But in taking Scotus at his best, I do not wish to indulge in the practice of benignant interpretation, an art in which the medieval scholastics were well adept. Rather the text of Scotus and the inner coherence of his thought will be my guide.

As was already stated, Scotus' fifth argument for infinity proceeds from the nature of the first eminent being, the most perfect being which excells all other beings in perfection. The actual existence of such a being is proved in the first article of the Ordinatio question that has been under consideration. The proof for infinity based on the most eminent being is as follows:

> I argue that it is incompatible with the idea
> of a most perfect being that anything should
> excell it in perfection, as has been pre-
> viously explained. Now there is nothing in-
> compatible about a finite thing being ex-
> celled in perfection; therefore, etc. The
> minor is proved from this, that to be in-
> finite is not incompatible with being; but
> the infinite is greater than any finite being.(15)

Now it seems to me that essentialism enters into this argument in the proof for the minor: "to be infinite is not incompatible with being." How is this compatibility of being and infinity known? A rather clear answer to this question is given in the second formulation of the proof from eminence. Here it is asserted that the compatibility of being and infinity cannot be proven a priori.

For, just as contradictories by their very nature contradict each other and their opposition cannot be made manifest by anything more evident, so also these terms (viz. "being" and "infinite") by their very nature are not repugnant to each other. Neither does there seem to be any way of proving this except by explaining the meaning of the notions themselves. "Being" cannot be explained by anything better known than itself. "Infinite" we understand by means of finite. I explain "infinite" in a popular definition as follows: The infinite is that which exceeds the finite, not exactly by reason of any finite measure, but in excess of any measure that could be assigned. (16)

Now I wish to acknowledge that Scotus' explanation of the compatibility of being and infinity constitutes a real difficulty for one who rejects the essentialist interpretation of his proof. According to Fr. Owens, infinity is the operative notion and special characteristic of the Scotistic proof. By this Fr. Owens means that in the last analysis the actual existence of God is proven from the concept of infinite being. Thus actual existence plays no operative role in the proof for God. (17)

This view of Fr. Owens appears plausible when one considers the proof quoted above for infinity. Favorable to the essentialist view is that part of the proof which states that the only way of showing the compatibility of being and infinity is by explaining the notions themselves. If such an explanation for the possibility of an infinite being is really acceptable, then the Scotistic proof should be quite brief. It could be formulated in this way. An infinite being can actually exist, as is seen from a consideration of the notions of being and infinity. But the infinite cannot be caused. Therefore, the infinite being actually exists.

The proof for infinity from eminence is reenforced by a series of further arguments. All these arguments have the intent of showing the compatibility of being and infinity. (18) In the light of this compatibility, Scotus proceeds to touch up Anselm's argument in the Proslogion.

God is a being conceived without contradiction, and he is such that there would be a contradiction, if a greater being could be conceived. But since God is a being which can be conceived without contradiction, he can actually exist in reality. The greatest conceivable being, moreover, cannot exist merely in the intellect. For then the existence of this being would be simultaneously possible and not possible. The existence of this being would be possible, because it is conceivable without contradiction. The existence of this being would be impossible, because it cannot exist in virtue of some cause. Therefore, God, the greatest conceivable being, actually exists (19)

The argument which results from Scotus' touching up of the ratio Anselmi is substantially the same as the argument I have formulated above from the compatibility of being and infinity. The greatest conceivable being is possible, for it can be thought without contradiction. But it cannot be caused. Therefore, it actually exists.

Clearly this argument does not start with actual existence. Rather it starts with the notion of the greatest conceivable being, and points out that such a being cannot be caused, and then concludes to actual existence. No wonder then that Fr. Owens appeals to Scotus' adaptation of the Anselmian argument as testifying to the essentialism of his proof.

Now there can hardly be any doubt that Scotus accepts his own adaptation of the Anselmian argument. He presents it and does not reject it. But the all-important question still remains: how much value does the Subtle Doctor accord this argument? This question Fr. Owens does not face. But I submit that it is decisively important. For Scotus himself clearly indicates in the text that he does not consider all parts of his extended proof to be of equal value. Some arguments are introduced as confirming and persuasive arguments. Fr. Owens' complete neglect of this matter, I believe, undermines his entire interpretation of the Scotistic proof.

Scotus' adaptation of the Anselmian argument is presented in connection with a series of four persuasive arguments, showing the compatibility of being and infinity. While the Subtle Doctor labors to increase the convincing character of these arguments, still he himself calls them 'persuasive.' This epithet means that they have value, but are not altogether conclusive. After presenting these persuasive arguments, Scotus writes: "In this way Anselm's argument in the Proslogion about the highest conceivable good can be touched up." (20) Thus Scotus' own adaptation of the Anselmian argument appears to be persuasive. It has the status of a secondary and confirming argument in the entire Scotistic proof.

Here it should also be remembered that Duns Scotus, an original thinker though he is, is a man of tradition. Hence we should not be surprised that he interprets favorably in his own way Anselm's argument and gives it a place, albeit a secondary place, in his extended proof.

But now let us turn our attention back to the argument for infinity from eminence. This time may I take the liberty of recasting the argument and presenting it in syllogistic form thus:

> Every finite being is surpassable in perfection.
> But the most perfect being is not surpassable in perfection.
> Therefore the most perfect being is not finite.
> Therefore the most perfect being is infinite.

Now as far as the minor premise is concerned, this argument does not involve an essentialism. For the most perfect being spoken of has been previously proven actually to exist and to be such that it cannot be surpassed in perfection. (21) But essentialism does seem to enter the proof of the major premise. For every finite being is surpassable in perfection, because being and infinity are compatible, and the infinite surpasses every finite being.

Now the way of showing the compatibility of being and infinity constitutes the crux of the problem. An a priori proof for the compatibility is expressly excluded in the Ordinatio text. How then does Scotus show the compatibility? By a conceptual consideration of the notions themselves. As he puts it, "Neither does there seem to any way of proving this (the compatibility of being and infinity) except by explaining the meaning of the notions themselves." (22) This statement seems to exclude a proof for the possibility of an infinite being in some way grounded in experience.

But to me it seems that this statement must be understood in the context in which it is given. Now it is given by Scotus to prove the premise: every finite being is surpassable in perfection. This premise is as strong as its proof. But how strong is the proof? It seems quite clear from the succeeding persuasive arguments that Scotus does not consider the proof conclusive. In other words, showing the compatibility of being and infinity merely by explaining the meaning of the notions, this is not a conclusive proof for the real possibility of an infinite being. Duns Scotus says: "Just as anything is assumed to be possible, if its impossibility is not apparent, so also all things are assumed to be compatible, if their incompatibility is not manifest." (23) This statement occurs in an argument which Scotus labels 'persuasive.'

According to my understanding, the argument for infinity from eminence is not presented as a conclusive proof. The nature of the most perfect being as such does not necessarily imply infinity. If the possibility of an infinite being is assumed, then the most perfect being must be infinite. In this context, Scotus can only show the possibility of an infinite being by explaining the meanings of the notions of being and infinity. But in other contexts, in other arguments (the first and second arguments for an infinite being), the Subtle Doctor does not and does not have to show the possibility of an infinite being in this way.

It is true that in the Ordinatio Duns Scotus does not expressly label the argument for infinity from eminence 'persuasive.' Neither does he apply this label in the De Primo Principio, although the text seems to suggest it. (24) But there can be no doubt that Duns Scotus does not consider the proof from eminence as his main argument for infinity. His main argument is the one from the infinite intelligibles of the divine mind. For this argument makes use of the four conclusions established as preliminary to the proof for infinity. (25)

The essentialist interpretation does not face up to the fact that Scotus accords different parts of his proof different values. This interpretation also destroys the unity of the entire proof. Fr. Owens states that the arguments for infinity could logically have preceded the part which treats of the coalescence of the primacies of efficient causality, final causality, and eminence in one nature. (26) But really if the essentialist interpretation of the argument from eminence is correct, all the preceding parts become unnecessary. If showing the compatibility of being and infinity merely by a consideration of the notions is a conclusive proof for the real possibility of an infinite being, if the Scotistic adaptation of the Anselmian argument is conclusive, then Duns Scotus has a proof which reaches the infinite being in short order. But when a merely persuasive character is accorded these arguments, then they can be given their proper and secondary place in the long and protracted effort of Duns Scotus to reach the infinite being. In this way, the unity of the entire proof can be maintained.

While the essentialist interpretation destroys the unity of the Scotistic proof, it also conflicts with Scotus' own statements in the very question in which the proof is presented. In the beginning of his Ordinatio presentation of the proof, Scotus tells us the kind of proof he is attempting. "Although the proposition 'An infinite being exists' can, by the very nature of its terms, be demonstrated by a demonstration of the reasoned fact, we are not able to demonstrate it in this way. Nevertheless, we can demonstrate the proposition by a demonstration of fact beginning with creatures." (27) I submit that if the essentialist view is accepted, the Scotistic proof ceases to be "a demonstration of fact beginning with creatures."

Furthermore, the essentialist interpretation of Fr. Owens conflicts with the whole nature of Scotus' metaphysics conceived as the science of the transcendentals. In particular, this interpretation discords with the clear Scotistic doctrine on the disjunctive transcendentals and the special fecundity attributed to these notions by Scotus in providing demonstrations for the existence of God. This point is capable of extended development. But it will suffice here to quote from Duns Scotus the law of the disjunctive transcendentals, a law which lies at the very heart of his metaphysics:

> In the disjunctive attributes, however, while the entire disjunction cannot be demonstrated from "being," nevertheless as a universal rule by positing the less perfect extreme of some being we can conclude that the more perfect extreme is realised in some other being. Thus it follows that if some being is finite, then some being is infinite. And if some being is contingent, then some being is necessary. For in such cases it is not possible for the more imperfect extreme of the disjunction to be existentially predicated of "being," particularly taken, unless the more perfect extreme be existentially verified of some other being upon which it depends. (28)

It hardly needs to be noted here that to predicate existentially a more imperfect extreme of some particular being is to make a judgment based on experience. Thus according to Scotus, the proposition 'some being is infinite' can be concluded from the proposition 'some being is finite.' The latter proposition is a primary truth of fact and experience.

As was already stated, the fifth argument against infinite regress in essentially ordered causes provides another apparently clear basis for the essentialist interpretation. I quote the argument in full:

> Then, fifthly, inasmuch as to be able to produce something does not imply any imperfection, it follows that this ability can exist in something without imperfection, because that which implies no imperfection can be asserted of beings without imperfection. But if every cause depends upon some prior cause, then efficiency is never found without imperfection. Hence an independent power to produce something can exist in some nature, and this nature is <u>simply</u> first. Therefore, such an efficient power is possible, and this suffices, for later we shall prove that if such a first

efficient cause is possible, then it exists in reality. (29)

Clearly, this argument does not involve an appeal to the experience of some effect. Efficient causality simply does not imply imperfection. Hence a first or altogether independent efficient cause is possible. The possibility of a first efficient cause is established from the concept of efficient causality.

But here again the question to be asked is: how much value does Duns Scotus accord this argument. The Ordinatio does not label it persuasive, but the Reportata Parisiensia does. (30) Here too it is to be pointed out that if Duns Scotus would consider this argument alone conclusive in establishing the possibility of a first efficient cause, he could jettison everything which precedes it and some of the argumentation which follows it.

Finally now, I will consider the very first statement of the Scotistic proof: some being is effectible. For Fr. Owens, this statement clearly testifies to essentialism.

The proposition 'some being is effectible,' of course, is not an existential, empirical, or fact proposition. It asserts the possibility of a fact, namely, an effect. But what is the evidence for this proposition? What is its justification?

Expositors of Duns Scotus have explained that this proposition of the possible is inferred by immediate inference from the fact proposition, something is an effect. This inference is made on the basis of the axiom of modal logic: ab esse ad posse valet illatio. This explanation, I believe, agrees with the various texts of Scotus. In the De Primo Principio, the Franciscan Doctor asserts:

> In this conclusion, and in some of those which follow, I could argue in terms of the actual thus. Some nature is producing since some nature is produced, because some nature begins to exist, for some nature is contingent and the result of motion. But I prefer to propose conclusions and premises about the possible. For once those about the actual are granted, those about the possible are

also conceded, but the reverse is not the case. (31)

The Subtle Doctor does not say that we know an effect is possible merely by understanding the meanings of being and effect. On the contrary, his explanation is: "once those (conclusions and premises) about the actual are granted, those about the possible are also conceded, but the reverse is not the case." This last statement quite clearly indicates that the justification of the proposition asserting the possible existence of an effect is the axiom of modal logic: ab esse ad posse valet illatio; a posse ad esse no valet illatio.

One way of showing the possibility of something to exist is to explain its constituent intelligible elements. Scotus does not consider this a sure-fire method, at least in general. Otherwise, his adaptation of the Anselmian argument would be more than a persuasive argument. Another way of showing the possibility of something to exist is to infer its possibility from its actuality. Something shown to be possible in this way can be called a real possible to distinguish it from a possible shown to be such according to the preceding method. Another way of showing the possibility of something to exist is to show that it is a prior and necessary condition for some real possible. Such is the possibility of the first efficient cause to which Scotus concludes. This possibility can, likewise, be called a real possibility, because it is inferred from a real possible.

At this juncture, the question can be asked: why does Duns Scotus argue from the possible? The answer to this question is well known and given by Scotus in several places. He explains that by arguing from possibles he can argue from necessary premises and thus fulfill a requirement of Aristotelian demonstration. (32)

In commenting on this answer, Fr. Owens asserts that for Scotus actual existence does not enter the probative force of his argument. It can be disregarded and is really eliminated from the starting point of the proof. (33) It is true that in the very argument for the possibility of a first efficient cause no proposition of fact enters. At least such is the case in the Ordinatio presentation of

126

the argument. It begins with the proposition of the possible: some being is effectible. But Scotus comments on his
own argument and particularly on this proposition. The
comments form his answer to the objection that his argument
is not a demonstration. In these comments, Scotus clearly
shows his concern about the evidence and justification of
the proposition: some being is effectible. As I explained
before, the proposition of the possible is justified by an
inference from a proposition of fact. Once this justification is accepted or presupposed, actual existence can be
disregarded and eliminated from the proof for the possibility of a first efficient cause.

It is to be noted here that in the Lectura in Primum
Sententiarum, the argument for a first efficient cause is
first presented in the order of actual existence. It begins
with the proposition: some being is non-eternal. Later the
objection is faced that the argument is not a demonstration,
because it begins with a contingent premise. The proof is
then worked out in the order of possibility. (34)

In commenting on Scotus' use of possibles, Fr. Felix
Alluntis suggests that the Scotistic proof may perhaps be
more effective in practice, if it is presented on the existential level, as it is developed in the Lectura Prima.
For the Subtle Doctor clearly considers this presentation of
the proof evident and valid. (35) This suggestion no doubt
has its merits for non-specialists and also for some special-
ists. Indeed, the fulfillment of the Aristotelian ideal of
demonstration does not seem to be a preoccupation of many
contemporary philosophers. But an issue which is contemporary is the question of necessary knowledge. Is there
such a thing as necessary knowledge? If there is, what is
its range? Can any existential proposition be necessary?
In facing these questions, a contemporary thinker may be
considerably helped by studying Duns Scotus' extended proof
for the existence of an infinite being.

Before concluding this paper, it appears appropriate to restate the basic question before us: is Duns Scotus'
proof for the existence of an infinite being essentialist
or not? I can only answer this question by making a distinction. The expression 'essentialist proof' can be taken
in the sense of a proof which proceeds only from proposi-

tions of the possible. These propositions are shown to be true merely by explaining the meanings of the terms making up the proposition. In this sense, Duns Scotus' proof is not essentialist.

The expression 'essentialist proof' can be taken in the sense of a proof which also proceeds from propositions of the possible. But these propositions are shown to be true by immediate inference from propositions of fact and are ultimately grounded in experience. In the context of a total proof, a proof of this sort can be associated with arguments which proceeds from possibles known as such from the meaning of terms. But these arguments have only the status of secondary, probable, persuasive arguments. They do not enter the main line of the total proof. If the expression 'essentialist proof' is explained in this way, I believe that Scotus' extended proof can be called essentialist. One might object to this appellation, because of a possible confusion with an essentialist proof in the first sense. The Subtle Doctor himself calls his proof for the existence of an infinite being a demonstration of fact beginning with creatures.

It should also be added here that Scotus holds to the validity of a proof which proceeds from existential propositions. But neither the premises nor the conclusion of such a proof are necessary propositions, even though the premises may necessarily imply the conclusion.

In my limited assessment of Scotus' extended proof for the existence of an infinite being, I do not wish to give the impression that it is without defect and needs no improvement. The proof may involve certain difficulties, which are not revealed by considering it from the standpoint of essentialism. The Subtle Doctor himself reworked his proof perhaps more than three times and does not seem to be altogether satisfied with it. Nevertheless, it is a great proof, the like of which does not exist in all philosophical literature. One general lesson that can be learned from it is this. The Christian metaphysical patrimony is not restricted to two alternatives in the effort to reach God: a proof for the existence of God which presupposes a real distinction between essence and existence, or a proof which is purely conceptual with no grounding in experiences.

The proof of Duns Scotus as a historical fact precludes such an impoverishment of the Christian tradition in metaphysics.

FOOTNOTES

(1)   "Existential Import in the Philosophy of Duns
        Scotus", Franciscan Studies, IX (1949), 274-313.

(2)   See ALLAN B. WOLTER, The Transcendentals and Their
        Function in the Metaphysics of Duns Scotus (St.
        Bonaventure, N.Y.: The Franciscan Institute, 1946),
        66-7.

(3)   Being and Some Philosophers (Toronto, Canada: Pont-
        ifical Institute of Mediaeval Studies, 1952), 84-96.

(4)   JOSEPH OWENS, "The Special Characteristic of the
        Scotistic Proof that God Exists", Analecta Gregori-
        ana, LXVII (October, 1953), 314.

(5)   Ibid., 320, 322.

(6)   Ibid., 316.

(7)   Ord. I d. 2 p. 1 q. 1, II 150-65.

(8)   Ibid., 151: aliquod ens est effectibile.

(9)   Ibid., 158-9.

(10)   Ibid., 159-60.

(11)   Ibid., 153-6.

(12)   Ibid., 150-215.

(13)   Ibid., 206-11.

(14)   Art. cit., 312-321-2.

(15)   Ord. loc. cit., 206. The translation presented here
        is taken from Philosophical Writings John Duns Scotus,
        tr. Allan Wolter (N.Y.: The Bobbs-Merrill Co., 1964),
        75.

(16)   Ord. loc. cit., 206-7. Translation taken from op.
        cit., 75-6.

(17)   Art. cit., 320 322.

(18)   Ord. loc. cit., 207-8.

(19)   Ibid., 208-11.

(20)   Ibid., 208-9. Translation taken from op. cit., 77.

(21)   Ord. loc. cit., 167-8.

(22)   Ibid., 207. Translation from op. cit., 75-6.

(23)   Ord. loc. cit. Translation from op. cit., 75-6.

(24)   John Duns Scotus, A Treatise on God as First Prin-
         ciple, tr. Allan B. Wolter (Chicago: Franciscan
         Herald Press, 1966), 119-21.

(25)   Ord. loc. cit., 174. The argument from infinite
         motion also seems to be rated as conclusive by
         Scotus.

(26)   Art. cit., 322.

(27)   Loc. cit., 148. Translation from op. cit. (see foot-
         note 15), 40-1.

(28)   Ord. I d. 39 q. 1, VI Appendix A 414-5. Translation
         from op. cit., 9. Distinction 39 is certainly an
         authentic source of Duns Scotus' thought. Vide
         Adnotationes of volume VI of the Vatican edition,
         36*-30*.

(29)   Ord. I d. 2 p. 1 q. 1, II 158-9. Translation from
         op. cit., 46-7.

(30)   Rep. Par. I d. 2 q. 2, XXII 65: Ad hoc etiam induxi
         duas persuasiones....Secunda est, esse effectivum
         nullam imperfectionem importat de se.

(31)   John Duns Scotus, A Treatise on God as First Prin-
         ciple, tr. Allan B. Wolter (Chicago: Franciscan
         Herald Press, 1966), 42-3.

(32)   Ord. loc. cit., 161; Rep. Par. loc. cit., 64-6;
        Lectura in Primum Librum Sententiarum I d. 2 p. 1
        q. 1, XVI 131-2; see footnote 31.

(33)   Art. cit., 315-6.

(34)   Loc. cit., 126-32.

(35)   "Demonstrability and Demonstration of the Existence
        of God", John Duns Scotus, 1265-1965, ed. John K.
        Ryan and Bernardine M. Bonansea (Washington, D.C.:
        The Catholic University of America Press, 1965),
        169-70.

Discussion

ALLAN WOLTER, O.F.M., PH.D.

Professor of Philosophy
Catholic University of America
Washington, D.C.

As Father Effler has well said there is an acceptable
and an inacceptable sense in which Scotus' proof of an
infinte being might be called essentialist. The acceptable
sense is that in which any basic answer to a question of the
form "Quid est?" (e.g. 'What is this?') could be said to be
giving some essential property or characteristic of the thing
in question. Putting it another way, we could say: Scotus
picks out what is essential or invariant about any actual
contingent fact or situation, viz. its possibility. In this
sense his proof for God's existence is essentialistic since
it consists in working out through a reductive analysis what
is required as a necessary or sine qua non condition of such
a real possibility, viz. the actual existence of an infinite
God.

The inacceptable sense is the claim of Father Owens
that no factual or existential data play an operative role
in the proof. It is this claim that Father Effler has
challenged and has shown in detail that Scotus is no metaphysical magician pulling real or live rabbits from a factual empty hat.

We could say there are three points at which factual
or existential information is injected either explicitly
or by implication into the Scotist proof. The first is the
fact of contingency or change that allows him to infer that
something can be produced. Father Effler has elaborated
this point at some length in his paper.

The second is the point brought up by Father John
Joseph Lakers yesterday evening in his discussion of Dr.
Cresswell's paper, viz. what Scotus requires for any notion
or essential description to be meaningful. One cannot
simply lump conceptual elements together and claim that the
combination is meaningful and that consequently it represents a 'real essence,' e.i. something that could without
contradiction be said to exist in the extramental or real
world. Any non-simple notion like 'rational animal' or
conceptual construct like 'the class of all classes' requires proof that it is not 'false in itself' (in se falsum),
proof that it does not contain incompatible elements so that
to assert it of some subject is equivalent to asserting
contradictory statements. Here Scotus has in mind the words
of Aristotle: "That is false as a thing which either is not

put together or cannot be put together, e.g. 'that the diagonal of a square is commensurate with the side' or 'that you are sitting'; for one of these is false always and the other sometimes; It is in these two senses that they are nonexistent." (Metaphysics, Bk. V, c. 29 1024b 17-22). For Scotus only irreducibly simple notions are self-justifying as it were. That is, one either has such a notion or not. And since such ideas cannot be derived by any inferential process from other better known notions, for only what is not irreducibly simple can proved to exist, one must have at some time encountered something or experienced a situation that gave rise to such conceptions. In Ordinatio I, distinction 2, n. 26 in the course of his discussion of whether a proposition such as "An infinite being exists" or "God exists" is self-evident, Scotus insists that none of our notions that are peculiar or proper to God are irreducibly simple. On the contrary, they are conceptual constructs whose meaningfulness must first be justified before one can appeal to them as evidence for the analyticity of any proposition in which they occur.

Evidence that any composite concept or conceptual construct is not "false in itself" or meaningless takes two forms for Scotus. The first and most obvious form of evidence is to find some object or situation that fits the concept in question (Oportet cognoscere partes rationis subiecti et praedicati uniri actualiter, ibid. n. 30). From the fact that such features are found to coexist, one can argue there is nothing incompatible about their combination and hence a concept constructed of such intelligible elements is not in se falsum. A second form of evidence that such complex concepts are meaningful would be any cogent proof of the compatibility of its elements. Such would be the case, if unio istarum partium demonstratur (n.29). If this can be done, then we no longer have what may just be a meaningless construct but an instance of what Scotus calls conceptus conclusi per modum complexionis (Collatio 13, n. 4, Opera omnia, ed. Vives, v. 5, p. 202). That is to say, if we have concluded to the truth of a certain proposition in virtue of some reasoning process, the subject and predicate of the conclusion can be combined as a single term. Assuming the conclusion to be true, it follows that the complex term is what Scotus calls a concept in the technical sense of that term. And this brings us to the third point where factual information is introduced into the Scotist proof, viz, in what he says about "infinite being" being a genuine concept.

In the so-called <u>coloratio</u> <u>rationis</u> <u>Anselmi</u>, we have
the genius of the Subtle Scot at its best. Since no proper
concept of God is <u>per</u> <u>se</u> <u>notum</u>, Anselm's argument, as he
interprets it, would not be what contemporary philosophers
would call a priori or 'ontological.' In fact, one could say,
it begins with what Anselm believed to be a fact of experience,
that the notion he had of God as "that than which a greater is
inconceivable" is a concept in the technical sense of that
term. At least that is how Scotus interprets him.

What is peculiar about the Aristotelian theory of
intellect to which Scotus subscribes is that it rejects the
possibility of the mind retaining contradictory opinions at
one and the same time (Cf. <u>Metaphysics</u>, Bk. 4, c. 3 1005b 23-
24; also Scotus, <u>Ordinatio</u> I, dist. 3, n. 231). In similar
fashion, Scotus argues that the mind cannot conceive incompatible elements at one and the same time. It may oscillate
between conceiving the one and then the other. One may even
give a name to something like a "square-circle," etc. and to
that extent one may speak of it as having a <u>quid</u> <u>nominis</u>,
but there is no true <u>quid</u> <u>rei</u> involved. One cannot "conceive
of it without contradiction." Contrariwise, if one can be
sure that one has a true idea or concept in the technical
sense of the term, one can be sure by definition that the
conceptual elements of the concept are not incompatible.
Consequently, Scotus' contention is that a genuine concept
of 'infinite being' is possible, i.e. these two notions do not
contradict each other: 1) <u>ens</u>, <u>hoc</u> <u>est</u> <u>cui</u> <u>non</u> <u>repugnat</u> <u>esse</u>
and 2) <u>infinitum</u>. The first includes the idea that the indi-
vidual subjects of which it can be predicated are able to
exist in the real or extramental world. The second excludes
by implication the idea that the subject in question could be
caused. If this combination is a true concept, i.e. conceivable without contradiction, then from this fact--note
Scotus considers this to be a fact that one can in principle
show to be true or false--it would follow that the concept
in question entails as a necessary condition of its existence
as a mental state (<u>qualitas</u>) the actual existence of God.

The argument here is similar in many respects to
Descartes' a posteriori proof, viz. that from the fact that
we have an idea of God as infinitely perfect and that this is
a positive notion and not just a negative concept of infinity
combined with the notion of thing (Scotus would add the
qualification that it must be not only positive but simple
and irreducibly simple at that); its origin as a mental state

in the human mind cannot be explained in terms of any encounter with experiential date or through any act of introspection of one's mental states for such are finite and imperfect. Hence, it must be something caused immediately by
God. Descartes' argument, note, is a causal one, and if one
grants the initial assumption--viz. that one has such a concept and is not simply deceived about what he does have--the
argument is valid. It is a straightforward argument from an
effect to a cause capable of accounting for the same. The
same point is made by Scotus here and, if his interpretation
of Anselm is correct, it was in Anselm's mind also, viz. that
our concept of God from which his existence follows by logical entailment is a genuine concept, i.e. does not contain
incompatible or self-negating elements. For the argument
boils down to this. One asserts of one and the same subject
that 1) it is capable of existing in the extramental world,
and 2) that it is not caused, and hence cannot be actually
non-existent or merely virtually existent in some actually
existing cause which could conceivably bring it into
existence.

Where Anselm assumes at the outset of his argument
that we have such a concept, and in his answer to Gaunilo
gives reasons for assuming the same, Scotus recognizes that
one must prove 'infinite being' is truly conceivable. His
proof that it is such, and hence is not a meaningless word,
rests on what he regards as a psychological fact, viz. that
the mind does not 'abhor' such a notion as the ear abhors
dissonance, but rather reaches out for such a notion and is
not satisfied with anything short of it. Whether he be
right or wrong, one thing is clear. Scotus was not excluding factual evidence from his 'coloratio' of the Anselmian
argument and by the same token was not presenting it as an
empty notion or factually asceptic idea from which the
existence of God might be inferred.

FATHER ANTONELLUS OSTDIEK, O.F.M., upon comple-
tion of graduate studies at the Pontificium
Athenaeum Antonianum in Rome, has been Profes-
sor of Dogmatic Theology and Liturgy at St.
Joseph Seminary, Teutopolis, Illinois. His
doctoral dissertation was entitled
Disquisitio comparativa in prologos Lecturae
Oxoniensis et Ordinationis I. D. Scoti.

SCOTUS and Fundamental Theology

ANTONELLUS OSTDIEK, O.F.M., S.T.D.

Introduction

In order to bring the topic of this paper (1) into focus, let me begin by saying that the term "fundamental theology" is used in the title in a rather generic sense. This discipline has included such a variety of elements in the past, such as apologetics and various elements of theories of knowledge and of ecclesiologies, and there is so much renewal going on in this field at present that a clear-cut definition can hardly be given. In general, if theology itself is the endeavor of the reflecting Christian to know and penetrate his faith, then fundamental theology is that endeavor initially reflecting on itself, attempting to lay down the foundations it needs. It will thus consider such topics as the philosophical and theological presuppositions, the sources of theological knowledge and the modes of its transmission, and something of the nature, subject, task, and method of the theological endeavor. What I have in mind, then, is not merely an apologetic, but rather an introduction to theology. (2)

To sharpen the focus a bit more, our concern is not Scotus and our fundamental theology, but Scotus and his fundamental theology. If Scotus is to speak today, we can not simply transplant him into our age, nor can we ask him our questions. We must rather allow him to speak for himself, that is, we must listen to him as he speaks to his own age, careful to accept his discourse on its own terms and merits, alert nevertheless for any crossing of the ways which he may have passed by unnoticed and which might open up to us new and unexplored paths, to use Rahner's figure of speech. (3) Only in this way can we truly philosophize or theologize with him in a way that will enable him to speak and guide our endeavors today.

At the outset, we ought to mention that Scotus has made himself heard in this way in recent years. For he has received attention, whether exclusively or in passing, in a

number of authors who have recently taken a fresh, historical approach to several of the perennial themes of fundamental theology. In regard to the philosophical aspects,
covering a cluster of questions including the relation between philosophy and theology, the relation of nature and
supernature, the object of the intellect, the theory of
knowledge, etc., we might mention the work done by Balic,
Wolter, Gilson, O Huallachain, and especially Vignaux. (4)
Questions relative to tradition and the sufficiency of
Scripture have been treated by Bakhuizen van den Brink, de
Vooght, Geiselmann, Oberman, Rosato, and Buytaert. (5) The
problem of faith and its apologetic in Scotus has been cast
in a new dimension by Aubert and Lang. (6) Finally, special mention should be made of the work of Josef Finkenzeller, Offenbarung und Theologie nach der Lehre des Johannes Duns Skotus. (7) In addition to covering most of
the above points, Finkenzeller's historical-systematic
study does a sympathetic job of organizing Scotus' thought
into an organic whole very much akin to some of the recent
trends in fundamental theology.

   Without intending to depreciate the many contributions
made by these studies, I would like to take a somewhat
different approach in this paper. Rather than canvas the
whole of Scotus' writings for his doctrine on particular
themes of fundamental theology, rather than construct such
themes into a scotistic fundamental theology, faithful to
Scotus though it be, I prefer to try to sketch his fundamental theology as Scotus himself elaborated it. Now, in
medieval school theology the prologue to the first book of
the commentaries on the Sentences of Peter Lombard served
as fundamental theology, or the introduction to theology.
Therefore it is to the prologue that we ought to look to
discover the contents and especially the thought-structure
of their fundamentals. This is what this paper on Scotus
proposes to do in an exploratory way.

Philosophical setting

Let us begin by recalling something of the background
in which Scotus wrote his prologue. At the end of the
thirteenth century the university world, far from being a
closed, static world, was open and alive to a wide variety
of influences. In the course of the century before Scotus,
Aristotle had made the last and most influential of his
"entrances" into the West. (8) In the first part of that
period his more philosophical works (physical, metaphysical,
psychological, ethical) had made their way into Latin
through the Jewish and Arab commentators; not long after-
wards they were translated directly from the Greek.
The impact of these works was far from being spent at the
time of Scotus; the assimilation of Aristoteliansim by
Christianity was still far from being complete. To be
sure, it can be said that the medieval theologians of this
period were commonly Aristotelians, due to the pattern of
their course of studies, (9) which gave them a thorough
acquaintance with Aristotle, a common language, many common
ideas and patterns of thought. Nonetheless, there were
endless degrees of acceptance and varieties of interpretation of Aristotle, all the way to the extreme form known as
Averroism, an exaggerated rationalism that claimed for itself complete independence and superiority over theology.
It was this Averroism that rocked the university world and
split it into warring factions, the philosophers and the
theologians, and finally evoked the condemnation of 1277.
(10)

Theological milieu

The scholastics of that period also enjoyed a common
fund of theological knowledge, drawn from the Scriptures
and the patristic writings as presented to them in the form
of various encyclopedic collections, especially the Sentences of Lombard, the common theology "manual" of that
time. But once again, there was no straight-laced uniformity in their theological formation. The Sentences actually

imposed no more than an accepted order of presentation for the most part. (11) In addition to the variety of positions taken within the commentaries on the Sentences, there was also a wealth of theological discussion and development in both the frequent ordinary disputations (quaestiones disputatae) and the extraordinary disputations (disputationes de quolibet). And all of this was constantly enriched by a free-flowing exchange of professors and students between the great universities.

The task at hand

Faced with a new-found Aristotelian philosophy with its consistent, completely rational view of man and nature and its theory of knowledge, and working in a vigorous theological milieu, the theologians had set about the task of reconciling and harmonizing that philosophy with the ancient Christian Faith, the task of elaborating a new theological synthesis. One of the most ambitious and complete attempts to date, that of St. Thomas, had been drawn into the wake of the condemnation of 1277 because of an affinity to some of the condemned propositions. For the time being his work had been put aside, (12) and the task of constructing the new Christian synthesis had to be undertaken anew. It was to this unfinished business that Scotus, like Henry of Ghent, Godfrey of Fontaines, and so many others of his day, addressed himself.

It is against this background that we must view the work of Scotus in attempting to understand his fundamental theology. The question then, is how did Scotus introduce his audience to theology as he set about elaborating his commentary on the Sentences in a world of theology at once unsettled, alive with a constant flow of discussion and dispute, profuse in ideas, searching for a new synthesis? What type of prologue did he write? At this point it becomes particularly relevant to note that in the prologue, which was presented with a greater degree of solemnity at the beginning of the school year, the commentator apparently enjoyed complete freedom as regards both the length of treatment and the choice of content. (13) In view of the fluid state of all theology, the prologue would then become a most promising area for theological initiative and

development, and eminently worthy of examination as it
stands.

THE PROLOGUES OF SCOTUS

Various forms

Actually, Scotus has left us more than one prologue.
The manuscripts containing a prologue to the first book of
the commentary have been classified into seven forms: the
Lectura in librum primum Sententiarum, the Ordinatio,
Reportationes I A through I D, and the Additiones Magnae.
(14) As far as the questions treated in these prologues
are concerned, these prologues can be further reduced to
two forms. The Lectura and the Ordinatio prologues have
the same set of questions, with the exception of the addition of question two in the Ordinatio (call these set II).
The prologues of the Reportationes and the Additiones
Magnae all have a different, essentially uniform set of
questions (set I). It seems to me that these two sets of
questions for the prologue manifest notably different
thought-patterns when placed side by side.

The questions found in the Reportationes, at least the
first, more elaborated questions, seems to follow an
abstract logical progression moving from general to particular. The first three questions ask whether there can be a
science which treats of God under the precise aspect of his
being God, whether man is able to know such truths about
God as God, and whether man can arrive at all truths about
God from natural things. The following question and the
final one deal with the scope of theology, and the remaining questions concern the oneness of theology and its
relation to other sciences. (15)

The questions of the other set (the Lectura and Ordinatio) are grouped into five parts in the Vatican edition.
The first part treats of the necessity of revelation.
Part two, which is missing in the Lectura, asks whether the
revelation necessary is sufficiently contained in Scripture.
Part three consists of three questions concerning the object and scope of theology. Part four has two brief questions about the scientific character of theology. The last
part seeks to determine if theology is practical or

speculative. (16)

The first impression one gets from this second set of
questions is that there has been a change of thought-
pattern from the first set, that of the Reportationes. (17)
And even though a further, detailed comparision reveals
that much more of the material of the first set has been
incorporated into the second type of prologue than a mere
comparative listing of the questions might lead one to
believe, the impression of a difference of thought-
pattern persists. This change, it seems to me, is not
simply the adoption of a different but equally abstract
pattern, such as the one which was also quite prevalent in
prologues of that time, viz. the division of the prologue
according to the four causes of Aristotle. (18) I believe
it is possible to find indications that the second type of
prologue is developing a thought-pattern that might be
called more organic, more discursive, more actual.

Dates of the Lectura and Ordinatio

Before going into a detailed analysis of this second
type of prologue, we ought to touch on the relative dating
of the two prologues in question.

The Ordinatio, a redaction that Scotus was preparing
for publication, is the last of Scotus' commentaries. In
general it depends on the Reportationes of the Paris
lectures, (19) which were begun in 1302, and therefore it
postdates them. According to contemporary practice,
Scotus probably worked on this redaction at the time of or
after his inception as master. (20) This would date it
roughly to 1305. The Ordinatio prologue itself yields no
internal evidence for a more exact determination of its own
date of composition, except for the well-known reference to
the crusade battle of Medjamaa el-Moroudji, December 23,
1299, in the second part. (21)

The Lectura antedates the Ordinatio, since the Ordinatio depends on it, (22) but an exact date can hardly be
given for the Lectura as yet. The difficulty lies in dating the Oxford lectures on the Sentences which it represents. I believe the most promising argument up to now, in
spite of its need of further clarification, is one from ex-

ternal evidence. It is based on the fact that Scotus took part in a disputation of Philip of Bridlington, who was regent master at Oxford in 1300-1301. (23) The exact nature of this disputation, whether it was Philip's magistral inception itself or a subsequent ordinary disputation during his regency, as also the nature of Scotus' role in the disputation, has not yet been definitively established. In accordance with the somewhat later statutes of Oxford University (pre-1350), two possible dates emerge: first, Scotus commented on the Sentences in the scholastic year 1297-1298 or 1298-1299 if the disputation in question is Philip's inception; (24) or second, in the scholastic year beginning in either 1300 or 1301 if it is an ordinary disputation. (25) The first possibility (c. 1298) seems more likely to me. (26)

There was, then, an interval of possibly as many as eight years during which this second type of prologue could develop from its prototype, the "primitive, pristine form" found in the Lectura, (27) into its more mature and elaborated form in the Ordinatio. I believe that the advanced structuring of the Ordinatio prologue, which I shall now try to trace, is one of the most significant aspects of this development and gives a certain uniqueness to Scotus' introduction to theology as found in its final stage of development in the Ordinatio.

THE PROLOGUE OF THE ORDINATIO

Part one

The prologue of the Ordinatio opens with what was one of the most burning issues of the day: the fight between the theologians and philosophers (the Averroists) over the necessity of supernatural revelation, (28) and, consequently, of theology. Admittedly, Scotus is not the first of his age to ask the question whether man in his present state has need of supernatural revelation. (29) What is new is the tone of actuality he gives the issue in his treatment and the masterly, painstaking manner in which he sets up the confrontation between the two positions.

In attempting to resolve the dispute, Scotus concedes what is valid in each position. Ultimately his own posi-

tion is that of the theologians. He accepts their three
most cogent arguments for the necessity of revelation: (30)
first, man's actual destiny (sharing eternally in the inner
life of the Trinity through knowledge and love) can not be
known from human nature and its capacities, since it is
based on God's free design of calling man to this higher
end; (31) second, the means to this end, their necessity
and sufficiency, are likewise unknowable from nature, since
the means necessary and sufficient on man's part are those
acts of man which God has freely chosen to accept as merit-
ing the end; (32) third, neither can man naturally come to
know pure spirits as he must (especially God as the beatify-
ing object). (33) Hence, for these three reasons man needs
a supernatural revelation. But Scotus is quick to point out
to the theologians that these arguments do not really prove
the necessity of revelation. They are merely persuasions,
based themselves on something accepted in faith. (34) For
as the philosophers are quick to rejoin, (35) an end above
nature can not be demonstrated by a reasoning process. The
best a theologian can prove is that one half of this disjunction must be true: the beatific vision of God is or is
not the final end of man. The theologians' proofs for the
first member turn out to be theological persuasions. (36)

To the philosophers, then, Scotus admits that the
necessity of a supernatural revelation can not be proved on
their terms. But he disagrees with them when they maintain
that nature is sufficient of itself to achieve its entire
perfection, (37) and that the so-called supernatural end, to
which man admittedly has a capacity, is really only natural
and can be discovered from an examination of nature and its
capacities. (38) Defining supernatural in relation to our
present fallen state, (39) Scotus concedes that man has a
natural capacity for supernatural perfection in as much as
he is able to receive such a perfection, but insists that
it is supernatural in the sense that it is not within man's
nature to be able to actively attain this perfection. (40)
As he puts it in regard to the final end, "concedo Deum
esse finem naturalem hominis, sed non naturaliter adipiscen-
dum sed supernaturaliter." (41) Furthermore, this natural
capacity is unknowable, (42) and hence the necessity of a
supernatural revelation if man in his fallen state is to
learn about his supernatural end. With this clarification

in mind of what he means by supernatural, Scotus then goes on to define what supernatural revelation is (43) and to explain to the philosophers how supernatural knowledge occurs in the human mind in accord with his theory of knowledge. (44)

This is a brief, and I hope representative, summary of the very complex argumentation of the first question. There are a number of related areas that simply can not be explored further here--Scotus' notion of revelation; his metaphysics of supernatural knowledge derived by applying his theory of knowledge to faith; the problem of the adequate object of the intellect (on which he adopts a theological position); the states of man, etc. Enough has been said to enable us to isolate the initial steps of thought in Scotus' prologue. I believe there is something of a double step here. The main step is this: Scotus sets out to establish the necessity of supernaturally revealed knowledge. To show this, Scotus argues from man's need as a rational being to know his final end. But in order to make this step acceptable to the philosophers, he has to go back a step, to explain the idea of the supernatural in a way acceptable to them, and thus, in effect, show them the possibility (from man's side) of the supernatural in general and of supernatural revelation and supernatural knowledge in particular.

Part two

The prologue then continues with part two, which contains one question: whether the supernatural knowledge necessary for the wayfaring man is sufficiently transmitted in Sacred Scripture. (45) This part of the prologue of the Ordinatio has a lot of vexing but intriguing aspects which will have to be skimmed over here. First, as far as I can ascertain up to now, this is the first time this question appears in any of the medieval commentaries or quaestiones disputatae; (46) indeed, it seems to appear only this one time in the writings of Scotus himself (it was lacking in the Lectura, the primitive form of the Ordinatio). The other topics treated in the prologue, on the contrary, were widely discussed at that time. Second, as already indicated, the date of this question can be quite accurately fixed to

the year 1300/1301, a number of years before the revision
of the Ordinatio. But this raises the difficulty of a
seeming lack of revision in certain parts of this question.
Third, compared to the rest of the prologue, this part
seems to fall short of the level of refinement and maturity
of the other parts as regards its literary style, its
spirit, and the internal structuring of its contents. (47)
To describe the contents briefly: as far as the structuring
is concerned, the contents seem to fall into two more or
less distinct units. The question and the opening arguments pro and con, the brief solution of the question, and
the response to the opening arguments constitute one unit.
(48) The other unit consists of the body of the question,
which comes between the opening arguments and the solution.
(49) The first unit deals directly with the question itself, if Scripture sufficiently contains the revelation
necessary for man. It gives a solution that is very
obviously correlated with the first part of the prologue,
with the three arguments of the theologians accepted as
valid. That is, the solution affirms that Scripture does
sufficiently teach the wayfaring man what he needs to know
about his last end, the means necessary and sufficient to
attain it, and something about immaterial beings. (50) The
body of the question, on the other hand, consists of ten
apologetic arguments given to prove the divine origin of
the Scriptures, the "truth of the doctrine of the Canon,"
in the terminology of Scotus. (51) The problem here is
that the text does not give an express indication of how
Scotus intended to unify into one part two related but
apparently distinct units. (52) Still, it is entirely
logical to presuppose that there is a connected line of
thought. Since Scotus apparently composed an entirely new
type of question about a topic certainly not discussed very
widely, if at all, and incorporated this into the prologue
of the Ordinatio, he must have intended to fill a gap he
saw in the Lectura in his line of thought. It is essential, then, that this part be taken in relation to the
other parts, especially the first one, in order to discover its internal unity.

The main point of part one had been to establish the
necessity of revelation on the basis of the three accepted
arguments. This necessity, however, allows no inference to

151

the fact. Scotus had very pointedly reminded the theologians that these arguments take their starting point from the contents of revelation. (53) Hence, we can add, they presuppose the fact of revelation, and any attempt to use these same arguments to eventually infer back to the fact of revelation would be to argue in a vicious circle.

It is in the ten apologetic arguments of the body of the second question that the substantiation of this fact of revelation can be found, at least implicitly. As mentioned earlier, these ten arguments are proposed in order to prove the divine origin of Scripture. This is actually a double statement which affirms that God spoke what is narrated in Scripture, as the third apologetic argument words it. (54) Thus these apologetic reasons have a double role in the thought-process, to show that God has de facto given a supernatural revelation, and that that revelation is contained in Scripture. Once this double step has been taken, Scotus can then move on to the solution of the original question of the second part, whether Sacred Scripture sufficiently contains those revealed truths that part one had shown to be necessary for the wayfarer.

It may well be that Scotus did not consciously intend to substantiate the fact of revelation, as suggested above. Together with his contemporaries he may simply have taken the fact for granted. In that case, the progression of thought would be: part one: the necessity (and possibility) of revelation; part two, in corpore: the fact that Scripture actually contains the revelation necessary; part two, in the solution: the fact that Scripture sufficiently contains the necessary revelation. The substantiation of the fact of revelation in the body of part two would then be implicit, rather than reflex. Be that as it may, I believe the progress of thought sketched for the first two parts would still remain valid in its essentials.

With that the first two parts are formed into an organic whole and the gap between parts one and three can be bridged. But before going on to part three, I would like to take up two issues that have been introduced relative to the second part by the authors mentioned at the beginning.

Digression

First, there is the manner in which some have interpreted this question as supporting a theory of the material
sufficiency of Scripture. (55) Others have already commented at length on this interpretation. (56) Suffice it to
say that this is simply not the same question as our question. (57) Scotus was not concerned with whether Scripture
contains all revealed truths. Likewise, the suggestion
that Scotus was here substituting a sufficiency of moral
precepts for doctrinal sufficiency (58) seems inadmissable
to me. The related problem of the concept of tradition
might also be mentioned here. (59) I would agree with
Buytaert's analysis, that the word tradition, whether in
the substantive or verb form, has its etymological rather
than our technical meaning in Scotus. (60) This meaning
is then further specified by each context. Consequently,
we can not without further examination of the context
attribute to Scotus a Tridentine usage of tradition and
traditions, whether this be in the pre-Geiselmann interpretation of Trent or in the newer interpretation. I
would rather suspect that there are elements of both view-
points present, without a conscious attempt on the part of
Scotus to analyze or harmonize them. (61)

Second, an area suggested by the research of Aubert
and Lang has to be mentioned here. It seems that Scotus
here brings together into new focus a number of lines of
development regarding faith and its apologetic. It was in
the course of the thirteenth and fourteenth centuries that
apologetics gradually emerged from its theological surround-
ings in the tract on faith in book three of the commentaries
on the Sentences. It first received separate treatment in a
number of treatises, but eventually found its way into the
prologue of the commentary. (62) The key figures in the
early attempts to work out a more or less systematic apologetic for the faith are William of Auxerre, William of
Auvergne, and William Peraldus. (63) Their apologetic
consists of two steps: first, there is only one true faith;
second: that faith is the Christian Faith. As proof of
this second statement, they adduced various apologetic
arguments of the type still familiar today. (64) The
development begun by these men found its most fruitful

continuation within the Franciscan School, especially the so-called middle school. The two most important names here are Bartholomew of Bologna and Matthew of Aquasparta, through whom the fledgling **apologetics** was first introduced into the school disputations. (65) Their ideas were presented in their quaestiones disputatae de fide in the late 1270's. To the earlier two-step apologetic they prefixed another step: that it is necessary for salvation to believe something unattainable by natural reason. (66) From this point the lines of development to Scotus become somewhat obscure. I believe they might be able to be traced through a number of Friars, Raymund Rigaldus, Jacques du Quesnoy, and Vital du Four; but to try to delineate the connections too sharply would be premature. (67) This would bring us up to Scotus' presumed period of theological study in Paris. Henry of Ghent's long introduction to his Summae Quaestionum Ordinariarum would also have to be taken into account.

The suggestion that the first two parts of Scotus' prologue represent a culmination of these threads of development (68) does not seem accurate, if taken in the sense that his prologue contains the same type of apologetic arguments in part two correspond in part to those found in Bartholomew and Matthew; (69) Henry of Ghent uses apologetic arguments (different ones) to prove the divine origin of Scripture; (70) the first step in the three-step apologetic of Bartholomew and Matthew is quite similar to Scotus' first question on the necessity of revelation, etc. Nevertheless, the total thought-structure is different. It is interesting to think that he might well have taken his inspiration from that apologetic and adapted its structure to his own use. Instead of the necessity of faith, he speaks of the necessity of supernaturally revealed knowledge in view of the problem facing his audience. Instead of the oneness of faith and the presence of that faith in Christianity, he speaks of the presence of revelation in Scripture, and then its sufficient presence there. The apologetic arguments are also used in a different way. They now form an apologetic for the divine origin of Scripture, whereas the immediate Franciscan predecessors had used them as an apologetic for the Christian Faith. We might add that the discussion on faith is more along the lines of a metaphysics of supernatural knowledge, as indicated earlier. The theological treatment of faith has still been left to book three. (71)

Parts three to five

To return to the main line of thought in Scotus' prologue so far we have isolated the essential steps in the thought-process of the first two parts, from the necessity of revelation to its being sufficiently contained in Scripture. This progression, I believe, is relatively apparent. From this point on, the continuation of this line of thought becomes quite obscure and difficult to establish as a conscious plan on the part of Scotus. There are, however, a few hints as to the direction to take.

The general topics of the last three parts do not offer much of a lead at first sight. Part three devotes three questions to the object of theology, asking if God is its first object; if so, under what aspect; and if theology concerns other things in relation to God. Part four in a very brief fashion dicusses theology as a science: whether the theology of God and the Blessed is a science, and whether it is a subordinating or subordinated science. The fifth part goes into great detail about the nature of praxis and practical science before taking up its second question, whether theology is a practical science.

There are, however, a number of underlying themes which tie these parts together in harmony with the thought-pattern described thus far. Many of these themes, such as the infinity of God, the doctrines of formal non-identity and divine ideas, the notion of the first object of the intellect and of science, etc., have already been discussed at some length by Gilson and Vignaux. (72) The point to be noted here is that Scotus views God's knowledge of himself and his decrees as the perfect theological knowledge. (73) It is a perfect, immediate and intuitive knowledge of his own essence and of all other beings in it. (74) God has decided to communicate this knowledge in varying degrees, to the Blessed and to man on earth. (75) The share in his knowledge that God has offered to man is to be found in public revelation, in Scripture. The truths contained in Scripture and those that can be elicited from these form

155

the subject of our theology. "Terminus autem praefixus a
voluntate divina, quantum ad revelationem generalem, est
illorum quae sunt in Scriptura divina...Igitur theologia
nostra de facto non est nisi de his quae continentur in
Scriptura, et de his quae possunt elici ex eis." (76)
Here, I believe, we find the thought-pattern continuing on
from the earlier steps of the necessity of revelation and
the sufficient presence of the necessary revelation in
Scripture. For what Scripture does is give us a share in
God's theological knowledge about himself and all else in
relation to him. Hence the truths contained in Scripture
or deducible therefrom form the content of our theology.
With that, the prologue has bridged over to the nature and
task of theology. Theology is conceived of as existing on
various levels with a communication or sharing from the
highest level to the lower ones. (77) By implication the
task of theology is to plumb the Scriptures for the truths
latent there. (78)

Part four continues: theology, though not a science in
the strict Aristotelian sense of the word, is the highest
wisdom. (79) And part five adds: it is a practical knowledge that is to lead man to his final end of the vision
and loving contemplation of God. With this, the thought-
structure of the prologue has come full circle. Beginning
with the final end of man, the prologue concluded to the
revelation necessary, its sufficient presence in Scripture,
its scope and nature as theology, a practical wisdom meant
to lead man to that end. There are other themes which
might be garnered from the prologue, such as the various
philosophical presuppositions, the various roles within
tradition, etc. To my mind, the thought-pattern that seems
to be taking shape in the Ordinatio is one of the most
significant facets of the prologue.

THE PROLOGUE OF THE LECTURA

General comparision with the Ordinatio

A comparision of the Ordinatio prologue with its prototype in the Lectura tends to confirm the suggestion that an
organic progression of thought is emerging in the Ordinatio.

This is not to say that Scotus radically altered the type
of matter treated or reversed his opinions in the Ordinatio.
(80) On the contrary, the Ordinatio builds on the Lectura,
there is a close parallel between the two prologues. The
list of questions treated is the same, except for the one
addition; the solutions follow the same general line of
thought; and most of the material of the Lectura has been
retained and incorporated into the Ordinatio prologue.
Thus there is a basic continuity between the two prologues.

This continuity, however, is not simply one of sameness.
With the Ordinatio we have reached a new level of development. This new level is due, not to radical changes, but
to the refinement and expansion of existing materials and
to the addition of new matter that carries the line of
thought further. (81) It is precisely these improvements
and additions that very frequently seem to give evidence
of the newly emerging thought-pattern. Thus the Lectura
negatively, by what it has not yet said. For that reason,
it is worth mentioning a few of the individual advances
briefly.

Particular points of comparison

There are a number of noteworthy improvements in part
one. The first has to do with the terms used to describe
the present state of man. The Lectura ordinarily uses
phrases such as "status viae," "in via," and "viator" for
this purpose. In order to avoid useless speculation about
whether man before the fall might have been able to have
natural knowledge of his capacity for the supernatural and
thus reason to his end, the Ordinatio sharply limits the
discussion to the fallen state and substitutes the phrase
"status iste." (82) Scotus thus stresses the insufficiency
of nature and strengthens the arguments of the theologians
for the necessity of revelation. The metaphysics of
supernatural knowledge also receives a more concise explanation. (83) Possibly one of the most valuable improvements in the first part is the addition of the prefatory
note on the value of theological reasoning which shows that
such reasons are persuasions based on faith. (84) This is
not only the mark of a more mature theological self-
criticism, but it also effectively precludes any misuse of

these persuasions to infer to the fact of revelation. It thus opens the gap that part two will have to fill.

Part two, as mentioned earlier, is entirely new in the Ordinatio prologue. It has no parallel in the Lectura. The incorporation of this new question into the prologue is the most cogent reason for seeking an over-all organic pattern in the prologue. In that pattern this question forms an essential link.

In regard to the final three parts, many of the remarks in the Ordinatio that seem to be indications, even though obscure, of the progression of an organic line of thought have no parallel in the Lectura, e.g., the themes of God as the voluntary theological object and of the degrees of communication of this theological knowledge. (85)

A much more detailed analysis and comparison of the thought of the two prologues would have to be made before a final position can be adopted. Provisionally, however, I believe that the lacunae of the Lectura tend to confirm the thought-structure I have tried to trace in the prologue of the Ordinatio.

CONCLUSION

By way of conclusion, I shall offer some observations
in three areas. First, as regards the main contention of
this paper. In view of the fact that Scotus worked in a
period of theological rebuilding much like our own and that
the prologue offered him every opportunity for theological
initiative, a study of that prologue as a whole is impera-
tive if we are to appreciate his fundamental theology. In
regard to its content, the prologue brings together a
number of common questions and some threads of new development. The result is far from being a mere collage. It
seems to me that Scotus has attempted, often in a groping
way, to organize this material into an organic whole, a
progressing thought-pattern sensitive to the needs of the
situation. Starting from a contemporary issue basic and
crucial to theology's very existence and right to exist, he
lays the foundations for the theological endeavor being
undertaken so as to meet those needs. In regard to the
thought-pattern I have tried to discern in his prologue, I
readily admit that my attempt is only exploratory. The
pattern of the first two parts seems clear to me, but from
there on I may have read too much into the mind of Scotus.

Second, if Scotus' age is akin to ours, what value does
his fundamental theology have for us today? I do not think
we can simply transpose his prologue as a whole into our
context. It certainly would not mesh with a more traditional type of approach, an apologetical approach. (86) If
the pattern I have attempted to trace in his prologue is
correct, then the prologue is much closer in spirit to what
might be called the newer trend in fundamental theology.
(87) But then transferring the prologue as such would not
be of great value, because there are many themes and notions that have progressed far beyond what Scotus could
have said about them. (88) Paradoxically, then, far more
could be gained by recourse to a work such as Finkenzeller's. Although his book uses more than the prologues
of Scotus and is offered as a study in the ecclesiology of
Scotus, its systematization comes very close to the structure of the newer type of fundamental theology. (89) As to

the particular elements of a fundamental theology, Scotus' prologue offers much food for thought: a starting point taken from a contemporary issue that lies at the very root of theology, in order to show contemporary man the possibility and meaning of supernatural revelation in terms he understands; the role of fundamental theology in showing the need and usefulness of theology; a method that is on the whole theological rather than philosophical; (90) a subordinate place for apologetics; a certain concrete realism and organic approach to his theme, as opposed to an abstract, artifical systematization.

Third, the most important suggestion I can offer is the need for further research in the area of medieval prologues, which give promise of being a rich source. Some of the themes that might well be worth exploring are: the concept of tradition and its continuity with revelation; (91) the origin and evolution of the notion of the sufficiency of Scripture; the role of the Church in regard to revelation and tradition; the function of the theologian; (92) and the evolution of apologetics.

FOOTNOTES

(1)   This paper is a summary and further development of
      some of the results of a comparative study of two of
      the prologues of Scotus (those of the Lectura in
      librum primum Sententiarum and the Ordinatio) which
      the writer presented as a doctoral dissertation in
      the theological faculty of the Pontificium Athenaeum
      Antonianum in Rome under the title, Disquisitio com-
      parativa in prologos Lecturae Oxoniensis et Ordi-
      nationis I. D. Scoti.

(2)   See H. Bouillard, "Human Experiences as the Starting
      Point of Fundamental Theology," The Church and the
      World (Concilium 6), New York 1965, 79-80. Also con-
      fer K. Rahner, Theological Investigations (transl. C.
      Ernst) I, London 1961, 17-18.

(3)   K. Rahner, Theological Investigations I, 7-8.

(4)   C. Balic, "Circa positiones fundamentales Ioannis
      Duns Scoti," Antonianum 28 (1953) 261-306; A. B.
      Wolter, The Transcendentals and Their Function in
      the Metaphysics of Duns Scotus, St. Bonaventure,
      N. Y. 1946; E. Gilson, Jean Duns Scot. Introduction
      a ses positions fondamentales (Etudes de philosophie
      medievale XLII), Paris 1952; E. Gilson, "Les
      maitresses positions de Duns Scot d'apres le Prologue
      de l'Ordinatio," Antonianum 28 (1953) 7-18; C. O
      Huallachain, "On Recent Studies of the Opening Ques-
      tion in Scotus' Ordinatio," Franciscan Studies 15
      (1955) 1-29; P. Vignaux, Philosophy in the Middle
      Ages: An Introduction (transl. E. C. Hall), New York
      1959, 146-160.

(5)   J. N. Bakhuizen van den Brink, "Traditio im theolog-
      ischen Sinne," Vigiliae Christiannae 13 (1959) 65-
      86; P. de Vooght, Les sources de la doctrine
      chretienne, Paris 1954, 30-31; J. R. Geiselmann, Die
      Heilige Schrift und die Tradition (Quaestiones Dis-
      putatae 18), Freiburg im Br. 1962, 232 and 263; H.
      Oberman, The Harvest of Medieval Theology. Gabriel
      Biel and Late Medieval Nominalism, Cambridge, Mass.

1963, 374 footnote 40; L. Rosato, "Ioannis Duns Scoti doctrina de Scriptura et Traditione," De Scriptura et Traditione (Pontificia Academia Mariana Internationalis), Romae 1963, 233-252; E. M. Buytaert, "Circa doctrinam Duns Scoti de Traditione et de Scripturae sufficientia," Antonianum 40 (1965) 346-362.

(6)   R. Aubert, Le probleme de l'acte de foi. Donnees traditionnelles et resultats des controverses recentes, Louvain 1958, 649 footnote 2, and 656; R. Aubert, "Le Traite de la Foi a la fin du XIII siecle," Theologie in Geschichte und Gegenwart (ed. J. Auer-H. Volk), Munchen 1957, 349-370; A. Lang, Die Entfaltung des apologetischen Problems in der Scholastik des Mittelalters, Freiburg im Br. 1962.

(7)   J. Finkenzeller, Offenbarung und Theologie nach der Lehre des Johannes Duns Skotus. Eine historische und systematische Untersuchung (Beitrage zur Geschichte der Philosophie und Theologie des Mittelalters XXXVIII), Munster Westf. 1961.

(8)   Confer Y. Congar, La Foi et la Theologie (Le Mystere Chretien. Theologie Dogmatique 1), Tournai 1962, 243; Y. Congar, "Theologie," Dictionnaire de theologie catholique XV, Paris 1946, col. 374.

(9)   Cf. H. Rashdall-F. M. Powicke-A. B. Emden, The Universities of Europe in the Middle Ages III, Oxford 1936, 153-159; L. Daly, The Medieval University 1200-1400, New York 1961, 132-133.

(10)   See the discussions of P. Vignaux, Philosophy in the Middle Ages, 84-90; E. Gilson, History of Christian Philosophy in the Middle Ages, New York 1955, 387-410.

(11)   P. Glorieux, "Sentences (commentaires sur les)," Dictionaire de theologie catholique XIV, Paris 1941, col. 1863-1864 and 1875.

(12)   M.-D. Chenu, Toward Understanding Saint Thomas

(transl. by A.-M. Landry and D. Hughes), Chicago 1964, 39.

(13)   Thus there is no trace of Lombard's prologue, "Cupientes...," in the prologue of Scotus. The freedom regarding length of treatment is indicated in a pre-1407 Oxford statute reflecting earlier practice: "...(lector Sententiarum) non replicet pluries quam semel ultra introitus librorum et cessaciones eorumdem; introitus enim et cessaciones librorum, ac recitacio locorum ad materiam propriam pertinens... pro replicacionibus minime computantur," S. Gibson, Statuta Antiqua Universitatis Oxoniensis, Oxford 1931, 195.

(14)   C. Balic, "De Ordinatione I. Duns Scoti disquisitio historicocritica," Ioannis Duns Scoti Doctoris Subtilis et Mariani Opera Omnia (ed. Commissione Scotistica) I, Civitas Vaticana 1950, 144*-145*. This work will be cited hereafter as "Disquisitio." Also see C. Balic, "Adnotationes," Ioannis Duns Scoti Doctoris Subtilis et Mariani Opera Omnia (ed. Commissione Scotistica) IV, Civitas Vaticana 1956, 2*.

(15)   As found in the Additiones Magnae, edited under the title of Reportata Parisiensia in L. Vives, Joannis Duns Scoti Doctoris Subtilis Opera Omnia XXII, Paris 1894, the questions of this set are:

1.   utrum Deus sub propria ratione Deitatis possit esse subjectum alicujus scientiae (ed. Vives XXII, 6a)
2.   utrum veritates per se scibiles de Deo sub ratione Deitatis possint sciri ab intellectu viatoris (XXII, 33b)
3.   utrum viator ex puris naturalibus possit scire omnes veritates scibiles de Deo (XXII, 45b)
4.   utrum illa scientia, quae est de Deo secundum se sub ratione divinitatis, sit cognitiva omnium (XXII, 50b)
5.   an Theologia sit una scientia (XXII, 51a)
6.   an sit maxime una (XXII, 51a-b)
7.   si Theologia sit distincta a scientiis Philo-

sophicis (XXII, 52b)

8. an haec sit prior aliis (XXII, 52b)
9. an sit subalternata alicui alteri scientiae (XXII, 52b-53a)
10. an Theologia sibi subalternet aliam (XXII, 53a)
11. an Theologia sit de omnibus (XXII, 53b)

(16) The list of questions in the prologue of the <u>Ordinatio</u>, edited in <u>Ioannis Duns Scoti Doctoris Subtilis et Mariani Opera Omnia I</u>, Civitas Vaticana 1950, is:

part 1: utrum homini pro statu isto sit necessarium aliquam doctrinam specialem supernaturaliter inspirari, ad quam videlicet non posset attingere lumine naturali intellectus (n. 1 ed. Vat. I, 1)

part 2: utrum cognitio supernaturalis necessaria viatori sit sufficienter tradita in sacra Scriptura (n. 96 I, 59)

part 3: utrum theologia sit de Deo ut de primo obiecto (n. 124 I, 89)
utrum theologia sit de Deo sub aliqua ratione speciali (n. 133 I, 92)
utrum scientia ista sit de omnibus ex attributione eorum ad primum eius subiectum (n. 139 I, 94)

part 4: utrum theologia in se sit scientia, et utrum ad aliquam aliam scientiam habeat habitudinem subalternantis vel subalternatae (n. 208 I, 141)

part 5: utrum theologia sit scientia practica vel speculativa (n. 217 I, 151)
utrum ex ordine ad praxim ut ad finem dicatur per se scientia practica (n. 223 I, 153)

(17) The intricate problem of the number and chronological order of the lectures represented by these forms still awaits a final solution. The policy of the Scotistic Commission has been to go ahead with the critical edition and leave this problem for gradual solution in the future. Confer C. Balic, "Disquisitio," 144*. Earlier attempts to clarify

the chronology of Scotus' academic and literary
career had been made by such men as A. Callebaut, A.
G. Little, L. Meier, and F. Pelster. Only recently
the discussion has been taken up again by C. K.
Brampton, "Duns Scotus at Oxford, 1288-1301," Franciscan Studies 24 (1964) 5-20.
In accord with a provisional chronology, Reportatio
I C represents lectures given at Cambridge (C. Balic,
"Adnotationes," 3*) apparently at the outset of
Scotus' teaching career, if we accept the notation
in the Oxford MS, Merton College library, cod. 66, f.
120vb as following a time sequence (cf. A. Callebaut,
"Le bienheureux Jean Duns Scot a Cambridge vers
1297-1300," Archivum Franciscanum Historicum 21
(1928) 608-611. The year 1297 might be given as a
conjectural date. The Lectura would come next,
dating from his lectures at Oxford (c. 1298), about
which more will be said later. Next we have the
Reportationes of his Paris lectures (beginning in
1302, according to the Worchester MS, Cathedral
library, cod. F. 69, f. 158v). The Ordinatio, the
revision still being prepared for publication at his
death, would be dated later than the Paris lectures
(c. 1305?). Chronologically then, the forms of the
prologue would occur in this order: set I, set II,
set I, set II.

(18)   Such a division of the Ordinatio prologue is indi-
       cated in an opening text that has now been classi-
       fied as an interpolated text in the Vatican edition
       (I, 1, line 13).

(19)   C. Balic, "Disquisitio," 160*-161*; C. Balic, "Re-
       latio ann. X-XI: 1947-49, Nuntia Scotistica (Ratio
       criticae editionis Operum omnium I. D. Scoti III),
       Romae 1951, 178.

(20)   Confer H. Rashdall-F. M. Powicke-A. B. Emden, The
       Universities of Europe in the Middle Ages I, Ox-
       ford 1936, 491.

(21)   Ord. prol. n. 112 (I, 77): "...et in brevi, Domino
       volente, (secta Mahometi) finietur, quia multum

debilitata est anno Christi millesimo trecentesimo,
et eius cultores multi mortui, et plurimi sunt
fugati." Concerning this battle, confer R. Rohricht,
"Etudes sur les derniers temps du royaume de
Jerusalem. B. Les batailles de Hims (1281 et 1299),"
Archives de l'Orient latin I (1881) 633-652; G.
Golubovich, Biblioteca Bio-Bibliografica della
Terra Santa e dell'Oriente Francescane I, Quaracchi
1906, 335-336. Scotus, who was stationed at the
friary at Oxford in July of 1300, as we know from
the notation of Bishop J. Dalderby, Liber Memorandum, f. 13r (quoted in A. G. Little, Franciscan
papers, lists and documents, Manchester 1943, 235),
would likely have learned of the victory in June or
July. Papal messengers arrived in Cambridge with
the news on June 6, 1300, as recorded in a contemporary chronicle. See Martini, Continuationes
Anglicae FF. Minorum for the year 1299, edited in L.
Weiland, Monumenta Germaniae Historica. Scriptorum
Tomus XXIV, Hannoverae 1870, 258. Scotus' hope-
filled words had to be written within a short time
of this announcement of the victory, since the
events of the following year would have dashed his
expectations of a speedy downfall of Mohammedanism.
That same chronicle continues: "(Terra Sancta) rursus
a Sarracenis recuperata est et occupata, anno
videlicet Domini 1301," ibid. This offers a rather
strong argument for dating the second question to
the year 1300/1301. But we would not be entitled to
apply this same argument to the rest of the prologue,
in view of the peculiar characteristics of the second
question (to be touched on later).

(22)   (C. Balic), Les commentaires de Jean Duns Scot sur
les quatre livres des Sentences. Etude historique
et critique (Bibliotheque de la Revue d'histoire
ecclesiastique I), Louvain 1927, 56-86; C. Balic,
"Disquisitio," 157*-160*.

(23)   Worchester MS, Cathedral library, Q. 99, Quaternus
VI, q. 20, f. 64va-65rb. See E. Longpre, "Philippe
de Bridlington, O.F.M. et le Bx. Duns Scot,"
Archivum Franciscanum Historicum 22 (1929) 587-588;

also A. G. Little-F. Pelster, Oxford theology and theologians c. A. D. 1282-1302, Oxford 1934, 309-310, 344-347 (ibid., 236 for the dating of this MS). Philip's inception as master had already taken place by July 26, 1300, according to J. Dalderby, Liber Memorandum, f. 13r, quoted in A. Little, Franciscan papers, lists and documents, 235.

(24)   In the case of participation in an inception, the pertinent requirements would be: a commentary on the Sentences begun within a year after admission and continued through a scholastic year (H. Anstey, Munimenta Academica, 395, quoted in A. G. Little, "The Franciscan school at Oxford in the thirteenth century," Archivum Franciscanum Historicum 19 (1926) 826; a two-year period of study during which the bachelor made objections and replies (those at inceptions included) in all the schools (S. Gibson, Statuta Antiqua, 50); of these objections and replies, only those made during the second year fulfilled the requisites for the master's degree (ibid., 51).

(25)   Apparently Oxford allowed those who were not yet bachelors to object and reply in the disputation of the masters (S. Gibson, Statuta Antiqua, 48. See also A. Little-F. Pelster, Oxford theology and theologians, 33-34). Admission to reading the Sentences in this case could have taken place in the Autumn of 1300 or thereafter.

(26)   The second possibility would seem to crowd the chronology quite a bit, and a confirmatory argument might be constructed from the with-holding of an opinion of Olivi in book one, distinction 26, of the Lectura (confer C. Balic, Les commentaires, 74), though his opinions had been freely quoted earlier in the book, e.g., distinction one, part three, question three. This might well be explained by a letter issued by the Minister General of the Franciscans, John of Murovalle, which decreed that all the works of Peter Olivi be collected and burned, and which excommunicated all friars retaining and

using them (cf. L. Amoros, "Series condemnationum et processuum contra doctrinam et sequaces Petri Ioannis Olivi e cod. Vat. Ottob. lat. 1816," Archivum Franciscanum Historicum 24 1931, 504). The probable dating of this letter to the Pentecost general chapter of 1299 might then be used to argue to a prior dating of the Lectura prologue. C. Balic, "The Life and Works of John Duns Scotus," John Duns Scotus, 1265-1965 (ed. J. K. Ryan-B. Bonansea), Washington, D. C. 1965, 11, still accepts what has been the more common opinion, dating the Oxford lectures to 1300/1301. On the other hand, C. Brampton, "Duns Scotus at Oxford...," Franciscan Studies 24 (1964) 18, dates them to 1298-1299 without qualification.

(27) This description of the Lectura is given by C. Balic, "Disquisitio," 157*-160*; C. Balic "Praefatio," Ioannis Duns Scoti Doctoris Subtilis et Mariani Opera Omnia XVI, Civitas Vaticana 1960, ix.

(28) Ord. prol. n. 5 (I, 4-5): "In ista quaestione videtur controversia inter philosophos et theologos. Et tenent philosophi perfectionem naturae, et negant perfectionem supernaturalem; theologi vero cognoscunt defectum naturae et necessitatem gratiae et perfectionem supernaturalem. Diceret igitur philosophus quod nulla est cognitio supernaturalis homini necessaria pro statu isto, sed quod omnem cognitionem sibi necessariam posset acquirere ex actione causarum naturalium."

(29) E.G., St. Thomas, Sum. Th. II-II q. 2 a. 3. Even closer is the single question of the prologue of Vital du Four (dated c. 1295): "utrum lex aliqua non humano ingenio inventa, sed divinitus revelata, sit homini necessaria, ut directus in suis actibus per talem legem possit consequi finem suum" (Prag MS, Univ. 2297, XIII D 5, f. 18ra. Cf. F. Stegmuller, Repertorium Commentariorum in Sententias Petri Lombardi I, Wurzburg 1947, 425). Compare this with Ord. prol. n. 1 (I, 1): "utrum homini pro statu isto sit necessarium aliquam doctrinam specialem

supernaturaliter inspirari, ad quam videlicet non
posset attingere lumine naturali intellectus."

(30) <u>Ord</u>. prol. n. 54 (I, 32), n. 66 (I, 41).

(31) <u>Ord</u>. prol. n. 13-16 (I, 9-11), n. 19-25 (I, 13-16),
n. 28-38 (I, 16-22).

(32) <u>Ord</u>. prol. n. 17-18 (I, 11-13), n. 26-27 (I, 16), n.
39 (I, 22).

(33) <u>Ord</u>. prol. n, 40-48 (I, 22-30).

(34) <u>Ord</u>. prol. n. 12 (I, 9): "...Unde istae rationes hic
factae contra ipsum alteram praemissam habent
creditam vel probatam ex credito; ideo non sunt nisi
persuasiones theologicae, ex creditis ad creditum."

(35) <u>Ord</u>. prol. n. 70 (I, 43).

(36) <u>Ord</u>. prol. n. 71 (I, 43-44): "...Et hoc modo rationes
praedictae ut sunt naturales concludunt de altera
parte contradictionis, hac vel illa; non determinate
de hac nisi ex creditis tantum."

(37) <u>Ord</u>. prol. n. 6-11 (I, 5-8).

(38) <u>Ord</u>. prol. n. 19-25 (I, 13-16).

(39) <u>Ord</u>. prol. n. 37 (I, 21): "...Saltem tamen respectu
viatoris pro statu isto est dicta cognitio supernaturalis, quia facultatem eius naturalem excedens;
naturalem, dico, secundum statum naturae lapsae."
This statement is a reply to the objection "quod
homo in statu naturae institutae potuit cognoscere
naturam suam, ergo et finem naturae...ergo illa
cognitio non est supernaturalis," <u>Ord</u>. prol. n. 35
(I, 21). Confer also n. 57-59 (I, 35-37).

(40) <u>Ord</u>. prol. n. 57-59 (I, 35-37), n. 28-38 (I, 16-22).

(41) <u>Ord</u>. prol. n. 32 (I, 18-19). In this connection,
confer the excellent article by A. Wolter, "Duns

Scotus on the Natural Desire for the Supernatural,"
The New Scholasticism 23 (1949) 281-317.

(42)   *Ord*. prol. n. 28-38 (I, 16-22) *passim*.

(43)   "Haec autem prima traditio talis doctrinae dicitur
revelatio, quae ideo est supernaturalis, quia est ab
agente quod non est naturaliter motivum intellectus
pro statu isto," *Ord*. prol. n. 62 (I, 38).

(44)   *Ord*. prol. n. 60-65 (I, 37-40), n. 94 (I, 57-58).
In the first of these places cited, Scotus explains
how supernatural knowledge is effected. In natural
knowledge, the agent intellect and the object (as
present in the phantasm) are efficient co-causes.
In supernatural knowledge, a supernatural agent takes
the place of the object (whether a natural or supernatural object) and moves the intellect to assent
even though it has no evidence from the object. In
the second citation, he explains how supernatural
knowledge is received in the human intellect. The
possible intellect and the revealed truth or object
are not immediately proportioned to each other.
However, by a natural obediential potency, the
possible intellect is immediately proportioned to and
open to the action of a supernatural revealer; by a
natural capacity it is also immediately proportioned
to and able to receive the supernatural form, i.e.,
the assent to the revealed truth, to which the
supernatural agent moves it. Thus, with a few deft
strokes Scotus has sketched what we might call a
metaphysics of supernatural knowledge. Note that he
does not describe it under the specific aspect of
faith.

(45)   *Ord*. prol. n. 95 (I, 59): "utrum cognitio supernaturalis necessaria viatori sit sufficienter
tradita in sacra Scriptura."

(46)   J. Finkenzeller, *Offenbarung und Theologie nach der
Lehre des Johannes Duns Skotus*, 66, writes: "Die
Frage wird vor und nach ihm (Scotus) in dieser Form
gestellt, da das Probelm des Verhaltnisses zwischen

Offenbarung, Schrift und Tradition, noch nicht im
Sinne der spateren Theologie prazisiert ist." He
rightly notes that the question of the sufficiency
of Scripture did not mean the same for the scholastics as it does for us. But until now I haven't
been able to verify that the question was placed before Scotus. Finkenzeller gives no references for
that. Nor can I find any verification in F. Stegmuller, Repertorium commentariorum in Sententias
Petri Lombardi I and II, or in P. Glorieux, La
litterature quodlibetique de 1260 a 1320 (I)
(Bibliotheque Thomiste XXI), Paris 1936. E. Buytaert, "Circa doctrinam Duns Scoti de Traditione et
de Scripturae sufficientia," Antonianum 40 (1965)
359 footnote 4, cites R. Aubert ("Le Traite de la
Foi a la fin du XIII siecle," J. Auer-H. Volk,
Theologie in Geschichte und Gegenwart, 359) as indicating that Raymond Penafort and his followers
and Raymond Lull had treated of this question.
Aubert's concern in the context is about a more
apologetic treatment of the faith. Scotus certainly
has forerunners in this. But whether they were also
concerned about the sufficiency of Scripture would
have to be examined further.

(47) The arguments in the body of the question have a
rhetorical style, e.g., frequent rhetorical questions, periodic constructions, exclamations and
invectives against the Mohammedans, that is in sharp
contrast to the concise, severe scientific style of
the rest of the prologue. The dialectical, critical,
impersonal spirit of the first part has given way in
these arguments to an apologetic attitude (the attitude is often unquestioning, and there are relatively few objections to the arguments presented). All
this suggests an interesting idea as to the origin
of this question. This part can be dated to the
year 1300/1301, when Scotus in all probability was
at Oxford. Could it be that he originally composed
it as a public sermon to meet the requirements at
Oxford for inception in theology? (Confer S. Gibson,
Statuta Antiqua, 50). There are known examples of
sermons preached at about the same time or slightly

earlier in which apologetic reasons similar to those
in part two are expounded (see A. Lang, Die Entfaltung des apologetischen Problems in der Scholastik
des Mittelalters, 131-133). In the process of re-
vising the Ordinatio he might then have incorporated
this question, without thoroughly re-working it.
This would help explain why the solution, which is
in itself a very simple statement, is a later addition, why the list of eight reasons given in the
beginning (Ord. prol. n. 100 I, 61) was not expanded
to include the ninth and tenth reasons added later.
These difficulties have also been noted by E. Buytaert, "Circa doctrinam Duns Scoti...," Antonianum
40 (1965) 360.

(48) Ord. prol. n. 95-98 and 120-123 (I, 59-60 and 85-
87).

(49) Ord. prol. n. 99-119 (I, 60-85).

(50) Ord. prol. n. 120 (I, 85).

(51) Ibid. The various phrases used by the individual
arguments, e.g., canonicity, authorship, authenticity,
etc., can all be reduced to this, that Scripture
comes from God and is a true font of revelation.

(52) That Scotus saw these two units as related is evident from the opening words of the solution: "Habito
igitur contra haereticos quod doctrina Canonis vera
est, videndum est secundo an sit necessaria et
sufficiens viatori ad consequendum suum finem," ibid.

(53) Ord. prol. n. 12 (I, 9). He even added marginal
notes to two of the accepted arguments, pointing out
the premise accepted in faith. Cf. Ord. prol. n.
14 (I, 10, line 15) and n. 18 (I, 12, line 18).

(54) Ord. prol. n. 106 (I, 67). In trying to establish
the authorship of the books of Scripture, Scotus
asks rhetorically, "Et prpter idem, quomodo asserunt
Deum locutum esse multa quae ibi narrantur, et hoc
personis quibus libri intitulantur, si talia non

acciderunt talibus personis?"

(55)   Thus P. de Vooght, Les sources de la doctrine
         chretienne, 30-31; J. R. Geiselmann, Die Heilige
         Schrift und die Tradition, 232 and 263. They then
         conclude that Scotus later changed his position when
         he wrote that some articles of faith, such as
         Christ's descent into hell, are not expressed in
         Scripture. See Ord. I, d. 11, n. 20 (V, 7-8) and
         Ord. IV, d. 17, q. un., n. 17 (Vives XVIII, 519).

(56)   Cf. L. Rosato, "Ioannis Duns Scoti doctrina de
         Scriptura et Traditione," De Scriptura et Traditione,
         243 footnote 9, and 248 footnote 26.

(57)   Thus J. Finkenzeller, Offenbarung und Theologie, 74;
         Y. Congar, La tradition et les traditions. Essai
         historique, Paris 1960, 146-147.

(58)   H. Oberman, The Harvest of Medieval Theology, 374
         footnote 40; L. Rosato, "Ioannis Duns Scoti...,"
         De Scriptura et Traditione, 249-250. For a critique
         of this position, cf. E. Buytaert, "Circa doc-
         trinam Duns Scoti...," Antonianum 40 (1965) 361-362.

(59)   Cf. J. N. Bakhuizen van den Brink, "Traditio im
         theologischen Sinne," Vigiliae Christianae 13 (1959)
         81; J. Geiselmann, Die Heilige Schrift und die
         Tradition, 263; and L. Rosato, "Ioannis Duns Scoti
         ...," De Scriptura et Traditione, 247-250.

(60)   E. Buytaert, "Circa doctrinam Duns Scoti...,"
         Antonianum 40 (1965) 347-358.

(61)   In all fairness, any reference to Scotus in relation
         to our current question on the sufficiency of Scrip-
         ture ought to allow for two sets of facts pointed
         out by E. Buytaert. On the one hand, there are many
         instances when Scotus speaks of truths which are not
         written as such in Scripture; he speaks of truths
         handed on orally without writing, often citing Jn.
         16:12-13 and Jn. 20:30 to bolster up these state-
         ments. On the other hand, he quotes Apoc. 22:18 and

says that our human theology concerns only those
things which are contained in Scripture or which can
be elicited from them (see Ord. prol. n. 204 (I, 137-
138); he also defines revelation as the prima traditio of supernatural knowledge (see Ord. prol. n.
62 I, 38). Buytaert concludes that Scotus might
therefore be plausibly invoked by partisans of both
sides of the one source/two source debate, "Circa
doctrinam Duns Scoti...," Antonianum 40 (1965) 358-
359 and 362.

(62) Cf. A. Lang, Die Entfaltung, 195; R. Aubert, "Le
Traite...," Theologie in Geschichte und Gegenwart,
367-368.

(63) For an account of the early development, cf. A. Lang,
Die Entfaltung, 129-130 and 196-198; M. Muckshoff,
Die Quaestiones Die putatae de Fide des Bartholo-
maus von Bologna, O.F.M. (Beitrage zur Geschichte
der Philosophie und Theologie des Mittelalters
XXIV), Munster i. W. 1940, 109-120.

(64) Cf. A. Lang, Die Entfaltung, 129-130.

(65) M. Muckshoff, Die Quaestiones Disputatae, 113 and
120.

(66) A. Lang, Die Entfaltung, 196. As found in Bartholomew of Bologna, Quaestiones Disputatae de fide, qq.
1, 2, and 5, the steps are: "utrum sit necessarium
ad salutem credere aliqua quae non possunt con-
vinci per naturalem rationem"; "utrum quilibet in
sua fide possit salvari, an solum sit una fides
tantum, in qua sit salus"; "supposito quod tantum
sit una lex sive fides, in qua sit salus, utrum
illa fides sit fides Christiana," M. Muckshoff,
Die Quaestiones Disputatae, I, 22 and 77.

(67) The links would be the last question of Quodl. IV of
Raymond Rigaldus (or perhaps of Jacques du Quesnov)
and the opening question of book four of the commentary on the Sentences by Jacques du Quesnoy and/
or Vital du Four. With that, the apologetic would

have entered into the commentary on the Sentences. For the leads concerning this, see V. Doucet, "Les neuf Quodlibets de Raymond Rigauld, d'apres le ms. Padoue Anton. 426," La France franciscaine 19 (1936) 234-236; R. Aubert, "Le caractere raisonnable de l'acte de foi d'apres les theologiens de la fin du XIII siecle," Revue d'histoire ecclesiastique 39 (1943) 35-36 footnote 1.

(68)   M. Muckshoff, Die Quaestiones Disputatae, 149-150.

(69)   Compare Ord. prol. n. 99-119 (I, 60-85) with Bartho-lomew of Bologna, Quaestiones Disputatae de fide, q. 5 (ed. M. Muckshoff, Die Quaestiones Disputatae, 84-89) and Matthew of Aquasparta, Quaestiones Dis-putatae de Fide, q. 3 (ed. Bibliotheca franciscana scholastica medii aevi I, Quaracchi, Florence 1957, 81-89).

(70)   Henry of Ghent, Summae Quaestionum Ordinariarum, a. 9, q. 3 and in corp. (photographical reproduction) (Franciscan Institute Publications. Text Series n. 5) I, Louvain 1953, f. 70 and 72P.

(71)   Ord. prol. n. 62 (I, 38).

(72)   Cf. E. Gilson, "Les maitresses positions de Duns Scot d'apres le Prologue de l'Ordinatio," Antonianum 28 (1953) 9-17; P. Vignaux, Philosophy in the Middle Ages, 147-160.

(73)   Ord. prol. n. 201 (I, 136).

(74)   Ord. prol. n. 200 (I, 135-136).

(75)   Ord. prol. n. 203-204 (I, 137-138).

(76)   Ord. prol. n. 204 (I, 137-138).

(77)   Cf. C. Koser, "Ensaio de metodologia teologica segundo ideias do Doutor Sutil," Revista eclesiastica brasileira 2 (1942) 369. Part four of the prologue excludes the relationship of subalternation between

theology as it exists on these various levels.

(78) Ord. prol. n. 123 (I, 87): "...circa quarum (truths
virtually contained in Scripture) investigationem
utilis fuit labor doctorum et expositorum."

(79) In determining that theology is not a science in the
strict sense, Scotus is speaking of the theology of
God and of the Blessed. Human theology would obviously fail to meet the four conditions of Aristotle.
Scotus' remarks about theology as wisdom, however,
are not expressly limited to the theology of God
and the Blessed. Cf. Ord. prol. n. 213 (I, 146).

(80) There are some instances in which Scotus has changed
his opinion, e.g., regarding the subdivision of
theology in part two and three of the Lectura and
Ordinatio respectively, the scientific character of
divine contingent theology in the second last part,
and the speculative nature of divine theology in the
last part. But these instances are of relatively
minor importance.

(81) Due to this expansion and addition of matter, the
prologue of the Ordinatio is nearly three times as
long.

(82) Cf. Ord. prol. n. 35 and 37 (I, 21). The concepts
of the supernatural, of the desire for the supernatural, and of supernatural revelation are accordingly more specific than they had been in the
Lectura. Cf. ibid.; also Ord. prol. n. 32 (I, 18-19)
and n. 62 (I, 38).

(83) Compare Lect. prol. n. 32-34 (ed. Vat. XVI, 13-15)
and n. 51 (XVI, 21) with Ord. prol. n. 60-65 (I, 37-
40) and n. 94 (I, 57-58). The notions of revelation
as found in these citations also offer an interesting point of comparison.

(84) Ord. prol. n. 12 (I, 9). An objection and reply
found later on in part one of the Ordinatio might
well have inspired this note. Cf. Ord. prol. n. 70-

71 (I, 43-44).

(85) Compare Lect. prol. n. 104 (XVI, 37) and Ord. prol.
n. 204 (I, 137-138).

(86) I might add here that the description of the prologue
by P. Vignaux, Philosophy in the Middle Ages, 155,
as a "philosophical introduction to theology" seems
incomplete.

(87) Y. Congar, La Foi et la Theologie and J. Feiner-M.
Lohrer, Die Grundlagen heisgeschichtlicher Dogmatik
(Mysterium Salutis I), Einsiedeln 1965, are examples
of this trend, which combines such themes as revelation, tradition, the role of the Church relative to
these, the development of doctrine, theology, and
faith, into the pattern of an interpersonal dialogue,
of invitation-response (God speaks, man accepts in
faith).

(88) This holds true especially as regards the relation
of Scripture and Tradition, the more personal nature
of faith, the development of doctrine, etc.

(89) The tables of contents of the works of Finkenzeller
and Feiner-Lohrer show a remarkable similarity in
their arrangement of thought.

(90) In addition to his general critique of the theological
arguments as persuasions, Scotus introduces various
themes taken from faith, e.g., man's end, supernatural merit, etc.

(91) For example, cf. Scotus' definition of revelation
as the "prima traditio," Ord. prol. n. 62 (I, 38)
and n. 69 (I, 42-43). This definition, which can
also be found in some of the Fathers, seems to imply
an organic continuity.

(92) These last two might possibly contain an incipient
idea of development of doctrine.

Discussion

AUGUSTINE MC DEVITT, O.F.M., S.T.D.

Professor of Theology
Holy Name College
Washington, D.C.

Since the general theme of our symposium is expressed in the title "Scotus Speaks Today," I shall limit my discussion of Fr. Antonellus' very capable and thoughtful presentation to what he suggested concerning Scotus' relevance today in the area of theology and its task.

A. In the first of this three final observations, our learned speaker pointed out that the Subtle Doctor treated of the nature of theology with an eye to the contemporary issue of whether theology had a right to exist. I think that it would be profitable for us to remember that, in wrestling with this basic question, Scotus never abandoned his pursuit of speculative theology. In this, I think he teaches us a valuable lesson. We are greatly concerned today--and rightfully so--with the validity of some of the basic premises on which the scientia fidei has traditionally rested: the validity of analogous knowledge of God, the limits to which demythologization may--and should--be carried, the meaningfulness of God to man, etc. We are being forced today to re-think our pre-theological principles. In the work of Scotus we can learn, I think, that our grappling with pre-theological problems must not distract us from the pursuit of that speculative theology whereby we may further explicate the truths of our faith. This continued attempt to develop revealed truth, even while re-investigating the pre-theological problems, demands that today's theologian be, like Scotus, a man of intense faith.

B. The balance which Duns Scotus strikes between the validating of principles and the pursuit of theology, is matched by an admirable balance in another area. The Doctor is careful to ground his theological consideration of divine revelation in a reasonable apologetic. In Part II of the Ordinatio Prologue, he speaks--in the body of the question-- of the truth of Sacred Scripture. He has shown that revelation is necessary because man has been called to supernatural glory; but the existence of this end of man is itself contained in revelation; in order, therefore, to avoid ways of arguing against heretics," i.e., ten reasonable criteria of revelation for the benefit of those without faith.

What is Scotus here saying to us? In the fundamental theology of our own times, there exists on the part of some a tendency to deny the relevance--or even the possibility--of a rational apologetic for our faith (Avery Dulles, S.J., Apologetics and the Biblical Christ, Westminster: Newman, 1963, deals with one aspect of this problem). One perceives, especially in some popular writers, a resurgence of a fideism or gnosticism, which takes man's faith completely out of the reasonable and into the intuitional. Scotus and his contemporaries may have employed criteria of revelation which have been out-dated in some aspects by modern scholarship; but their conviction that faith, and therefore theology, is a human--and reasonable--activity, is especially cogent in our day.

C. I think that one of Fr. Antonellus' very valuable contributions in his paper was his delineation of the Doctor's fundamental thought-structure in the Ordinatio Prologue: revelation is necessary to man because God has created him for glory; Sacred Scripture sufficiently advises man of his ultimate goal, of the means he must use to attain to it, and of the existence of immaterial beings; theology explains and explicates revealed truth; it is a wisdom, rather than a science strictly so-called; and it leads man to his final glorious end.

It seems to me that Scotus' discussion of revelation and theology here reflects in its entire spirit, the mystical trend in Franciscan theology. In the mind of the Subtle Doctor, the keystone of theology is man's glory, the free gift of a loving God; revelation is necessary, and theology is possible, not only because God is ultimate truth, but basically because He has in fact called man to glory. Fr. Antonellus has observed that this emphasis on God's loving initiative is reminiscent of the Prologue of Vital du Four. We may add that Alexander of Hales seems to have had in mind this same idea when he stated that "Doctrina sacra dicitur divina seu theologica, quia a Deo et de Deo et ductiva ad Deum" (Summa Theol., q. 1, cap. 2 ad objecta; Quaracchi, 1924, I, 5).

This emphasis on God's loving action as the point from which theology begins, and toward which it leads, seems characteristic of the Seraphic tradition, which stresses God's immanence among His creatures. St. Thomas, in the second of the two Quaestiones which comprise the Prologue to his Commentary on the Sentences, does point out that man's mind can apprehend (though not comprehend) revealed truths by the help of God's grace (Commentum in Libros IV Sententiarum, Prologus, q. 2, art. 1; Vives, 1878, XXX, 11). But the Angelic Doctor does not lead his reader to the recess of God's love, as to the wellspring of theology.

Modern theology, with its accent on God's proximity to His creatures (the virtually constant divine presence in salvation history, man's "supernatural existential," the sacramentality of the natural order), has a forerunner in the Franciscan spirit. The Scotistic view of things may prove to exert a strong influence on the theological synthesis with theologians hope for in the future.

As Fr. Antonellus has pointed out, it is primarily the spirit of Scotus' Prologue which is of value today. Formed, as it is in its specific questions, by the exigencies of the Middle Ages, the Scotistic consideration of theology does not answer all the needs of our own time. But its general character--realistic, existential, properly theological--is something of great value to today's theologian.

D. While I was reading Scotus' Prologue, there occurred to me a question which I should like to submit to the consideration of this gathering. In the third part of the Ordinatio Prologue, the Subtle Doctor treats of the problem of the manner in which one should organize the science of theology: he asks whether Christ is theology's first object, i.e., the subject of attribution. He presents the opinion of St. Bonaventure and of Robert Grossatesta, who held that Our Lord is the subject in which theology is focused. Scotus, however, rejects this opinion, asserting that theology's subject of attribution is God Himself under the aspect of His divinity.

In the light of Scotus' general Christocentrism, based on his teaching of Jesus' absolute primacy in creation, it seems rather strange that our Doctor does not consider Christ to be the focal point of our knowledge concerning God.

E. Finally, I should like to say a brief word concerning the general tendency of theology in the Franciscan School, a tendency which, catching the spirit of St. Francis himself, bears the marks of Plato, St. Augustine, the Victorines, and St. Bonaventure. In this tradition, theology is viewed as a living wisdom, rather than a merely speculative science; it is mystical in that it emphasizes God's role in man's attainment of his final end; it stresses the proximity of nature and grace. At the same time, it upholds man's inherent dignity by stressing God's immanence in His creation; and it emphasizes the practical value of theology--God's word as preached and as lived.

It seems to me at this point, that Duns Scotus is not as deeply immersed in this tradition as is St. Bonaventure. It also seems to me that one of the tasks of our future study of the Subtle Doctor will be a more precise determination of his relation to this tradition. Is it possible that he achieved a balance between this and the Thomistic tradition? And if so, then has he outlined for us a path along which we may travel in our theology today?

FATHER S. YOUREE WATSON, S.J., completed his
graduate studies in philosophy at the
Gregorianum in Rome. At present he is Associate Professor of Philosophy at Spring Hill
College, Mobile, Alabama. He is author of
various papers, articles, and essays published
in collections, and of a booklet entitled A
Brief Account of the History of Philosophy.

Dissimilarity and Distinction in the Philosophy of DUNS SCOTUS

S. YOUREE WATSON, S.J., M.A.

Distinction, it is clear, is a condition of dissimilarity, but is the converse true: Is dissimilarity a
condition of distinction? This is the question we seek to
answer here with the help of John Duns Scotus. However,
in order to be able to grasp what Scotus has to say concerning this problem we shall first have to consider two
other matters, which at the outset may not seem to be
closely related, namely: 1) Scotus' doctrine on imperfect similarity and 2) his doctrine on universals.

Part I. Imperfect Similarity

Scotus' Analysis of Imperfect Similarity

Scotus holds that two things cannot be imperfectly
similar unless at least one of the two is composite, for
if two simple things were imperfectly similar, this would
mean that that by which one would be similar to the other
would be strictly identical with that by which it would be
dissimilar. This, Scotus believes, would involve a contradiction.(1) Hence, whenever two things are imperfectly
similar, we can distinguish, in one of them at any rate,
at least two distinct "parts," by one of which it is similar, by the other of which it is dissimilar, to the other
thing. Scotus, therefore, holds that imperfect similarity
is not an irreducible "given."(2)

Thus, for example, that by which blue differs from
red cannot be unqualifiedly identical with that by which
blue is like red. This means that there is a distinction
between the objective ground of generic color and the objective ground of the specific difference which adds a
further determination to color as such, a distinction, in
this case, between that which makes blue color color and
that which makes blue color blue and not red.(3) The fact
that there is material identity between "colored thing"
and "blue thing" or even between "color" and "blue" ("color"
understood) does not imply that that which makes blue
color to be color and that which makes blue color to be

blue are formally the same, that is to say, one and the same "form" or, better, "formality."(4)

As the similarity and dissimilarity here are objective, so too must be the distinction. This so-called "formal distinction" is, as we know, a distinction between inseparable constituents of one and the same being. If Scotus denies that this distinction is real the only reason is that he calls "real" only those distinctions which are between res (things), realities capable of separate existence. A formal distinction is real in the more common usage of this term, however, for it is extramental. (5)

Now, doubtless the primary reason why Scotus was led to accept and develop certain of his predecessors' teaching on the formal distinction was theological--concerned with the dogma of the Trinity.(6) Another reason was, it appears, the result of his search for an explanation for the plurality of our concepts of individual things.(7) But still a third reason--and it is this with which we are presently concerned--was his analysis of the implications of imperfect similarity.(8)

Actually, the distinction between color and its difference, treated above, is not the best example of a formal distinction. For Scotus seems to have considered the union between color and its difference even closer a than that which is found between a generic nature and its specific difference, which would constitute the more typical example of a formal distinction. But the argument for the latter distinction is the same. Rationality cannot be simply identical with animality, for animality is that by which a man and a brute are similar and rationality (in the man) is that by which they are dissimilar. Now, animality and rationality are not things, but formalities; hence they are, in Scotistic terminology, not really, but only formally, distinct.

One might argue that that by which man essentially differs from the brute is his human soul. This statement rightly interpreted may be correct, but the problem recurs. For, as it happens, the human soul itself, is imperfectly

similar to the brute soul. This is manifested by the fact
that while it has operations similar to those of the brute
soul, it has other operations which are dissimilar, so
that we must conclude that the human soul itself is composite of that by which it is similar to the brute soul
and that by which it differs from it. Indeed, we may
speak of the "animality" and "rationality" of the human
soul in much the same way we speak of the animality and
rationality of man as a whole. If the human soul is to
be considered as a sort of "difference" between man and
brute, it is not the ultimate difference. Ultimate differences must be wholly dissimilar, since any similarity
between them would imply a distinction in each (or at
least in one) between a common element and a differentiating element: the element of otherness, difference,
dissimilarity, which, as we shall see, in Part II of this
essay, Scotus identifies with the principle of individuation.(9) The ultimate differences are said to be primarily diverse, for they are the source of the diversity,
that is to say, the dissimilarity, of the beings in which
they are found.(10)

The similar, like the dissimilar, constituents of
two imperfectly similar material beings could, of course,
be integral parts, capable, though not as parts, of separate existence. Thus, we might say a man is similar to
a chicken in having two legs, which are parts that no one
would consider as formalities. But we are quickly driven
to abandon the concrete order for the world of formalities
if we are to offer a plausible solution to the problem
at issue. For if a human limb can be said to be similar
to the leg of a fowl, it is certainly not perfectly similar. It is, therefore, imperfectly similar. But, according to the theory we have been propounding, this is equivalent to partially similar, partially dissimilar. What
would be perfectly similar about the two legs? Surely not
any two concrete, that is, integral, parts. Rather the
legs are similar in shape, similar in function too, though
it is in great part the similarity in shape which makes
possible the similarity in function.

Now, shape--to confine ourselves to this example--
may be considered an accident modifying the substance

through the accident extension. But we cannot stop here.
Since the similarity in shape is not perfect, we are forced
to distinguish in each shape between that by which it is
similar and that by which it is dissimilar to the other
shape. But what does this presuppose? That every shape
is composite of that formality by which it is like any
other shape and that formality by which it is unlike it.
Grant this and it follows that every shape must be composed
of as many formalities as there are different kinds of
shape. The number of constituent formalities will, in
consequence be staggering. We do not recall seeing any
passage in which Scotus confronts this particular aspect
of the problem. Yet as an uncompromising metaphysician,
he would not have hesitated to accept the consequences of
principles which he held to be true, no matter how unexpected and how contrary to popular beliefs these consequences might be.

In conclusion, we should observe how the outcome
of his analysis of imperfect similarity reinforced Scotus'
doctrine on the formalities. For this analysis has led
him to the same belief in the reality and hence extramental distinction of the formalities to which other reasons,
as we have seen, also strongly inclined him. Here again
the formal distinction provides what he considers the only
safeguard of the objectivity of human concepts.

Criticism of Scotus' Analysis of Imperfect Similarity

Let us state at the outset that the mere fact that
Scotus' analysis seems to lead us into the necessity of
positing a very large number of formalities is not a telling argument against it. After all, scientists assure
us that the number of atoms--not to mention the number of
subatomic "particles"--in a grain of sand is enormous.
Why, then, boggle at the number of Scotus' "metaphysical
atoms"?(11) Of course, the principle of economy must be
given its due even in philosophy.(12) If Scotus' position
is to be taken as a mere hypothesis, then a different hypothesis offering a simpler explanation is doubtless to be
preferred.

However, Scotus' position is not proposed as merely

hypothetical, but rather as the conclusion of rational argument based on self-evident principles and certain facts. We must question, therefore--if question we must-- only the correctness of the reasoning, the truth of some alleged fact, or the evidence of some principle. As Scotus' logic seems impeccable and his facts correct, let us have a look at his principles. The one which seems most vulnerable is that which affirms that imperfect similarity implies composition. At least this calls for further analysis, and to this we must now devote ourselves.

It would be a contradiction for two things which are perfectly similar to be simultaneously dissimilar in any part or respect. Likewise, it is impossible for two things to be perfectly similar in respect to one part and in any way dissimilar in respect to the same part. If part x of being A is just like part y of being B, then x cannot without contradiction be at all unlike y. But the same does not necessarily hold for imperfect similarity. This, it seems, is ill-defines as "partial similarity, partial dissimilarity," as the "partial" strongly suggests part and so begs the question. Rather it would appear that so far from being incompatible with dissimilarity, imperfect similarity actually implies (imperfect) dissimilarity and vice-versa. Consequently, there would seem to be no contradiction in their being two simple realities which are imperfectly similar. Ipso facto they would also be imperfectly dissimilar. Likewise, in the light of this analysis, there appears no reason why there could not be two (imperfectly) similar complex realities in which no part of one would be perfectly similar or utterly dissimilar to any part of the other.

This sounds plausible enough, and Scotus himself would certainly grant that imperfect similarity implies dissimilarity, that that which is imperfectly similar must ipso facto be imperfectly dissimilar. However, he would also insist that one thing cannot be imperfectly similar to another unless it is in some real respect (in the last analysis, some formality) perfectly similar. And that he may just possibly be right is suggested by the fact that as soon as we note that two things are imperfectly similar (two human faces, for instance) we are led to look for that in regard to which they are similar (ultimately perfectly similar) and that in which they differ.

To take a relatively clear example, when we have
noted that a polygon is similar to, and yet not perfectly
similar to, a circle, we instinctively ask: In what is it
similar? Actually, of course, we can indicate a "perfect"
similarity: the polygon is perfectly like the circle in
that both are plane figures; that is to say, they are similar in a certain set of characters which each possesses
and which is the basis of our calling it a figure. Let us
symbolize this set of characters as f. On the other hand,
the polygon is not exactly like the circle. It is dissimilar inasmuch as it possesses a set of characters, x, which
the circle does not possess and lacks a set of characters,
y, which the circle does possess. Now, we must ask: Are
or are not the sets of characters f and x, which we have
attributed to the polygon truly objective? Are they found
"in" it or only in our thinking about it? And if "they"
are objective, how can they be just one set of characters?
The concept f is adequately distinct from the concept x.
(The fact we must judge that nothing can have x without
also having f does not prove that the two are not distinct.) How, then, can that which the concept f represents in the real order be unqualifiedly identical with
that which the distinct and differing concept x represents,
supposing that the two concepts are representative and
that to "represent" means to manifest what something, or
some part of some "thing" is like?

In the light of all that has been considered, it
does not seem that the tendency to ground all similarity
in some perfect similarity and, conversely, all dissimilarity in some utter dissimilarity, is a merely subjective
mode of thought. However, all that has been established
so far is, at most, that the distinction between two imperfectly similar beings implies some utterly dissimilar
elements. As this does not rule out the possibility that
there may be distinct beings which are perfectly similar,
we cannot yet make the general affirmation that all distinction is grounded in dissimilarity.

We shall now proceed to a consideration of the
second problem mentioned at the beginning of this paper,
namely, that of universals. If this consideration will
not provide us with full justification for the general

affirmation just spoken of, it should at least supply us
with rather strong evidence in its favor.

Part II. The Common Nature and Individuation

Problematic

What precisely is the problematic back of Scotus'
teaching on universals, or as he himself prefers to say,
on the common nature and individuation? It is rooted in
the relation between distinction and dissimilarity. A and
B are distinct if one is not the other, whether A and B
are wholes or parts of wholes, whether they are capable of
separate existence or not.(13) They are dissimilar if one
is unlike the other, that is, if A or B has some characteristic, trait, attribute, note, or what-you-will which the
other does not have, or if A or B is some characteristic,
trait, etc., which the other is not. No doubt, dissimilarity implies distinctness, for dissimilarity, the negation
of the relation of similarity, like similarity presupposes
two distinct terms. Dissimilars, therefore, will always
be distinct. Yet the two terms, "dissimilar" and "distinct"
as ordinarily used, do not evoke the same concept. The
truth of this can be recognized merely by a bit of reflection on common usage. We note, for instance, that "dissimilarity" admits of degrees, whereas "distinctness" does
not. A Chinaman and a Dane are likely to be far more dissimilar than identical twins of any race and nationality,
but they are not more distinct. Two peas in a pod are
just as distinct as an angel and a pebble, but they are
not nearly so dissimilar, so unlike.(14)

The difficulty begins with the question we asked
at the beginning: Granted that dissimilarity implies distinctness, does distinctness correlatively imply dissimilarity? Is some minimal degree of dissimilarity a condition of distinctness? Naturally, if there cannot be two
perfectly similar things, then "similar" can only correctly
signify imperfectly similar. Now, what is imperfectly
similar to another thing must also be imperfectly dissimilar.

One thing cannot be another thing. This is obvious. A lion cannot be a lamb, nor this lion, that lion. But if everything is distinct from everything else, how is it ever necessary or even helpful to employ the word "distinct"? Distinction, it would appear, could be taken for granted, if everything were red, it would be inane to say, "This is red."

The need for the term arises from the relationship of concepts to things. Two or more concepts may refer to one thing. Thus the concepts Frenchman, merchant, and husband may all refer to one particular individual named Jean Duval. Hence, such questions as the following are meaningful and, indeed, often useful: "Is the pen on the counter the pen you lost?" That is, "Do these two concepts: 1) pen on the counter and 2) pen you lost refer to one and the same thing? Does one and the same thing correspond to both?

Conversely, one concept may refer to two or more things. But as a concept is usually able to refer or signify only inasmuch as it represents its referents and since a representation can represent only that to which it is in some way similar, it follows that the things represented by one concept must be similar not only to it, but to each other, it being evident that two things similar to a third thing in the same respect must be similar to each other. Actually, however, it is rather the other way round: because things are similar to each other they can be represented by one concept. Because this tea rose and that jonquil are similar in certain respects they can be represented by the one concept flower and the one concept yellow. To be sure, the term "represents" must in the present context be taken in a very broad sense, so as to include not only absolute, but also relational characteristics.

After this little effort to clarify our use of the words "distinct" and "dissimilar" and the implications of that use, let us return to the heart of the problematic: Does distinctness imply dissimilarity? Scotus' answer was strongly influenced by the Aristotelian teaching on natures. According to this each member of a given species must have a nature (or, from differing points of view, an essence or substance) exactly like every other member of that species. For natures or essences, Aristotle says, are like numbers: change anything and you get a new number, a new nature. The problem arises: How can there be two or more natures of one kind or species? What differentiates one from the other? If it is easy to imagine two horses which will differ in their accidents, at least in the accidents of time and place, how is one to conceive of two "horsenesses" or "equinities"--which certainly cannot be imagined--when horseness, as such, furnishes no foundation for the multiplication of itself. "Equinity," as Avicenna has said and Scotus repeats after him, "is only equinity."(15) That which has equinity can have something else, and this "something else" can furnish a basis for distinction. A subject can have various "forms." But equinity is a "form" and a "form" unlike a subject can have nothing. Two subsistent equinities would, it seems, coincide like congruent triangles in geometry, would, so to speak, collapse into one. In other words, it appears impossible that two such equinities should exist. It would be a paradigm case of "a distinction without a difference." What we need is some principle or source of individuation to differentiate this individual from that individual of the same species, and thus make possible the multiplication of perfectly similar natures. What is this principle of individuation? Can it--in material beings at any rate-- be matter, somehow connected with quantity, as Aristotle seems to say? This was the precise question which in the context of the whole problematic described, presented itself to the Sutble Doctor. Let us now give an account of his solution.

Scotus' Position on the Problem of Universals

Scotus' position on the problem of universals, or in more precise terms, on commonness or community and individuality, may be summarized as follows: Although each member of a given species has its own individual nature numerically distinct from every other, all these natures are perfectly similar. Since two things cannot agree and disagree in respect to the same, that by which two members of the same species differ must be something other than the natures themselves. And since a quidditative difference would mean a different nature, the difference which

194

distinguishes one member from the rest must be a non-quidditative addition which has the function of making this nature this nature and that nature that.(16) This added entity (Thomists might say "principle of being") is Scotus' famous "haecceity" (haecceitas, literally "thisness").(17)

Scotus arrives at his doctrine on the haecceity only after rejecting various alternative principles or sources of individuation, including that of Aristotle. No aggregation of accidents, he holds, can serve this purpose, much less quantity alone; nor can matter itself play this role. Existence (esse) too is excluded. All accidents, including quantity, presuppose a substance which is already individual. Moreover, in regard to accidents, as well as in regard to matter and existence, we must seek for a principle of individuation. We must inevitably ask ourselves what makes this accident this accident, this matter this matter, this existence, this existence. These, no more than the nature itself, are as such individual.(18)

Now Scotus, as we know from the first part of this essay, also holds that two things cannot be similar and dissimilar in regard to the same. Correlating this thesis with the Aristotelian one that there can be no dissimilarity between two natures pertaining to the same species, Scotus was logically forced into holding that in every individual member of a species the (specific) nature and the haecceity, namely, that by which the individual is like the other individuals of the species and that by which it is dissimilar to these, must be extramentally distinct. John's nature, for example, will be just like Paul's except that John's nature is united to a particular haecceity and Paul's is united to a different, hence differentiating, haecceity. As there is question in each case of only one "thing," nature and haecceity are only formally distinct. (19) Hence, they are most intimately and inseparably joined in the being in which they are contained as one (unitive).(20) It is clear that Scotus' teaching on universals is intimately connected with his doctrine on formalities. If one considers the latter as exaggeratedly realistic, then, naturally, he will consider the former to suffer from the same defect.

Although in this necessarily limited essay we have wished to avoid as far as possible any extensive textual analysis, we judge it useful at this point to consider briefly some passages from the important Question 6 of Book II, Distinction 3 of the Ordinatio inasmuch as these will not only clarify the doctrine we have just summarized, but also bring out rather well the close connection between this doctrine and Scotus' analysis of imperfect similarity presented and discussed earlier in this essay.

In the first passage which we shall cite, Scotus introduces the notion of individuation by a differentiating addition. He writes:

> Every inferior includes in itself something which is not included in our understanding of the superior, otherwise the concept of the inferior would be as common as the concept of the superior and then what is essentially inferior would not be essentially inferior, because it would not fall under (the extension of) a common superior notion; therefore, something is necessarily included in the comprehension of an individual which is not included in the comprehension of the nature.(21)

There is an analogy according to Scotus between the relationship of a species to a genus and that of an individual to a species. For just as a species must add something to the comprehension of the genus, if the concept of the species is to be distinguished from that of the genus, so the concept of an individual must add something to the concept of the species if we are to be able to distinguish intellectually between an individual and its species. And as the specific difference is said to "contract" the generic ratio, so too the individual difference "contracts" the specific ratio.(22)

A little further on in the same question Scotus tells us:

> Every difference of differing things is reduced to some primarily diverse elements, otherwise there would be differences without and in differing things; but it is individuals which properly differ, because they are diverse, yet have something in common. Therefore, the difference between them is reduced to some primarily diverse elements.(23)

Here we have Scotus clearly saying that in two beings which differ; that is, which are not only distinct
but dissimilar,(24) there must in the last analysis be elements which are utterly dissimilar.(25) Back of this statement is latent the principle we have discussed in the first
part of this paper; namely, that two things cannot be similar and dissimilar in respect to the same. Hence, if the
"differences" (i.e., the differentiating elements) of two
differing beings are not wholly dissimilar, they can each
be broken down (reduced) to at least two constituent elements, one of which will be perfectly similar to a corresponding element in the other. Let x be the difference in
being A, y the corresponding difference in being B. If x
and y are not wholly dissimilar, there must be something--
some formality--in x by which it is similar to y and likewise something--some formality--in x by which it is dissimilar to y, and so of y in regard to x.

In the end we must come to an ultimate element in
each of two differing beings which is wholly unlike any
element in the other. These are the "primarily diverse
(primo diversa).(26) They are said to be primarily diverse in opposition to those beings which contain them but contain with them other elements similar to each other, and
which in consequence are diverse in a secondary or deriv-
ative way. They are dissimilar, but not in every respect,
not without qualification, not simply (simpliciter) dissimilar like the primarily diverse.

The passage cited above continues as follows:

These primarily diverse elements are not the nature in the one and the other, because things do not
formally agree and really differ in one and the same,
although one and the same reality can be really distinct from another reality and yet be in formal accord
with it.

Since there is question here of differing individuals, of two members of the same species, their respective
natures are the source of their similarity. These same
natures, therefore, cannot be the reason for their diversity, since that by which two things are in formal accord
or likeness (their perfectly similar forms or formalities)
cannot be that by which they really differ. Scotus goes on
to the point he is above all trying to make, namely, the
need for haecceities:

There is a great difference (27) between being distinct and being that by which anything is in the first place rendered distinct. And so, therefore, it will be with unity; hence over and above the nature in this and in that, there are some primarily diverse elements, by which this and that differ--that element in that thing, and this element in this thing.

The beings A and B are really distinct, but that by reason of which they are distinct is not their natures, for these are similar, nor simply their whole realities, for these are partly similar, but their haecceities, the "this-ness" of this and the "thatness" of that. These are wholly diverse and the foundation for the distinction of the beings as wholes and of their natures as parts of these wholes.

Still further on in the same question (n.14) Scotus states that from the fact that ultimate specific differences are primarily diverse it does not follow that the beings which have these differences are primarily diverse; that is, have nothing common (nothing in one perfectly similar to anything in the other). He adds that in one sense any distinct beings are as diverse as elements which distinguish them, for the beings as wholes, as well as the distinguishing "parts" are equally imcompatible (one is not and cannot be the other), but in another sense the beings are not as diverse (where "diverse," be it noted, must mean dissimilar) as the distinguishing elements, for the beings contain common (i.e., perfectly similar) elements, which are potential in respect to the differentiating elements. The differentiating elements agree in nothing, but this cannot be said of the differentiated beings.(28)

We pointed out, above, the analogy which Scotus draws between the relationship of a species to a genus and that of an individual to a species. We note that this is operative also in regard to diversity. Just as two opposed specific differences, e.g., rationality and irrationality, taken most formally, have nothing in common and so are primarily diverse as kinds, so also the haecceities which oppose the individuals within a species have nothing in common. But the similarity ends here, for whereas each specific difference is itself duplicatable in many individuals,

198

which would have this or that specific difference in common, no haecceity is duplicatable, so that no two haecceities, even of individuals of the same species, have anything in common.(29)

The textual analysis of the preceding pages should suffice for our purposes here, but there remain many points of Scotistic doctrine which call for further explanation and discussion. To begin with, we note that though Scotus holds that a nature is not of itself individual, and hence that individuation needs to be explained, his point of view is not that universality is self-intelligible and so needs no explanation.(30) Although Scotus does hold that the common nature--not the universal--has priority over the individuality,(31) he does not hold that the common nature could exist apart from the particulars of which it is the nature.(32) (Its concept, of course, may exist in the intellect.) In this, it seems that Scotus does not differ from St. Thomas, for whom the natura communis or absolute considerata has esse only in singulars and in the mind.(33) The common nature for Scotus is not the universal. As he insists, it is only negatively--not, like the mind-fashioned universal, positively--indifferent to individuality. Much less does Scotus hold that the common nature is numerically one in many individuals. In fact, he explicitly rejects this doctrine.(34) Rather his idea is that without the haecceities we could have only one individual of a particular kind, since without these there would be no source of the "many," no objective basis for the distinction of individuals within a species. Hence a plurality of individuals in one species would be impossible.(35)

Scotus concludes that a given nature like humanity is not of itself (because it is what it is) incompatible with any particular singularity. He does not mean that a nature could exist in the real order apart from individuals. Nor does he mean that this nature might by divine power have been united to another individuality. Since it is precisely the haecceity to which it is inseparably united that makes a nature this nature,(36) a nature united to a different individuality would be another nature, numerically distinct from this nature. Basically what Scotus means is simply that there is nothing in the content of the nature of a particular being which implies this individuality or which is incompatible with another individuality.(37)

Does, then, Scotus' doctrine on the common nature merely consist in the affirmation that because each creature's nature is distinct from the haecceity which individualizes it, beings can be produced with perfectly similar natures? This is, no doubt, an oversimplification, but it expresses a great part of the truth provided we remember that perfect similarity in respect to nature is itself a type of unity or oneness. It is unity of kind or species, as opposed to plurality of the same. That is one which is undivided in itself, divided from everything else. Now, a nature is not divided in itself, for it is one, not two natures, and it is divided from every other nature--humanity, for example, is not catness or treeness. Rover and Fido share a common specific nature; dogness, wherever found, is one and the same nature in opposition to, say, catness.(38) A dog and a cat do not have this specific unity, though they share a common generic nature and so possess generic unity. They are one in animality and in this they are opposed directly to all those living things which lack it.(39)

When we speak of "natures" we are speaking of similarities. A "nature" is an attribute or set of attributes in which many things are or could be similar. Similarity, which as we have seen presupposes distinctness, is the unity of a class (species, genus); the unity of an individual (numerical unity) is something quite different; in fact, it implies the negation of similarity inasmuch as it consists in the absence of that distinctness which is the presupposition of similarity.

We are trying to explain what is meant by saying two distinct beings have the same nature. Perhaps an illustration may help us to understand. We speak of two things as having the same pattern rather than two perfectly similar patterns because when we are concerned with pattern as such; that is to say, with a certain kind of pattern as opposed to other kinds of pattern, the distinction between the individuals in which the pattern is exemplified is irrelevant. The scientist (who studies "natures") is interested in the molecular structure of, say, salt as differing from that of other compounds, not with this molecule or these grains of salt, much less with the number of salt cellars--or salt mines--in the world. He is concerned, we may say, with dissimilarity, which is the otherness of patterns as patterns, not with distinctness, which is the "otherness" of individuals as individuals. The former has to do with comprehension, the latter with extension, so much so that we can say that the unity of a species is a unity of comprehension (the unity proper to a predicate), while the unity of an individual (numerical unity) is a unity of extension (the unity proper to a subject). A species is one because its members are without dissimilarity of essential content; an individual is one because it is without distinctness as regards this content; that is, it is not two or more instances of this content. (40)

However, a rather obvious difficulty presents itself against Scotus' doctrine on the common nature. Is not the unity of a specific nature merely the unity of the one concept which represents and can refer to or signify every member of that species, and thus is it not something which exists only in the mind? The unity of this concept is indeed manifest. What is not so manifest is the fact that the individual natures must really be such that they can be represented by this one concept. Now, that which makes this representation possible is, of course, the perfect similarity of the natures. Then, this similarity must be real. The mind does not construct it, but discovers it. It is not the least of Scotus' merits that he has emphasized the reality of this similarity.

Scotus calls the unity of the common nature a "lesser unity," lesser, that is, than the unity of an individual. Is it lesser because similarity is a less strong bond of unity than that found in the individual, or is there another reason involved? In not a few passages Scotus takes an approach which leads to a different interpretation of "the lesser unity." In these passages "the lesser unity" becomes the unity of the nature in a determined individual in contrast with the greater unity of the supposite. This latter is identified with numerical unity (somewhat confusingly, for one can count distinct instances of a nature even if these are not distinct ratione sui). The unity of a nature is here the unity of a formality, of a part of a whole. Its unity is less than that of the supposite, for though it is

intrinsically undivided (<u>indivisum</u> <u>in</u> <u>se</u>), it is not <u>of</u>
<u>itself</u> divided from other natures of the same species
(<u>divisum ab omni alio</u>); whereas the supposite <u>is</u> thus
divided from other supposites, namely, by reason of something intrinsic to itself: its haecceity.(41) This brings
us to Scotus' doctrine on the <u>de</u> <u>jure</u> uniqueness of the
individual.

     Scotus, as we have noted, holds that a common na-
ture is multipliable. A specific nature, like humanity,
is multipliable. A generic nature, like animality, is in
a sense even "more multipliable," since every instance of
humanity (rational animality), as well as of irrational
animality, is at the same time an instance of animality.
In other words, a generic nature is multiplied not only,
like a specific nature, in an indefinitely large number of
individuals, but also in two or more species, each of which
will have its own series of individuals.(42) But this
"multipliability" of which we have been speaking is not too
easy to understand. We are impelled to ask: What precisely is multipliable? or to put the question in more technical terms: What is the referent of the concept <u>common</u>
<u>nature</u>? In our answer let us take as example the common
nature <u>humanity</u>. The referent in this case could be <u>any</u>
inferior of the universal concept <u>human</u> <u>nature</u>; that <u>is</u>,
any individual human nature, for this is multipliable in
the sense that it is duplicatable or, better--if we may
coin a word--"replicatable." The human nature of, say,
Paul, is such that replicas or copies can be made of it--
perfectly similar in themselves, but with differing individual determinations.(43)

     Yet there must, thinks Scotus, be something in
each individual over and above the common nature--something
which cannot be duplicated, which is unique not only <u>de</u>
<u>facto</u>, but <u>de</u> <u>jure</u>. For Scotus the haecceity is, as <u>it</u>
were, the extreme of unity. An haecceity is not only not
divided; it is indivisible. Whatever is simple (even
though not "simply simple") is indivisible physically, but
an individuality is not even divisible into so-called subjective parts.(44) There cannot be other realities like it.
(45) In fact, we cannot even conceive two or more of "it."
Or, rather, this would be true of one who <u>could</u> conceive an
individuality of haecceity. This, unfortunately, is beyond
us, for though we can and do conceive individuals as such,
their respective individualities <u>in</u> <u>themselves</u> cannot be
known by us in this life.(46)

That which is one is not only undivided in itself,
it is divided from everything else. Now, an individuality
is not, of course, separated from the being it individuates,
which it "divides" from other individuals; rather it is inseparably united to this. But if, as we have noted, similarity is a great bond of union, dissimilarity, conversely, divides. Hence the pure difference of an individuality
or haecceity dividing it from everything else is a source
of its high unity.

Criticism of Scotus' Position on the Problem of Universals

It is, of course, not possible here to criticize
in detail Scotus' teaching on universals. But there is one
point which we ought to discuss inasmuch as it directly concerns the principal theme of this paper, namely, the relation between dissimilarity and distinction. Scotus, as we
have seen, holds that the haecceity or individual difference is not quidditative. Now, this presents a problem to
us, for it seems to run counter to our claim that the Scotistic haecceities are principles of distinction because
they are principles of dissimilarity. For it would seem
that only quiddities could be similar or dissimilar. Certainly Scotus would not be on the side of those who claim
that similitude and dissimilitude may be predicated of existence or the act of being (esse).

Let us inquire more deeply into the intention of
Scotus when he rejects the quidditative character of the
haecceity. If it can be shown that in doing so he is denying only that it has the character of a specific quiddity,
but not that it has an individual character or quiddity,
then the problem will be solved. This is, in fact, what
we hope to show in the few pages remaining.

Let us first take a very general approach. The disjunction between the quidditative (or essential) and the existential orders seems to be adequate.(47) Whatever does
not concern the question: "Is it?" pertains to the question: "What is it? To be sure, if "What is it?" is taken
as equivalent to "What kind of thing is it?" (i.e., "To
what class of things does it pertain?" or "To what other
things is it similar? or "What is its definition?"), then
the disjunction between the question "Is it?" and "What is

it?" is not complete. But if the "what" is taken as signifying the whole character of a thing, not excluding its
unique, unrepeatable characteristics, then it would seem
that a thing's individuality would be included in what it
is. Otherwise the principle of individuation would be reduced to the mere fact of individuation or distinction from
everything else; and this at least comes close to making
existence the source of individuation, a position, as we
have said, explicitly rejected by the Subtle Doctor. In
any case, Scotus' principle of distinction (ratio disting-
uendi) is not the mere fact of being distinct, but the
reason, the ontological ground of this fact.

One of the main reasons why Scotus calls the haecceity non-quidditative is doubtless his acceptance of the
Aristotelian principle that any change in quiddity means a
change in species; in consequence of which a quidditative
haecceity would be equivalent to a specific difference.
There could not be so much as two individuals in one and
the same species. Each individual, like a Thomistic angel,
would exhaust its species. This was not Scotus' own view
of the matter, (48) so to avoid confusion--we would say--he
rejects a quidditative haecceity. We observe, however,
that to escape the basic difficulty it suffices to limit
Aristotle's principle to specific quiddities. So limited,
it would assume the quite harmless form: Any change whatever in quiddity (specific) means a change in species.

Another reason Scotus gives for refusing to admit
that haecceities may be quidditative in character is that
anything quidditative is duplicatable, and hence that only
a non-quidditative haecceity can render a being non-dupli-
catable and so truly individual. But is it the case that
every quiddity is duplicatable? Again, this would seem to
be true only of specific quiddities, and so one may wonder
if this is not the "quiddity" Scotus had in mind in the
passages in question. The reason why a specific quiddity
can be duplicated is that it does not yet have all the determination it needs for actual existence.(49) Consequently, two or more things, perfectly similar in regard to this
specific quiddity, can, nevertheless, be distinct by reason
of diverse (dissimilar) additions fully and finally determining the quiddity in each case. These complementing entities serve as principles of individuation, which by their
dissimilarity make possible the distinction of the beings

of which they are the respective ultimate determinations.
And because they are ultimate determinations (ultima realitas formae), they cannot themselves be diversified and so
multiplied by the addition of any further determinations.
(50)

It is diversifying additions which make possible
the replication of a given nature or quiddity.(51) Hence
as nothing can be added to a nature or quiddity which is
already fully determinate, this is, in consequence, not
duplicatable but individual in the strict sense of the
term.(52) We see, then, that the full determination of a
nature or quiddity is not merely that determination which
specifies it and is expressed in the definition. It includes also the individual determination or "whatness";
that is, those aspects (formalities) of an individual substance by which it differs from every other individual substance of the same species.

It seems clear from the foregoing considerations
that Scotus in conformity with his basic principles could
have held that haecceities have individual "quiddity" at
least in the sense that haecceities are dissimilar and differentiate by reason of their dissimilarity. The question
remains did he hold this? Actually, we feel an affirmative
answer is at least strongly suggested by all we have seen
so far, and in particular by Scotus' analysis of imperfect
similarity. However, it will, we think be useful to give
briefly a few more explicit indications of his views on
the matter.

We may note first of all that the haecceities,
which distinguish individual from individual, are said to
be primarily diverse. Now, while the word "diverse" is not
without ambiguity in Scotus' writings, it cannot here mean
merely distinct, for the whole context, notably the comparison of the function of haecceities with that of specific
differences, indicates that it means dissimilar.

Another indication of Scotus' real opinion can be
found in his doctrine on our knowledge of the singular.
According to Scotus we do have conceptual knowledge of
singulars, but because we cannot know haecceities in themselves, the unity of our singular concepts is "as it were,
per accidens," being compounded of the concept of a common
nature plus the concept "individual, numerically one, in-

communicable, etc." We never have <u>distinct</u> knowledge of
the singular in this life. "For we never come across anything which by its very nature is contradictorily opposed
to being in another."(53) Note the implication: We know
the fact of individuality, numerical oneness, incommunica-
bility. We infer that some ground for these must exist, but
we do not know <u>what</u> it is. If we did know what it is--its
nature (<u>ratio</u>)--we would then see why it would be contradictory for this or that individual difference to be in
another.(54)

More direct evidence is to be found in Question 13
of the <u>Metaphysics</u>. Scotus here writes: "From what has
been said it can be concluded that a nature is this by some
substance, which is a form" (i.e., is individualized by
something substantial,(55) which is formal in character--
(56) a "formality"). Somewhat later he adds: "A species
is not a genus for this reason, namely, that it is not predicated of many things differing in species, but only of
things differing numerically, because the individual form
added on to the nature of the species does not bring about
a specific difference, but only a numerical one....The species does not predicate in its integrity the whole nature
of the individual, just as the genus does not predicate
that of the species....The individual cannot be defined by
the (individual) difference, since a definition is a universal predicate and the whole nature of the individual is
not such that it can be predicated of many....Definition
is a speech indicating the universal <u>what is</u>, not the <u>what
is</u> of the individual."(57)

The words "form" and "individual form" applied to
the haecceity certainly suggest that this has a character-
a quiddity in this very general sense. The comparison of
the individual difference with the specific adds strength
to the suggestion. This is still further reinforced by
the statement that the entire "nature" (<u>natura</u>) of the individual is not expressed by the species; <u>i.e.</u>, is not
contained in the specific quiddity. Finally, we have the
explicit distinction between the specific quiddity and the
individual quiddity. Another explicit reference to individual quiddity occurs much later in the same question in
connection with our knowledge of the singular. Scotus
writes: "Yet the singular for its part is intelligible,
since it is a <u>what</u>, but it is not intelligible by us now
(<u>in via</u>) by a positive, simple act of the intellect."(58)

It seems then, that Scotus, at least in his Meta-physics, does identify the haecceity as an individual quid-dity. The Metaphysics appears to be an early work, but in the Ordinatio, which represents his mature thought, he continues to speak of the haecceity in a manner that indicates rather clearly that he conceived it as the source of the dissimilarity and, as a consequence, of the distinction of individuals. What is strongly suggested by Scotus' teaching on imperfect similarity is, we believe, implied by his doctrine on the common nature and individuality, namely: distinction presupposes dissimilarity.

Part III. General Conclusion

Scotus, in order to safeguard the objectivity of human knowledge, has emphasized the reality of similarity, and hence, indirectly, the reality of ots foundation: distinctness. Yet for a different reason he has emphasized even more the fact of dissimilarity, the "reality" of diversity, of difference, over and above mere distinctness. (59) Similar beings are distinct beings, but what makes them distinct is not their similarity, but rather their dissimilarity. As they are only imperfectly similar, they must also be dissimilar; and that by which they differ is, in a true sense, more important than the mere duplication of what is similar. What counts most is not mere distinction, but diversity. If there could be only two statues in the whole world, the Moses of Michaelangelo, let us assume, and one other, which would be preferable for that other: a replica of the Moses or, say, the Hermes of Praxiteles-- or even a statue of notably less beauty? Surely, it is better to have the music of both Bach and Gershwin rather than that of two Bachs duplicating each other. It may have been some such line of thought that encouraged Scotus to stress not only the diversity of species by reason of their unique specific differences, but also and especially that of individuals by reason of those differences--which render each thing unique.

When we reflect on Scotus' appreciation of the rich diversity in the universe, his insight into the peculiar goodness and beauty of each of God's creatures, we are not surprised to learn that he was specially beloved of the poets' poet, Gerard Manley Hopkins, who always sought to grasp as far as possible the individuality of each being he encountered, who like Scotus, never forgot that "there lives the dearest freshness deep down things."

See <u>Ord</u>.I,d.2,pars 2,qq.1-4,n.398; II,354.

(1) Cf. GRAJEWSKI,O.F.M., MAURICE J.: <u>The Formal</u> <u>Distinct-</u><u>ion</u> <u>of</u> <u>Duns</u> <u>Scotus</u> (Washington 1944), pp.97-100.

(2) Scotus' position on this point is directly opposed by
conceptualists like Ockham, who writes: "Est major conven-
ientia inter Socratem et Platonem quam inter Socratem et
istum asinum; non propter aliquid aliquo modo distinctum,
sed seipsis plus conveniunt" (cited from P.Vignaux: <u>La Pen-</u>
<u>see au Moyen Age</u>, Paris, 1948, p.165; English translation:
<u>Philosophy in the Middle Ages</u>, New York, 1950, p.168. Cf.
the words of a contemporary nominalist, W.V.O.Quine: "There
is not...any entity whatever individual or otherwise, which
is named by the word "redness," nor, for that matter, by
the word "househood," "rosehood" "sunsethood." It does not
follow, of course, that <u>all</u> who oppose Scotus on this matter are either conceptualists or nominalists!

(3) "Make" is, of course, not to be understood as suggesting efficient causality. When we say "that which makes blue
color <u>color</u>" we mean no more than that by reason of the
presence of which blue color is rightly denominated color.
As this is present "in" the blue color, the denomination
is intrinsic.

(4) Cf. <u>Ord</u>.I,d.2,pars 2,qq.1-4,n.407; II,358: "...Est
... in albedo aliquid realiter unde habet rationem coloris,
et aliquid unde habet rationem differentiae; et haec realitas non est formaliter illa realitas, nec e converso formaliter, immo una est extra realitatem alterius--formaliter
loquendo--sicut si essent duae res, licet modo per iden-
titatem istae duae realitates sint una res." See also <u>loc.</u>
<u>cit.</u>, n.419; II,366. <u>N</u>.<u>B</u>. Our references to Book I of
Scotus' <u>Ordinatio</u> are to the Vatican edition: <u>Joannis Duns</u>
<u>Scoti Opera Omnia</u> (Vatican City, 1950-). References to
Books II-IV and to all the other works of Scotus are--un-
less otherwise indicated--to the Paris or Vives edition:
<u>Joannis Duns Scoti Opera Omnia</u> , 26 vols. (Paris, 1891-95).
For the sake of uniformity we shall use the title <u>Ordinatio</u>
even when referring to earlier editions, which employed a
different name. The abbreviations: "Ord." and "Metaph."
refer respectively to the <u>Ordinatio</u> and to Scotus' <u>Quaest-</u>

iones Subtilissimae super libros Metaphysicorum Aristotel-
is. The Roman and Arabic numerals which follow the semi-
colon in references to Scotus indicate the volume and page
of the edition cited.

(5) For a full treatment of Scotus' doctrine on the formal
distinction see the work of Maurice J. Grajewski cited in
Note 1, above. For a brief account see the author's "Problem for Realism: Our Multiple Concepts of Individual
Things and the Solution of Duns Scotus." Essay in John
Duns Scotus, 1265-1965. Ed. by John K. Ryan and Bernardine
M. Bonansea (Washington, 1965), pp.64-68. The present essay,
incidentally, is the fulfillment of the hope expressed in
the earlier essay (note 3, pp.62-63) of soon being able to
publish the results of investigations concerning two other
problems for realism with which Scotus dealt.

(6) Scotus did not see how one can avoid a contradiction
if he does not posit some minimal, but extramental distinction between the divine nature and that in each Divine Person by which He is distinguished from the other divine Persons. If outside the mind, in reality, the Father is adequately identical with the divine nature and if the Son is
also adequately identical with the same divine nature, how
can we avoid saying that the Son is the Father and the
Father, the Son? Cf. Ord.I,d.2,pars 2,qq.1-4,nn.388-410;
II,349-61.

(7) See "Problem for Realism...", referred to in Note 5,
above.

(8) The question of similarity has, of course, been much
debated by philosophers and not only in connection with
the problem of universals, though this aspect was predom-
inant in ancient and mediaeval times. For an interesting
and stimulating treatment of the history of the problem
especially in modern times, see R.I.Aaron: The Theory of
Universals (Oxford, 1952). Cf. R.W.Church: An Analysis
of Resemblance (London, 1952).

(9) Here we pass over certain serious difficulties which
we must discuss later on.

(10)In Metaph.,VII,q.13,n.18; VII,418, we are told that
that by which one individual "primo distinguitur ab alio
individuo, ita quod id in hoc individuo, et aliud in illo,

sint primo diversa,...proprie vocatur differentia individualis vel singularis, cum differentia sit, qua differunt a
se singula." The diversity of the differentia individualis" is, so to speak, total, for "ex se diversum...a quolibet, sive opposito, sive differentia disparata" (ibid.).

(11) We are indebted to an esteemed confrere, Father J.
Benedetto, recently deceased, for this apt comparison.

(12) Anticipating Ockham, Scotus himself tells us: "Plu-
ralitas nunquam ponenda est sine necessitate" (Metaph. IV,
q.2,n.23; VII, 171).

(13) Scotus sometimes opposes "numerically the same" (idem
numero) to "distinct." However, it seems to us that the
concept distinct, though presupposed to the concept number,
is independent of this. The sheerly distinct, without any
common denominator whatsoever, are not countable. But two
"things" can be counted, as well as two roses or clocks.
In other words, only instances of a universal are countable,
so that until we recognize the similarity of this and of
that at least in "thingness" or in "objectivity," we shall
not be able to arrive at the concept two, but only at that
of distinct or other.

(14) Phenomenologically speaking, we must say that distinctness seems to presuppose dissimilarity rather than
vice-versa. It appears we know that red is not green, for
example, before we know that this (red) is not that (green).
The perception of the dissimilarity of red and green leads
to the perception of this and that. If there were no dissimilarity at all apparent in my field of consciousness,
how could I ever have come to think of this and that?

(15) See Ord. II,d.3,q.1,n.7; XII,48-49.

(16) Cf. Ord. II,d.3,q.6,n.12; XII,135: "Illa realitas
specifica constituit compositum, cujus est pars, in esse
quidditativo, quia ipsa est entitas quaedam quidditativa;
ista autem entitas individui est primo diversa ab omni entitate quidditativa, quod probatur ex hoc, quia intelli-
gendo quamcumque entitatem quidditativam, loquendo de quidditativa entitate limitata, non habet in quidditate intellecta, unde ipsa sit haec; ergo illa entitas, quae de se
est haec, est alia entitas a quidditate vel ab entitate
quidditativa; non potest ergo constituere totum cujus est

pars, in esse quidditativo, sed in esse alterius rationis!"
Cf. Ord.II,d.3,q.6,n.16; XII,146; ibid.,n.19; XII,147; and
ibid., n.30; XII,155. In Ord. II,d.3,q.7,n.3; XII,160, we
read: "Omnis quidditas quantum est de se communicabilis
est." See also ibid.,nn.3-5; XII,160-62.

(17) Scotus sometimes uses the term "haecceitas," and this
became very common in the history of Scotism. More often
he uses some other expression; e.g., "entitas singularis"
(Ord.II,d.3,q.6,n.15; XII,144: and III,d.14,q.3,n.9; XIV,
529), "realitas individui" and "entitas individui" (Ord.
II,d.3,q.6,n.12; XII,135; cf.ibid.,n.13; XII,135), "entitas individualis" (Ord.II,d.3,q.6,n.30; XII,155).

(18) See Metaph.VII,q.13; VII,404-26. Scotus also refutes
here the position that individuation can be due to a relation to the agent and the view that it could be based on a
mere negation.

(19) Cf.Ord.II,d.3,q.6,n.15; XII,144: "Sed haec est formaliter entitas singularis, et illa est entitas naturae formaliter, nec possunt istae duae realitates esse res et res,
sicut possent esse realitas unde accipitur genus, et realitas unde accipitur differentia ex quibus realitas specifica accipitur, sed semper in eodem sive parte sive toto,
sunt realitates ejusdem rei formaliter distinctae.

(20) See Metaph.VII,q.13,nn.19-20; VII,420.

(21) "Omne inferius (We follow here the reading of the
Quaracchi ed.,II,260) includit in se aliquid, quod non includitur in intellectu superioris, alioquin conceptus in-
ferioris esset aeque communis, sicut conceptus superioris
et tunc per se inferius non esset per se inferius, quia
non subesset communi, et superiori; ergo aliquid per se includitur in ratione individui, quod non includitur in ratione naturae" (loc.cit.,n.2; XII,128).

(22) See, e.g., Ord.II,d.3,q.6,n.30; XII,155: "...naturam
quae contrahitur, scilicet per illam entitatem individualem."

(23) As the next two passages to be quoted are continuous
with the present, it will be convenient to give here the
Latin original of all of them..."Omnis differentia dif-
ferentium reducitur ad aliqua primo diversa, alioquin non

esset status in differentibus; sed individua proprie differunt, quia sunt diversa aliquid idem entia; ergo eorum
differentia reducitur ad aliqua primo diversa. Illa primo diversa non sunt natura in illo et natura in isto, quia
non est idem quo aliqua conveniunt formaliter, et quo differunt realiter, licet idem possit esse distinctum realiter, et conveniens formaliter. Multum enim refert (sic:
differt?) esse distinctum et esse quo aliquid primo distinguitur, ergo sic erit de unitate; igitur praeter naturam in hoc et in illo, sunt aliqua primo diversa, quibus
hoc et illud differunt, illud in illo, et hoc in isto..."
(loc.cit.,n.9; XII,133).

(24) Scotus recognizes the fact that while two things can
be more or less dissimilar, they cannot be more or less distinct. Cf. Ord.II,d.3,q.1,n.5; XII,9-10: "Omnis diversi-
tas numeralis inquantum numeralis (i.e., every distinction
as such) est aequalis."

(25) Cf. Metaph. VII,q.13,n.22; VII,422: "Ad sextum,
quidquid per se inest uni individuo, cujus simile inest
alii individuo, inest per naturam communem, quia differentiis singularibus non inest commune aliquid."

(26) See note 10, above.

(27) We have assumed that "refert" is a misreading for
"differt" (see Latin text in note 23) and translated accordingly.

(28) See Metaph.VII,q.13,n.1; VII,403. Cf. Ord.II,d.3,q.6,
n.14; XII,136.

(29) But could it not be said that at least they have
"haecceity" or "thisness" in common? Doubtless Scotus
would deny that these common nouns formed from demonstra-
tives indicate anything more than a similarity of function,
that, namely, of individualizing. We know that in the
present context the Subtle Doctor is concerned almost exclusively with similarity in intrinsic content.

(30) Cf. Ord.II,d.3,q.1,n.10; XII,55: "Universalitas non
convenit rei ex se, et ideo concedo, quod quaerenda est
causa universalitatis."

(31) Cf. Metaph.VII,q.13,n.19; VII,420: "In Socrate enim

non solum secundum considerationem intellectus, sed secundum ordinem naturalem perfectionum unitive contentarum, prius est animal quam homo, et homo quam hic homo, quod patet ex operationibus propriis." This, of course, is nothing other than the natural priority of the determinable over that which determines it.

(32) Cf. Metaph.VII,q.13,n.23; VII,424: "...quia non est universalis nisi in singulari."

(33) St. Thomas has a rather full treatment of the natura absolute considerata in Quodlibet VIII,a.1. From the text it should be clear that we agree with Bettoni when he writes: "The Scotistic solution of the problem of universals is thus substantially within the framework of moderate realism." Efrem Bettoni, O.F.M.: Duns Scotus: The Basic Principles of His Philosophy. Transl. and ed. by Bernardine Bonansea, O.F.M. (Washington, 1961), pp.57-58. This, to be sure, is a controverted matter. For interpretations differing from ours see Etienne Gilson: Jean Duns Scot. Introduction a ses positions fondamentales (Paris, 1952), pp.110-13; 446-51; and Joseph Owens, C.SS.R.: "Common nature: A Point of Comparison between Thomistic and Scotistic Metaphysics." Medieval Studies 19 (1957) 1-14.

(34) See Metaph.VII,q.13,n.10; VII,410; q.18,nn.4-5; VII, 455; Ord.II,d.3,q.1,nn.8-9; XII,54-55; q.6,n.10; XII,133. Scotus sums up the matter very neatly in Metaph.VII,q.13,n. 21; VII,421, where he writes: "Respondeo, si loquamur realiter, humanitas quae est in Socrate, non est humanitas quae est in Platone, et est realis differentia ex differentiis individualibus unitive contentis, inseparabilibus hinc inde."

(35) Cf. Metaph.VII,q.13,n.1; VII,402-03: "Si...natura esset hoc aliquid de se, repugnaret sibi multitudo, et tunc natura non posset esse in multis....Item, si lapis de se formaliter esset hic lapis, omnis lapis esset hic lapis. Consequentia patet, quia quidquid inest naturae ex se, inest ei in quocumque invenitur." No doubt, it would have been less controversial if Scotus had said: If the concept stone were to include thisness (this thisness! Cf. Ord.II,d.3,q.4,n.3; XII,93), then only one stone, namely, this one, could correspond to it; that is, there could be only one stone. But Scotus has more in mind. He holds that to the "abstract" concept stone there must correspond something in this stone, which, because it is that

214

by which this stone is similar to all other stones, must
be extramentally distinct from the "thisness" by which
this stone differs from all other stones.

(36) See Ord. II,d.3,q.1,n.10: XII,55.

(37) A nature is one in the sense that its instances are
perfectly similar; it is not one in the sense that they
are not distinct. Two reds of the same hue, intensity,
saturation, etc., are not two colors in the sense of two
different (-differing) colors; they are two colors in the
sense of distinct instances of the "same" color. Color is
such that it can be thus multiplied.

(38) The unity of the common nature, the "unity less than
numerical," is in most respects identical with what is more
frequently referred to as specific unity. See, for example, Metaph.VII,q.13,n.21; VII,421. Yet we should add that
Scotus has achieved a fresh insight into specific unity,
that is, into the implications of the traditional doctrine
on species.

(39) Not Scotus alone, but the Scholastics generally,
speak of substances as being unum or idem specie or genera.
St. Thomas, for example, tells us that "diversa supposita
sunt unum quae communicant in una ratione speciei" (In X
Metaph., lect. 4,n.2005) and, by way of illustration:
"Socrates et Plato sunt idem humanitate" (ibid.,n.2002).

(40) One of Scotus' arguments in favor of the existence
of a unity less than numerical unity consists in an appeal
to the unity of the object of one type of sense activity.
See Ord.II,d.3,q.1,n.4; XII,9.(Cf. Metaph.VII,q.13,n.11;
VII,411.) Now, this unity is pretty obviously a unity of
kind, that is, of similarity. Scotus also argues (ibid.,
n.5; XII,9-10) that if this lesser unity were not given,
then any two beings according to their whole realities
would be primo diversa; in other words, they would be
wholly dissimilar. The lesser unity of the common nature
must, therefore, be a unity of similarity. Finally, Scotus'
argument (ibid.) from the unity of the generator and the
generated again indicates that the lesser unity is merely
one of specific likeness or similarity.

(41) Cf. Ord.II,d.3,q.6,n.10; XII,133: "In eodem ergo
quod est idem numero, est aliqua entitas, quam consequitur

minor unitas quam sit unitas numeralis, et est realis, et
illud cujus est unitas talis formaliter, non est de se
unum unitate numerali. Concedo ergo, quod unitas realis
non est alicujus entitatis existentis in duobus individ-
uis, sed in uno."

(42) This is why Scotus calls generic unity "unitatem mi-
norem unitate speciei" (Ord.II,d.3,q.6,n.10; XII,133).

(43) The common nature, it is clear, is not something
apart from its instances, but any one of these instances
considered in its pure suchness. Cf. Metaph.VII,q.13,
n.23; VII,424: "...non est universalis nisi in singulari."

(44) In rejecting various candidates for principle of individuation Scotus writes: "Contra...omnia ista est, quia
quodlibet istorum est communicabile; ergo de ipso est quae-
rendum, per quid fit hoc, vel per quid repugnat sibi divi-
di in partes subjectivas" (Metaph.VII,q.13,n.17; VII,418).
Scotus defines "subjective parts" as "tales...quarum quae-
libet sit ipsum" (loc.cit.; VII,417). Between the specific
and the individual unities there is one difference: "Tan-
tummodo est differentia in hoc, quia illa unitas naturae
specificae minor est ista unitate (of the individual), et
propter hoc, illa non excludit omnem divisionem, quae est
secundum partes subjectivas, sed tantum illam divisionem
quae est partium essentialium; ista autem excludit omnem"
(Ord.II,d.3,q.6,n.11; XII,134). See also: Metaph.VII,
q.13,n.18; VII,418; Ord.II,d.3,q.2,n.2; XII,78; q.6,n.9;
XII,132.

(45) Of course, this is true of the individual thing too
and per se inasmuch as the thing--the whole--contains unitive the non-replicatable haecceity. See the clear account
in Ord.II,d.3,q.6,n.10; XII,133-34.

(46) See, below, pp.22-23 and nn.53-54.

(47) The distinguished Scotist scholar, Father Allan
Wolter, O.F.M., has suggested to the author that it would
be better to speak of the essential rather than of the
quidditative character of the haecceity. Because of the
common, close association of "quiddity" with "species" and
"definition," this would, no doubt, be wise. However,
those who identify "essence" and "quiddity" would still

216

have their difficulties. Our discussion in the text (which antedates Father Wolter's suggestion) is meant directly for them, but should be a _fortiori_ acceptable to those who give "essence" a wider reference.

(48) Scotus' opinion on the individuality of angels is expressed in _Ord_.II,d.3,q.7,n.4; XII,160: "...simpliciter possibile est plures Angelos esse in eadem specie." For his argument for this and his answer to objections see the whole of q.7.

(49) _Cf. Metaph_.VII,q.13,n.19: "Cum etiam (a nature) nunquam fiat in rerum natura nisi dum determinato gradu." Only a fully determinate reality, which must include individual determination can exist.

(50) Cf. Ord.II,d.3,q.6,n.12; XII,135: "Quoad hoc, ista realitas individui est similis realitati specificae, quod est quasi actus determinans illam realitatem speciei quasi possibilem et potentialem, sed quoad hoc dissimilis, quia ista nunquam sumitur a forma addita, sed praecise ab ultima realitate formae." Shortly before Scotus had suggested that the haecceity, like certain specific differences, "sumitur ab ultima abstractione formae" (_ibid_.), but it comes to the same, since he holds that abstractions are grounded in an extramental distinction of formalities. Since a given matter is for Scotus a "thing," it too must have its haecceity. When, therefore, he wishes to include also this function of individualizing the matter, Scotus calls the haecceity, not _ultima realitas formae_, but _ultima realitas entis_. See _Ord_.II,d.3,q.6,n.15; XII,144.

(51) If two things were perfectly alike in _all_ respects, how could intelligence--even infinite intelligence --distinguish one from the other? That position from which an absurdity flows cannot be true. But might not the source of differentiation, and thus the principle of individuation, be an external relation? The question arises, for example, in regard to position in time and place. T⸱ whole matter is beset with obscurities, but as regards position in time and place, it seems to us more reasonable to say that things must be distinct prior--at least by nature--to their occupying distinct positions. For, unless one postulates an absolute space and time, the positions themselves can, it seems, be distinct only by reason of

the prior distinction of the bodies, the static and dynamic relations of which define those positions in place and time. Scotus, for his part, rejects the idea that position can be a principle of individuation. Cf. Metaph.VII, q.13,n.24; VII,425: "Hoc non est hoc per locum, quia si cognosceret hoc, inquantum hoc, etiam distingueret ab illo, posito quod simul essent, imo quocumque posito, stante hoc." Also loc.cit.,q.15,n.5; VII,437: "Haec albedo ponatur simul in loco cum illa albedine, manet ergo haec et haec, illa et illa, quia haec non est haec, per hoc esse in loco."

(52) Precisely because it is in itself fully determinate, the divine nature is of itself singular and has no need of, and will not allow of, a distinct principle of individuation. See Ord.II,d.3,q.6,n.16; XII,145 and n.30; XII,155. Cf. Ord.II,d.3,q.7,n.5; XII,161-62: "Dico igitur, quod omnis natura, quae non est de se actus purus potest secundum illam realitatem, secundum quam est natura, esse potentialis ad realitatem illam qua est haec natura."

(53) Metaph.VII,q.15,n.8; VII,439.

(54) For Scotus' teaching on our knowledge of the singular, see Metaph.VII,q.13, esp. nn.23-26; VII,423-26; also q.14,n.5; VII,433. Cf.Ord.II,d.3,q.6,n.16; XII,146. This matter is competently treated in Sebastian J. Day, O.F.M., Intuitive Cognition. A Key to the Significance of the Later Scholastics (St. Bonaventure, N.Y., 1947), pp114-24.

(55) For Scotus, we note, the haecceity was a logical, not an ontological accident. See Ord.II,d.3,q.4,n.19; XII, 111. Cf. loc.cit.,n.20; XII,112.

(56) If sometimes Scotus speaks of the haecceity as "material" rather than "formal," the reason is simply that the haecceity is the foundation of the "thisness" which constitutes a subject as such, in opposition to a predicate. Now, in logic subjects are taken "materially." Ontologically speaking, it's a different story, and this is why Scotus much more commonly affirms the formal character of the haecceity. See Metaph.VII,q.13,n.18; VII,418-19; ɵ Ord.II,d.3,q.6,n.13; XII,135.

(57) N.13; VII,412-13.

(58) <u>Metaph</u>.VII,q.13,n.25; VII,425.

(59) Cf. <u>Ord</u>.II,d.3,q.7,n.10; XII,169: "...in principal-
ibus autem entibus, est a Deo intentum individuum princi-
paliter...."

(60) We are reminded of a scrap of dialogue in T.S.Eliot's
<u>The Cocktail Party</u>:

       Edward: ...Mine is a very unusual case.
       Reilly: All cases are unique, and very similar to
                others.

Discussion

JAMES P. REILLY, JR., PH.D.

Editor, *Franciscan Studies*
General Editor, Ockham Edition
The Franciscan Institute
St. Bonaventure, New York

In his commentary on the Sentences, St. Bonaventure observes that one may produce a book, and presumably a paper, in four ways: 1) as a scribe, 2) as a compiler, 3) as a commentator, and 4) as an author. The program committee of this symposium, unlike St. Bonaventure, has not been so restrictive. At least, the role they have assigned me, namely, discussant, is not clearly defined. Indeed the latent ambiguity of the term could even tempt me to assume the role of an author, and thus, using Fr. Watson's paper simply as a point of departure, to present in my turn another paper on the problem. However, unlike the naive Bachelors of Roger Bacon's time who incurred his wrath for expounding Sacred Scriptures instead of reading them, I will not run the risk of angering you by identifying the role of the discussant with that of the author. Rather I shall assume that my role as discussant is comparable to the role of the commentator described by St. Bonaventure: "Aliquis scribit et aliena et sua, sed aliena tamquam principalia, et sua tamquam annexa ad evidentiam." (1)

Fortunately, Fr. Watson has made my task relatively easy. His presentation of the problem of dissimilarity and distinction in the philosophy of Duns Scotus is lucid and thorough. Everyone will agree, I am sure, that he has chosen correctly in deciding to develop his resolution of the problem in terms of its relationship to Scotus' teaching on imperfect similarity and his doctrine on universals. Furthermore, it is clear that Fr. Watson considers the resolution of this problem to be of fundamental importance for a proper understanding of Scotus' Realism. If nothing else, certainly his repeated stress on the centrality of Scotus' doctrine of formalities to the resolution of the problem, should alert us to the importance of this issue. Indeed, in a previously published article, "A Problem for Realism: Our Multiple Concepts of Individual Things and the Solution of Duns Scotus," he had promised just such an examination as we have had today: "We hope sometime in the near future to publish our investigations concerning two other problems of realism with which Scotus dealt. These problems can be approximately expressed in the following two questions: 1) What is the precise objective foundation for our judging that two things are imperfectly similar? and 2) What is the exact relationship between

221

distinction and dissimilarity? Both questions are, we believe, more fundamental than the usual questions asked about Scotus' teaching on universals." (2) It is these questions in effect, which Fr. Watson has attempted to answer this afternoon.

With regard to the first question, namely, the foundation of imperfect similarity, Fr. Watson contends, that according to Scotus, imperfect similarity is founded upon the relationship between similars, one of which, at least, must be composite. In short, imperfect similarity is not an irreducible given. For example, the brute soul and the human soul are imperfectly similar, because the human soul is a composite of those formalities by which it is both similar and dissimilar to the brute soul. Now, even though the human soul is a sort of difference between man and brute, it is not the ultimate difference. According to Scotus, the ultimate difference must be wholly dissimilar, otherwise the ultimate differences themselves would be similar, and thus would imply a further distinction between their common element and their differentiating element. Consequently, imperfect similarity cannot be based upon the ultimate difference, hacceitas, but rather it is based upon that formality which the two things in question have in common.

At this point in his paper, Fr. Watson proposes a critical analysis of the position of Scotus, and it is precisely here that some questions must be raised.

First of all, Father seems haunted by the principle of economy, or perhaps more graphically, by the shadow of Ockham's razor. While it is true that the necessity for positing a very large number of formalities is not in and of itself a telling argument against the position of Scotus, nevertheless it would seem legitimate to ask: Can the position of Scotus escape the charge of subjectivity, if formalities are multiplied virtually ad infinitum?

Secondly, Fr. Watson has subjected to analysis that principle of Scotus which he regards as most vulnerable, namely, that imperfect similarity implies composition. Because imperfect similarity implies imperfect dissimilarity, it is possible, he says, to conceive of two simple realities which are imperfectly similar, and

are, by that fact, also imperfectly dissimilar. Having
stated this possibility, he then goes on to say that,
though plausible, this constitutes no real objection to
the position of Scotus. After all, Scotus would grant
that the imperfectly similar implies the dissimilar, and
that what is imperfectly similar must be, by that fact,
imperfectly dissimilar. Yet has he not already concluded,
that according to Scotus, one of the two must be composite? How then can two simple realities be imperfectly
dissimilar? What precisely does the term simple mean in
this context, if indeed the possibility cited is compatible with Scotus' stated position?

Finally, Father affirms also that according to
Scotus, one thing cannot be imperfectly similar to another
unless it is in some real respect (i.e., some formality)
perfectly similar. But what exactly is understood by perfect similarity. Is it the same as that which is common?
Granted that there can be degrees of similarity, can there
also be degrees of commonness?

In answer to his second question, namely, what is
the relationship between distinctness and dissimilarity,
Father has developed his answer in terms of three main
points of the Scotistic doctrine; these are: common nature, universals, and hacceitas. There is no need to redo,
even summarily, what has already been done so well and in
detail. What is, however, worth repeating, is the answer
to the question posed in the opening line of Fr. Watson's
paper: "Distinction, it is clear, is a condition of dissimilarity, but is the converse true: Is dissimilarity a
condition of distinction? If I have understood him correctly, Father concludes that according to Scotus, it is
hacceitas which is the basis of distinction and dissimilarity. It is here that Scotus locates the principle of
dissimilarity and distinctness, because hacceitas is non-
quidditative in character; hence it is not able to be mul-
tiplies, and is, therefore, unique. In short, though similarity implies distinctness, and thus similar beings are
distinct beings, what makes them distinct is not their
similarity, but rather their dissimilarity. And it is
hacceitas which is the ultimate ground of dissimilarity.

Fr. Watson, however, is not content with the
Scotistic resolution. In particular, he suggests that one

weakness is the Scotistic insistence on the non-quidditative character of hacceitas. For example, Fr. Watson believes that because there seems to be an adequate disjunction between the essential and existential orders, whatever does not pertain to the question "Is it?", must pertain to the question "What is it?", provided that the
"What" signifies the character of a thing, not excluding
its "Thisness." But will the inclusion of "Thisness" in
the "What" serve as an adequate ontological ground for
the dissimilarity of this "Thisness" from that "Thisness?"

Another objection, according to Fr. Watson, is
that like the similar, the dissimilar must in some sense
be quidditative. Thus: What this is is something like
what that is. But has not Scotus emphatically denied
that hacceitas, the source of dissimilarity, is in any
way similar to anything else? Indeed I find it difficult
to understand what would constitute the similarity of dissimilarity.

Finally, Fr. Watson speculates whether Scotus might
not have been well-advised to have rejected the Aristotelian premise, namely, that a change in quiddity means a
change in species, and to have adopted instead the position
which would have allowed for slight quidditative modifica-
tions between two individuals who, nevertheless, would belong to the same species. In effect, then, Father is op-
ting for a quidditative hacceitas. But what now becomes
the ultimate determining principle? Does not this view
of hacceitas open the gate to a possible infinity of new
formalities? Furthermore, how, for example, will the definition of man remain unaffected, if quidditative modifi-
cations flowing from a quidditative hacceitas are added to
the nature. Would it not seem that the net result would
be that each individual would exhaust the species?

Before concluding these brief remarks, however, I
must observe that, as Fr. Watson has pointed out, the
teaching of Scotus on formalities, common nature, and individuation are better known than the problematic back of
them. In his paper, Father has courageously faced up to
the extremely difficult task of elucidating the structure
of the underlying Scotistic problematic. Undoubtedly a
clearer understanding and a firmer grasp of the real problem which Scotus was attempting to resolve, will further a

more fruitful dialogue between ourselves and the Subtle
Doctor. Although certainly in his state of blessedness
Duns Scotus has no further need of dialogue, we, who are
still wayfarers, have need of a continuing dialogue with
the thought of this great Franciscan master.

DR. JAMES F. ROSS is a graduate of the Catholic
University of America and of Brown University.
He has been Instructor and Assistant Professor
at the University of Michigan. At present he
is Associate Professor of Philosophy and Chairman of the Department of Philosophy at the
University of Pennsylvania. He has written
numerous papers, articles, and reviews for
journals. He is author of the book <u>Philosophi-
cal Theology</u>, Bobbs-Merrill, 1967.

An Application of a

SCOTISTIC Principle

JAMES F. ROSS, PH.D.

General and Circumstantial Introduction:

There is a surprising modernity about the major aspects of Duns Scotus' philosophy. This was noticed by Charles Saunders Pierce at the turn of our century and can be confirmed by reexamination of Scotus' work in the light of present day analytic philosophy and logic.

The logic of modalities, spread throughout his work, indicates that Scotus and his contemporaries had already turned much of the ground reworked by Lewis and Langford in their distinguished treatment of the logic of possibility and necessity. (1) Moreover, Scotus had given careful thought to what is now called "the logic of epistemic modalities," the logical structure of expressions involving verbs for believing and knowing; an area recently subjected to formalized analysis by J. Hintikka. (2) Even more importantly, Scotus had applied his sophisticated conception of logical operators (both modal and epistemic) to solving central metaphysical problems, thereby achieving a major advance in natural theology beyond all his predecessors (except perhaps Avicenna, who seems to have thought in a like vein). (3)

Scotus' original and profound conception of certain epistemological problems which turned out to be historically pivotal and which occupy our attention right now puts him in the front rank of the classical writers who have to be taken seriously today. When I speak of today, I have in mind not just the contemporary philosophical scene among scholastics and neoscholastics; rather, I am referring primarily to the analytic philosophers whose heritage grew mainly from the British empiricists and Kant through the logical atomists and the Vienna circle and on into the "ordinary language" tradition of Austin and Wittgenstein.

Specific Introduction:

This paper is chiefly a commentary upon Article Two of Question Four of the Opus Oxoniense Distinction Three; here Scotus presents a modernization of certain key Augustinian arguments from Contra Academicos. (4)

The interest of his arguments lies a) in his conception of the grounds for certitude in our knowledge of

228

self-evident truths; b) in the endorsement of a certain
class of beliefs about one's own states as being privileged,
and hence certain in a way most other contingent beliefs
are not; c) in a conception of what epistemic certainty
consists in; a conception which has its roots in Plato and
which by way of the 14th century disputes gave rise to and
identified both Rationalism and Empiricism; and d) most
importantly of all, in the Empirical Cannon, the principle
Scotus uses to solve two basic epistemological questions:
1) what are the grounds by which inductive inference is to
be justified; 2) in what way can we possess certitude in
perception? Responding to what he considers the exaggerated
and inaccurate "illuminationism" of Henry of Ghent, Duns
Scotus insists that 1) Henry's interpretation of St.
Augustine leads to skepticism by requiring that a person
shall never be able to know whether the intelligible
species he possesses represents only itself or some object
independent of it; and 2) that St. Augustine claims certainty for much more than Henry allows; namely, for "self-
evident" principles, and for "things known through sense
experience" and for "our own actions." Augustine's rejec-
tion of skepticism requires a rationale for each class of
certitudes, and it is to this that Scotus devotes Article
Two; a rationale is provided which makes no commitment to
illumination and instead, indicates that certainty is possible without special divine illumination.

A. Knowing per se nota truths.

        The terms of self-evident principles are said to be
identical in such a way that it is evident "that the one
necessarily includes the other." I wonder what Scotus
meant by "it is evident?" If he meant that "it is self-
evident that," then his analysis is circular; (we would
get nowhere saying that self-evident propositions are such
that it is self-evident that the subject includes the predicate or vice versa). Hence we must keep a sharp eye for
an explanation of what it means to say a proposition is
self-evident. On the other hand, if "it is evident that..."
is the basic concept, we need some indication of it. (5)
But we need not quibble here; perhaps Scotus merely wants to
insist upon the first claim; that self-evident truths have
identical terms. Yet how would he have squared this claim
with those propositions which he himself called "self-

evident" but which do not have a plurality of distinct
terms which could be called identical: e.g., "Some contingent things exist." (6) What does one do about the difference between self-evident propositions which are necessarily true and those which are contingent? Obviously being
per se nota is not the same as being necessarily true.

    Things become clearer if we first assume that
Scotus is (in Article Two) explaining the certitude of our
knowledge of first principles in general in terms of the
necessary truth of some self-evident principles. For Scotus
cannot possibly be giving the entire explanation of our
certitude about first principles, unless he was mistaken to
call any contingent truth a self-evident first principle
(and if he was so mistaken, it was no minor error since the
claim is repeated often). Evidently, then, we shall have to
supply some elements of the theory which Duns Scotus left
out. On the other hand, the ground for our certitude of
analytic (necessary) first principles (the subclass
Scotus uses to illustrate the existence of certitude concerning first principles) is to be found in the identity of
their terms. So, we had better ask just how the supposed
identity of the terms would explain our certitude about
such principles; and, then, what shall we substitute for
"necessary truth" or "identity of terms" as the ground for
our certitude about those self-evident principles which
happen to be contingent (the part of the theory we need to
supply)?

We are told:

> Quantum ad certitudinem de principiis dico sic,
> quod termini principorum per se notorum talem labat
> identitatem ut alter evidenter necessaric alterum
> includat; et ideo intellectus componens illos
> terminos ex quo apprehendit eos, habet apud se
> necessariam causam conformitatis illius actus ad
> ipsus terminos, quorum est compositio, et etiam
> causam evidentem illius conformitatis, et ideo
> necessario patet sibi conformitus, illa, cujus
> causam necessariam et evidentem apprehendit in
> terminis,....(7)

Father Wolter's translation of the central passage, beginning "et ideo" is:

"The intellect uniting these terms in a proposition, from the very fact that it grasps the terms, has preset to itself the necessary cause, and what is more -- the evident cause, of the conformity of this proposition with the terms that compose it. This conformity then (the evident cause of which the intellect perceives in the terms) cannot help but be evident to the intellect." (8)

We cannot, however, take "illus actus" to mean "proposition" because we are thereby required to talk about a conformity between a proposition and its terms, even while Scotus also talks about "uniting these terms in a proposition" of which the terms must in some way be constituents. Less confusion is generated if we stay with Scotus' talk about a conformity between the act or the judgment which results from the composition (treating the terms respectively as subject and predicate). Not all the confusion disappears but at least we do not have to talk about conformity between a proposition and its constituitive parts; nevertheless, is it better to speak of a conformity between an act or a judgment and the terms which become subject and predicate in it? In any case, the identity of the terms and the fact that the intellect apprehends this identity provide "the necessary and evident cause" of the truth of the resulting judgment. Yet, how does this explain our certitude about first principles?

Even more baffling is the claim:

"Such terms then cannot be combined in a judgment without being true and so it is that one cannot perceive this proposition (e.g., two white objects cannot exist without a relationship of similarity between them) and perceive its terms without also perceiving the conformity of the proposition to the terms, and therefore, perceiving the truth." (9)

There is something profound and yet something flagrantly erroneous about this. The error lies in "Such terms cannot be combined in a judgment without its being true," "non potest stare compositio talium terminorum quin sit vera." (10) For a judgment may be affirmative or negative. To every true affirmative judgment there corresponds a false negative judgment containing all and only the subject and

predicate terms of the former. Hence there is no set of
terms which cannot be combined in a judgment which is false.

Yet if, in defense of Scotus, we interpret the judgment to contain the presence or absence of negations as an
integral part (thus making all the parts of the expression,
both categorical and syncategorematic, into "terms" in it),
then the difference between a self-evident and a non-self-
evident truth would lie exactly in the distinction between
what is necessarily true and what is contingently true.
But this would be entirely unsatisfactory 1) because Scotus
actually considered some contingent truths to be self-
evident (and hence they could have been false); 2) because
not every analytic truth (even a truth with its predicate
identical with its subject) is self-evident to those who
understand its terms; and 3) because not every necessary
truth is analytic (has the requisite conceptual inclusion
between subject and predicate). We must, therefore, reject the claim that the terms of a per se nota proposition
cannot be combined into a false judgment.

Scotus intended to make it evident that from "P is a
first principle," it would follow logically that "If S understands and believes P, P is self-evident to S"; and from "P
is self-evident to S" it would follow logically that "If S
believes P, S is certain that P." And his reason for believing that these are the logical relations lay in these
two facts: 1) first principles are supposed to be things
knowable, than which there is nothing more reliably or
justifiably believed; 2) if we take all these things we
know whose knowledge cannot be acquired by our believing
something which is more reliably believed, we can eliminate
(in a manner of one seeking axioms) all but those things
which are cognitively underivable (independent) propositions, which one can know but whose knowledge cannot be
acquired through anything more reliably believed, is the
set of first principles of human knowledge.

These first principles, since they are not cognitively derived from something else, carry their own guarantee of truth; for whatever is known must be guaranteed as
well as be true. Hence, if P is such that nothing known is
better guaranteed and such that it cannot be logically deduced from anything cognitively independent and as well
guaranteed (and this is required by our hypothesis that at

least the contingent first principles are logically independent of all other first principles), then P, in order to
be known at all, must carry its own warrant, its own
guarantee, its own evidence.

Scotus attempts to explain what the self-evident of
these principles consists in: showing that what renders a
self-evident principle to be self-evident is exactly what
provides our certitude in believing it.

At first we restrict discussion to what is both
self-evident and necessary, though we must eventually consider what is self-evident and contingent. Within this
restriction, a judgment formed with all and only the exact
terms (i.e., the same meanings) and with the same or
equivalent logical constants belonging to a given self-
evident proposition can never fail to be true. These propositions are self-guaranteeing, not merely because they
cannot fail to be true when believed; that, would be a
totally insufficient condition ever to assure knowledge.
In addition to its truth, what is known must have a certain
status as "guaranteed" or "warranted."

That status as "warranted" is required for what is
known can be proved from the fact that for any necessary
truth, no matter when someone happens to believe it, he
believes something which could not fail to be true when believed; and yet, he might have come upon his true belief by
accident, by guess, through prejudice, or in some other way
which would leave him unjustified if therefore without knowledge; hence, the mere fact that something I believe cannot
fail to be true does not entail that I have knowledge of it,
much less that I have certitude. So how does a self-evident
principle guarantee itself or carry its own grounds for belief?

Duns Scotus proposes that the identity of terms
which constitutes the conformity between terms and proposition (and hence renders the proposition true) (11) is also
the warrant which the belief carries with it. Thus he says:

> "...I argue that there is some kind of repugnance
> existing between intellections in the mind, even
> though it is not exactly a formal opposition. For
> if the intellect possesses the knowledge of 'whole'

and 'part' and combines them in a proposition, since
they include the necessary reason for the conformity
of the proposition to the terms, if the intellect
were to think this proposition false, two mutually
repugnant acts of knowledge would coexist, even
though the opposition is not precisely formal."(12)

Scotus again speaks loosely; he does not mean that
any proposition involving the terms 'whole' and 'part' as
its subject and predicate terms will be self-evident; for we
could combine those terms into: "the whole is never greater
than any part"--which would be false. He means: if the intellect combines "whole" and "part" and "greater than" into
any well-formed proposition involving no further categorical
terms, then the resulting proposition will have its truth
value determined entirely by the relations (or lack of them)
between the concepts attached to the constituitive terms.
He intends that any well-formed proposition constructed entirely from syncategorematic arrangements of all and only
the categorical terms which enter into the statement of some
necessary truth will itself be either necessarily true or
formally contradictory. It is not true (as Scotus may
appear to imply) that every proposition formulated in terms
of "whole," "part," and "greater than" will be true. Nor is
it the case that every proposition so formulated (unless it
includes only these terms) will even be a priori. Furthermore, Scotus is not saying either a) that the identity of
the terms is necessary for a necessary truth or b) that
wherever the identity of terms is present, a self-evident
truth is present. He is not claiming the first, because
some necessary truths, e.g., "It is possible that something
exists" are not of the simple categorical form where identity of subject and predicate is a relevant consideration.
He does not claim the second (b) for two reasons: (i) because a very complex and non-primary necessary truth may
have identical terms whose identity is not easily recogniz-
able outside the context of a deductive demonstration of
that principle from first principles; (ii) because we can
formulate a self-contradictory proposition in which an over-
all negation joined to identical terms actually constitutes
the contradiction: "it is false that bachelors are un-
married." Mere identity of the terms does not even guarantee that we have a true or a consistent proposition. But
leaving these niceties aside, what is Scotus' real point?

Scotus wants to say that if you were to understand the terms "whole," "part" and "greater than" as they occur in "Every whole is greater than any of its parts" and yet if you were to "think this proposition false, two mutually repugnant acts of knowledge would coexist." (13) If you were to understand the terms "whole," "part," and "greater than" you would surely understand such of their conceptual relationships as determine the truth or falsity of the judgment in question. There is some kind of incompatibility in the assumption that one "understands" the terms but errs in a belief which is entirely constituted by a conceptual relationship among those terms. Consider an example: "A man is a man." How could one understand the term 'man' in both uses and not see that the proposition is true? Would not his erring in judgment constitute a misunderstanding of the relationship among the terms? This is what Scotus intends: that because a man who understands the terms could be right in believing that the proposition in question is false, only on the supposition that incompatible acts of knowing are simultaneously occurring, it follows that one who errs about such a belief as "Every whole is greater than any of its parts" must misunderstand the terms used in it and that, hence, he does not err in his belief about the proposition I know to be true, but rather primarily misunderstands it. It follows that one cannot both understand what is claimed and err in belief concerning a necessary per se nota principle: the truth or falsity of a necessary principle is constituted by the conceptual relations among the terms; one's understanding what is claimed is equivalent to one's recognizing the conceptual relation; one's disbelieving the proposition requires the absence of awareness that certain conceptual relations obtain, and hence, requires a misunderstanding of what is claimed.

Now this undoubtedly provides an explanation of what carries the "certainty" in our knowledge of propositions which are analytic. Among some first principles, self-evidence is constituted by the fact that one could not understand what is claimed and fail to perceive its truth. Understanding of what "man" means requires belief that a man is a man. (This suggests that there is a much closer relationship between conceptualization and judgment than the Aristotelian doctrine of abstraction has traditionally provided). If understanding the terms involves seeing at least the main logical relationships among them, then one cannot understand a necessary first principle and not see its truth; in fact such a principle merely states a relationship which must be actually recognized if the principle is understood. Moreover, one can assert honestly that a necessary first principle is false only if one misunderstand some first principle or mistakes something which is not a first principle for one.

Furthermore, we can supply Duns Scotus with a ready answer to the question as to why all necessary truths are not self-evident since all are constituted true by conceptual relations; some necessary truths are constituted true and necessary by conceptual relations among their terms which are so abstruse that no one would be said to have mis-understood the proposition if he denied it; it would merely be a case of his not having understood; some truths are conceptually incomplex in such a way that to have a grasp of the terms and not to see that what is claimed is true is both understood: One can upon consideration fail to see that "A man is a man" is true, only by misunderstanding. But most necessary truths are considerably more complex, so much so that some failures to believe result from not having understood, but do not require misunderstanding; incompleteness in our recognition of conceptual relations is not the same as distortion.

Let is be concluded that Duns Scotus exprofesso provides a treatment of the relationships between the self-evident and the necessary and tries to show that self-evident necessary truths are distinguished by the fact that what makes them true (the relations of identity between the subjects and predicates) is itself the same as the ground for believing them which is provided and is actually recognized intellectually by each person who understands them. Hence, our certitude about such principles is easily explained.

What is not adequately accounted for is the fact that some principles are self-evident but not necessarily true, and yet such that they are only a sub-class of the propositions which cannot ever be the object of a false belief or judgment. For example, "Some contingent things exist" is said to be self-evident but not all of: "Some judgments are made"; "Someone holds a belief"; "Someone has made a false judgment." Some of these are ¡neither¡ self-evident nor necessary and are still such that they cannot be

an object of false belief or judgment. We can consider all
such principles to be pragmatically first since the very
occurrence of such a judgment serves to make it true; if its
truth is not already accounted for; and hence such a judgment cannot be false on the assumption that someone holds
such a belief. Now if one understands the concepts in such
a proposition sufficiently to see what is its point, one
cannot in believing such a proposition thereby come to a
false belief about it. Therefore, to a believer the propositions carry a guarantee. But should they be called
self-evident too even though they have their truth as a
necessary condition for their being believed by anyone at
all? No; for that requirement is fulfilled by all necessary truths as well. So, it will not be sufficient to say:

> "A true proposition P is self-evident if and only if
> it is logically impossible that someone both under-
> stands P and believes P to be false without a
> semantic or pragmatic onconsistency."

Further insufficiencies are discolsed by the two
examples a) "Someone has made a false judgment" and b)
"Someone holds a false belief" (which are only samples from
a class which is infinitely large and pleasantly paradoxical).
These examples conform to the criterion above offered for
self-evidence; and they are contingent propositions. But it
is a contingent matter that there is someone who can believe
them; for if God alone existed, neither would be true and
neither could be believed.

There are difficulties enough with what is involved
in "understanding" a proposition, since a person may understand a proposition without knowing everything it implies or
everything which implies it. (What then is it to "understand" a proposition? But more directly there are further
difficulties with the criterion of self-evidence when we
ask why God could not believe (a) or (b) if He alone existed.
Although somebody's believing (a) or (b) would make (a) or
(b) true, and although it is even so that God's believing
(a) or (b) it would have to be on the basis of something else
he knows (i.e., that Socrates exists and errs in some belief).
Hence the mere fact that no one could mistakenly believe (a)
or (b) does not render (a) or (b) self-evident to everyone
who comes to consider whether or not to believe (a) or (b).
Both propositions require grounds (beyond their constitutive

concepts) for or against believing and neither provides such grounds. The mere fact that you will not go wrong in believing something is not a reason for believing anything since it is possible that what keeps you from going wrong about (a) or (b) may be the very fact that you will have gone wrong about something else. The same defect shows up in the case of a necessary truth: no one who believes a necessary truth can be mistaken in that belief; yet not all necessary truths are self-evident. Therefore the inability of anyone who believes the proposition to be in error about it does not render it self-evident; the inability to err, this alone, is not sufficient for self-evidence or even for knowledge. Something else is required: namely, a specifiable relation between the grounds for believing and the resulting correctness of the belief.

Could some proposition be self-evident and yet not true? This is equivalent to asking whether 'being self-evident' analytically involves 'being true' so that "P is self-evident" entails "P is true." We know that the metalanguage predicate "is true" applies only contingently to certain propositions, e.g., "There exists something whose existence is logically contingent." Now if we say that 'being true' is analytically involved in 'being self-evident,' then the metalanguage predicate "is self-evident" applies only contingently to those contingent propositions which are self-evident.

On the other hand, if 'being self-evident' involves 'being true' only conditionally we get quite different results. Suppose that to be self-evident a proposition must only be such that if true it carries its own warrant for justified belief. Then a self-evident contingent proposition could be false. The diastrous results of this way of describing things may appear sufficient to guarantee that 'being true' is analytically involved in 'being self-evident'. But that way of describing things is puzzling too. Take some particular self-evident but contingent proposition. It could have been false. It would not have been self-evident if it had been false. Yet the proposition did not change when it became true, and certainly nothing about what was to be believed or what would have been grounds for believing it changed either. This leads to the oddity that a proposition can be changed from being self-evident to not-being-self-evident or vice versa, with no alteration of the proposition itself.

Moreover, the self-evidence of some propositions precludes their being believed when they are flase. Consider, "Some contingent being exists," P. When P is false, P cannot be believed. Moreover some false contingent propositions cannot be believed simply because their true contradictions are self-evident to us. Without attempting to offer a more complete analysis of the relationship between 'being self-evident' and 'being true' and between these and the conditions where a proposition is believable, we can conjecture that there are some mistakes you simply cannot make.

In this context consider: A "Someone has a false belief." Suppose God alone exists. God cannot believe A. Yet, if someone believes A, A will be true. It would of course not be a sufficient condition for self-evidence that a proposition be such that if someone believes it, it will be true, as we have said before. But it is surely a necessary condition of the self-evident (and of the "necessary" too) that no one can believe it and thereby come to hold a false belief.

Consider B "Some contingent being exists"; is it really true that if anyone should believe B, his belief would be true? What if God alone had existed, would that condition be fulfilled? If God were to have believed B, would B be true? Our answer to this depends upon our invoking a logical technicality, fully familiar to Duns Scotus and a consequence of the well entrenched formal logic of his time. We cannot simply say "yes, because a conditional with a necessary false antecedent is true," since the antecedent "God believes B" is not necessarily false. (It is in fact true because there is some contingent being). Suppose the antecedent were "filled out" to read "God believes B and not-B is true", then our whole conditional would read "if God believes B and not-B is true, then B would be true." Then we would say that the whole conditional is true because the antecedent is necessarily false. And so it turns out that for anybody at all, if one were to believe B, B would be true. (This is a case where the paradoxes of strict implication are of positive value.) Hence we can conclude that we have found a necessary condition for what is self-evident, a property which is actually possessed by a number of contingent truths: that if a proposition is self-evident, no one can err in believing it; and yet this does not entail that no one could have erred in believing it, since its

239

self-evidence may be a contingent property as well.

Duns Scotus saw where the additional conditions must be sought, namely, in the fact that a self-evident proposition carries its own adequate reason or justifying grounds for being believed, as is clear from his attempt to show that the realized identity of the terms in necessary first principles is both a justifying reason for one's belief and that which renders the belief true.

B. Privileged contingent judgments.

Following St. Augustine's frequent insistence, Duns Scotus accords the highest degree of certitude to various classes of beliefs about one's own subjective states, both sensory and active. In terms reminiscent of recent discussions, Scotus thinks our knowledge of some of our own states is "privileged" in a way that some empirical knowledge is not. These beliefs are guaranteed because their very occurence presupposes that we have "privileged access" to all the grounds for or against holding them, grounds which fulfill three conditions: 1) their simple occurrence is both sufficient and necessary for the truth of the belief; 2) their occurrence is logically necessary but not sufficient for our having such beliefs; and 3) their occurrence is always an adequate reason for the belief. For example, if I think an orange looks lopsided to me, then it is certain that an orange looks lopsided to me; it is certain in the sense that I could not have been in error or have been unjustified under these conditions. (The earlier examples of propositions which were contingent such that no one could have been in error though believing them and yet not self-evident, were all examples where one could have been unjustified, without adequate grounds, in his belief.)

The assumption that there must be grounds for what is known leads to the consequence that in some cases a belief cannot even be held without the grounds which turn out to be sufficient both for its truth and for the justification of the belief. "Regarding the third type of knowledge, viz., of our own acts, I say that we are as certain of many of these as we are of the first and self-evident propositions..." (14)

Scotus quotes Aristotle's endorsement of the claim that it is immediately evident to us whether or not we are awake, when we are awake. "According to him (Aristotle), then, the fact that we are awake is as self-evident as a principle of demonstration." (15)

"And just as our certitude of being awake is like that of self-evident propositions, the same is true of many other acts in our power such as 'I understand' or 'I hear' and other such acts which are being performed." (16) (Notice the stipulation that the act in fact is actually going on.)

While Duns Scotus is much less profuse with examples than was St. Augustine, he is in another way more explicit than his predecessor, pointing out that it does not lie within the power of the mind to withhold assent to such propositions or to cast about for evidence of further confirmation, though this is possible where a "probable" judgment is concerned. The guarantee of the truth of such beliefs is identical with the conditions which must actually obtain in order for a person to hold such a belief; and these very conditions are the grounds for his believing. This is what Duns Scotus is trying to show in the case for all self-evident truths. For example, you cannot look white to me unless certain sensory states obtain such that the sensory states actually constitute a situation where you look white to me; moreover, these same sensory states are the grounds for my belief. So, too, I cannot think you actually look white, to me at T unless you do appear to me to be white at T. Since the connections between grounds and beliefs are such that the latter could not be false when the former obtains (i.e., you cannot look white to me when my belief that I think you actually look white is false), and since such grounds are always justifying, the most stringent conditions for certitude are satisfied.

Further, Scotus calls attention to the fact that even if the senses are deceptive, when one sees (in the phenomenal sense of this term) one does so irrespective of the perceptual reliability of the senses. This is the "appearance" or "seeming" sense of "see" which St. Augustine emphasizes.

241

C. Certitude.

Duns Scotus commits himself to an ideal of certitude which has its origins in Plato; an ideal which, after Descartes' dreams, became the Holy Grail for epistemologists. Scotus speaks of "infallible certitude." He says he wants to show "whether it is possible to have infallible certitude naturally: 1) of self-evident principles and conclusions, 2) of things known by experience, and 3) of our actions."(17)

But what is certitude? What is infallible knowledge (another phrase he employs)? Scotus does not mean that it is ever the case that when Jones judges that P, it is logically impossible that Jones should have made a false judgment instead. He knew, as we do, that given that Jones' judging that P was itself a contingent event, it is possible that that event should not have occurred and some other judgment (that Q, for instance) should have occurred, a judgment that is false. (Of course we do not say that every intellectual being could have made a false judgment for any of its true judgments; God would be an exception.) Infallible knowledge or certitude is not characteristic of knowledge which could not have been replaced with error; rather it is characteristic of belief which under certain supposed conditions could not have been in error and could not have been unjustified.

Scotus considers 'certitude' to be not merely a psychological state, but an epistemological or evidential state, a state where the falsity or lack of justification in one's belief or judgment is incompatible with the circumstances under which the belief is held.

But what shall we say of the "circumstances" which absolutely preclude both the falsity and the lack of justification of one's belief? We can generally characterize "certitude" or "scientific knowledge" as follows:

> S has certitude that P if and only if: S knows that P and it is not logically possible that S should believe that P and have the grounds for believing P that he actually has, when it be true either that P is false or that S actually lacks sufficient justification for believing that P.

We can define the self-evident derivatively from this, as follows:

A proposition $\underline{P}$ is self-evident to $\underline{S}$ if and only if: $\underline{S}$ simply understanding the terms of $\underline{P}$, the structure of $\underline{P}$, and what one is committed to in believing $\underline{P}$, provides $\underline{S}$ with grounds which guarantee that $\underline{S}$ has certitude that $\underline{P}$.

In other words by reversing what people usually assume to be the order of concepts we can achieve a definition of "self-evident" in terms of 'certain.'

Scotus does not explicitly state this criterion, but the arguments in each case he examines rest upon the derivation of some contradiction (either logical or pragmatic) from the assumption that what is believed is false or that the believer lacks justification for his belief. For instance, consider his argument that for a person to understand the terms of a necessary first principle and to err in his belief about it is inherently contradictory. The grounds for belief in a first principle is the person's understanding of the terms. Given what grounds he has by hypothesis, we derive an absurdity from supposing that he disbelieves the first principle or that his belief is false. So, too, in each of the cases he examines. Certitude is shown to result from a logical relation between the grounds actually possessed by one who makes a judgment and the two states required for knowledge a) true belief, and b) justification of belief.

A self-evident proposition is one which is so structured that its simply being understood provides the subject $\underline{S}$ with certitude about it. This description of the self-evident in terms of certitude accords well with Scotus' two main statements on the matter: The first is taken from Ox. I, d.2, q.2, no. 3:

"Est igitur omnis et sola illa propositio per se nota quae ex terminis, sic conceptis ut sunt ejus terminis, nata est habere evidentem vertatem complexionis."

243

He says in the same place:

"Nam propositio non dicatur per se nota quia ab
aliquo intellectu cognoscatur per se; tunc enim si
nullus intellectus actu cognosceret, nulla propositio esset per se nota; sed dicitur per se nota
quia, quantum est de natura terminorum, nata est
habere evidentem veritatem contentam in terminis,
etiam in quocumque intellectu concipiente terminos."

Again, Oxoniense, I, d.2, q.2, No.2:

"Dicitur igitur propositio per se nota, quae per
nihil aliud extra terminos proprios qui sunt aliquid
ejus habet veritatem evidentam."

It is definitely a mistake to assume that 'identity'
of terms is what always constitutes the "veritatem evidentam."

Duns Scotus devotes little attention to the matter
of the justification of belief when he discusses knowledge
of necessary truths and of our own subjective states. He
over emphasizes the inerrancy characteristics and under
emphasizes the justification characteristics. Yet we can
see why: the issue in the cases he considers is not that
which divides knowledge from what is merely true opinion but
rather that of whether a mistake, a false belief, is possible.
That one's understanding of what is claimed and one's sensory
experience provide justification for one's holding the beliefs in question is regarded as beyond doubt since these can
easily be shown to be the only relevant grounds for such beliefs. Surely when all the evidence or grounds which are
relevant to (and contribute to) the justification of a given
belief are actually present, the person so situated is
maximally justified in his belief. This condition is
obviously fulfilled in the case of first principles, as
Scotus most ably demonstrated, and in other cases as well,
for example, the case of privileged subjective states.
But still the underplay of "justification" is misleading,
unless explained.

Duns Scotus does not restrict the concept 'knowledge'
to those things of which we can be certain in the special
sense we have explained. Rather like C. I. Lewis, the 20th
century American who bears the greatest resemblance to him

244

in doctrine and technique, Scotus acknowledges what we now
call "empirical knowledge"; knowledge which involves belief which, though justified and true, is still so related
to the grounds that are present to the believer that he
could have been in error even given the grounds at hand.
Not all knowledge involves certitude. Knowledge is of two
sorts: that which is certain and that which is merely
empirical. The merely empirical is founded upon what is
certain, and yet sometimes we can go from what is merely
empirical and not certain in itself to what is certain as
well. This is explained in his discussion of the relation
between certainty and experience to which we turn below.

       The two sorts of knowledge differ not in whether or
not what is believed is true; for in both cases the judgments must be true. Nor do they differ in whether or not
one's belief is fully justified or reasonable; for in both
cases the judgments must be fully justified and not accidentally related to the presence of justifying grounds or
evidence. Rather they differ in the logical relationship
between what is believed and the grounds or evidence the
person actually has for his believing what he believes. In
the case of certainty, a contradiction or pragmatic absurdity can be constructed from the conjunct supposition that
the believer has the justifying grounds he actually has and
that his belief is either false or unjustified. In the case
of merely empirical knowledge (e.g., that my automobile has
an engine in it), the grounds and evidence are so related to
what I believe that is is possible that those very same
grounds should have been present to me under circumstances
where my belief that the automobile has an engine would have
been false, though it in fact is not false. Epistemic
certitude is constituted by the logical relation (between
grounds and belief) which precludes the presence of grounds
which justify belief and the simultaneous falsity of what is
believed.

       What then is the relation between a) the necessary,
b) the certain, and c) the self-evident? Not everything
which is self-evident is necessary; not everything necessary is self-evident; not everything of which we are certain
is self-evident; but everything which is self-evident is
something of which we can be certain.

In fact, we can describe the self-evident as that subset of things of which we become certain from a mere understanding of what is conceptually and pragmatically involved in believing them.

Not everything of which we are certain is necessary; not everything which is necessary is something certain. There are three distinct concepts with overlapping domains of application. Nevertheless, our certainty regarding truths which do not carry their own warrant is dependent upon our being certain of truths which do carry their own warrant. Thus certainty in human knowledge is possible only because there are some true beliefs which provide their own grounds, beliefs which nature cannot provide us without simultaneously furnishing us with the justification for believing them. Among the self-evident and, therefore, first principles of all science, some are necessary and some are contingent.

Whatever is self-evident is something someone can be certain of; but not everything we can be certain of is a necessary truth; not all necessary truths are beliefs we can be certain of. The self-evident is a subset of those things of which we can be certain and is essential as a source for our certitude about whatever is certain but not self-evident. Hence, the self-evident truths provide a bridge between the necessary and the contingent in human knowledge (some truths of both sorts being self-evident) and provide the bridge by which certainty about what does not guarantee itself (the not-self-evident yet certain) can be achieved. Let us turn now to the discussion of certitude in experience.

D. Certitude in empirical knowledge.

Scotus' inquiry into knowledge based upon experience has three facets. 1) He shows that, at least sometimes, one can have certainty in perceptual reports about particular states of affairs; 2) he shows how one can have certainty that the process, which we now call "induction," by which one reasons from the observed cases of a given sort to the general principles or necessities of nature, is reliable as a way of acquiring knowledge; and 3) he declares that certainty is possible about some of the generalizations which result from the exercise of what we now call induction.

It is one thing to decide whether or not we have
certainty about particular perceptual judgments, e.g. that
there is a chair in my study; it is apparently another to
decide whether we have certainty about the process of induction itself (the enterprise of judging unobserved cases
upon a finite sample of cases actually observed); and it
appears to be still a third thing to determine whether, on
the basis of induction, we have certitude about a particular
generalized or universalized truth.

As will be explained below, a distinctive feature of
20th century discussion has been the discovery that these
apparently different problems are in important respects the
same. Duns Scotus, too, treated all three as fundamentally
one problem and employed a single principle in his replies.
Nor was his an identification of the problems through inept
division; rather, it was through insight which anticipated
one of the major achievements of his successors.

Duns Scotus does not claim certitude for all perceptual judgments; not even for all true perceptual judgments;
nor even for all true perceptual judgments which provide
knowledge. 'Certitude' about what is believed is not a
necessary condition for every state of knowledge or for
every veridical perception, though certitude about what is
believed is necessary for scientific knowledge, and one's
capacity for certitude about first principles and about
one's own subjective states is a prerequisite for any perceptual knowledge at all.

When we talk of knowledge based upon experience we
must take "certitude" to name an epistemic state which may
be acquired but which is not always given along with the
immediate grounds for the particular judgment. By contrast,
self-evident judgments carry the grounds for our certitude
in the very conceptual acts by which they are understood;
but other judgments about which certitude is acquired do not
provide the certitude, they merely share in it.

It is the 'sharing' and 'conferring' of certitude
about which Scotus inquires when discussing experimental
knowledge. Certitude in a particular perceptual judgment,
e.g. "That wall is white" is the result not of the grounds
which justify our making that particular judgment (e.g.,
"that it looks white to me now") but is conferred through

the concurrence of other justified perceptual judgments.
Thus Scotus uses a "concurrence" or "confirmation" principle
which resembles basic elements in several other epistemolo-
gies. E.g., Carneades (213-129 B.C.) uses the principle,
"acceptable propositions that stand in the relation of concurrence are more reasonable than those that do not." (18)
Our own contemporary Roderick Chisholm employs the principle
that: "If h is confirmed by the set of all those propositions e such that e is empirically acceptable for S at t,
then h is acceptable for S at t." (19) And finally, uses
the principle that: "...if h is a member of a set of concurrent propositions each of which is acceptable for S at t,
then h is evident to S at t." (20) This proposition is very
much like Scotus' claim:

> "Regarding such an object (that something is white
> or hot the way it appears to be), either the same
> things appear opposite to the different senses or
> do not appear so, but rather all the senses knowing
> such an object make the same judgment about it. If
> the latter be the case, then we have certitude of
> this thing perceived by the senses in virtue of the
> aforementioned principle, namely: 'What occurs in
> most instances by means of something that is not a
> free cause is the natural effect of this thing." (21)

Now it is not the quoted general principle (what I
call the Empirical Cannon) to which I here call attention;
rather observe the doctrine that when the senses concur in
their reports, certitude is the result. This is like the
Chisholm principle that when acceptable beliefs concur,
something is thereby rendered evident. (22) Duns Scotus
makes a stronger claim than Chisholm; being 'evident' is
compatible with being 'false' (provided it is not a case of
what is directly evident) in Chisholm's picture of the
matter; for Scotus, certitude about P is not compatible with
the falsity of P.

In view of Scotus' argument to support his view by
means of the Empirical Cannon, his claim, which is stronger
than is common nowadays, is not implausible; and our assessment of it must depend upon our assessment of the Empirical
Cannon itself. If Scotus is correct in his stronger claim,
then the representative 20th century claim is too weak. (It
is interesting that contemporary critics consider it too

strong.)

The reasoning of Duns Scotus is that concurrence of
the senses yields certitude because the fact that the sense
reports confirm one another can be accounted for only
through their being alike, effects of a cause whose nature
is to produce those effects, and hence, of a cause which
must be as conceived through its effects. Suppose something
looks square, feels square, tests out as square, etc. These
are its appearances, which can be related as a concurrence
of sense reports. Is the object really the way the concurrent appearances suggest?

To say it is square is to say more than that it
looks square. It is to say that it has the property of being square; that is, that it has at least those real dispositions which cause its appearing square to normal observers under normal conditions (an infinite number of possible
observations and observers). Now since the regular result
of observation under standard conditions is that it looks,
seems, or appears square, we must account for this concurrence of the sensory phenomena. The concurrence is surely
not the result of chance; (the regularity of the phenomena
precludes that, and the regularity is attested by the experienced and remembered concurrence of the phenomena);
surely, the concurrent reports are not the result of a free
cause -- we are dealing with a natural object. Therefore
they must result from their natural cause, the cause which
by nature produces the effect: namely, the disposition of
the object. But what is the natural cause of the concurrent appearing to be square? It is analytic, that the
natural cause of concurrent appearing to be square is the
physical property, being square. Hence it follows strictly
that in the case of concurrent sense reports that the object
looks square, the object has the property of being square,
the conditions of observation being "normal." The concurrence of the senses provides certainty about the state of a
physical object.

While a particular perceptual judgment by itself may
lack certitude, even though it be something known, a regular
concurrence of such judgments about physical objects may
back up some "physical object judgment" to the point that it
could not have been in error, given the grounds at hand; e.g.,
the judgment: "This is a chair here in the study" may be

249

something about which one has certitude by way of true perceptual judgments which individually and apart from the concurrent set are not certainties.

Perhaps it is obvious now why I have called Scotus' a priori premise concerning the natural causal connection between regular phenomena and their non-random and non-voluntary origin the "Empirical Cannon." It is the principle which is the foundation of empirical certitude based upon concurrent sensory testimony, the principle which explains why concurrence among the true reports renders them certain. Further Scotus shows how the principle can be used along with other a priori knowledge to identify the source of error or confusion when the reports of the senses are not concurrent. He says:

"But if the judgment of different senses differs in regard to what is seen outside, for instance, if sight says that the staff which is partly in the water and partly in the air is broken, or if sight says, as it invariably does, that the sun is smaller in size than it really is, or in general, that everything seen from a distance is smaller than it is in reality, in all such cases we are still certain of what is true and know which sense is in error. This we know by reason of some proposition in the soul more certain than any sense judgment, together with the concurrent testimony of several of the senses." (23) (The proposition more certain than any sense judgment is the Empirical Cannon.)

The situation may be imagined where one actually sees the stick in the water and it looks bent. Sight is not defective; for we do see the stick and the water; moreover the stick does look bent. Would we be right to believe that it is? Can we discover that we would not be right to accept this appearance as displaying the reality? We can, by means of two things; the concurrent reports of a variety of perception experiences, e.g., how it looks after we take it out, how it feels while in the water, how it behaves when we use it to poke a rock; and certain a priori propositions each of which is "so evident....upon analysis of its terms that the intellect could not call it into doubt, even if its terms were derived from erroneous senses. Indeed, the opposite of this proposition includes a contradiction. Now both sight and touch attest that the stick is harder than the water and that the water gives way before the stick." (24) This is known to be so on the basis of concurrent sense reports and other perceptual knowledge.

What then of the stick, is it broken or bent in the water? We know that it is not, despite the appearance to the contrary, because of the analytic truth "The harder object is not broken by the touch of something soft which gives way before it."

"And so when reason judges that the senses err (that things are not as they look or seem), it does so in virtue of two kinds of knowledge. The first is a knowledge for which the intellect requires the sense only as an occasion and not as a cause--a knowledge in which it could not be deceived even if all the senses were deceived. The other is a knowledge acquired by the oft-repeated testimony of one or more senses which is known to be true by reason of the proposition so frequently quoted, namely: 'Whatever occurs in most instances, etc.'" (25)

When Scotus speaks of a sense as being deceived, he merely means that on that occasion the state of things is not as the sense in question makes it appear or seem. To postulate that on that occasion things are not at all the way they appear by way of the senses. The hypothesis that all the senses are deceived on all occasions is utterly absurd for Scotus, as long as we suppose that the sense reports exhibit the regularity we in fact encounter in our experience. For the relation of that regularity of reports to the actual state of the world is not a matter of chance; it is a matter of strict necessity as we indicated above. If the relation between reality and appearance is not random and not the result of a voluntary cause, the regular appearances must stand to the actual world as natural effect of natural cause; this is the same as saying that things really do have the properties which correspond to their concurrent and regular appearances: those physical properties or at least the dispositions to produce such regularities of appearances.

The line of reasoning which extracts certitude about physical object statements from a concurrence of sensory phenomena has at least three major suppositions: a) that what happens must be accounted for; b) that what does not account for itself must be related to whatever else actually obtains either by nature, or by chance, or through voluntary agency; c) that a short-term concurrence of sensible phenomena (in the context of a longer run of remembered perceptual experiences and analytical propositions) is sufficient to display the absence of chance or random coincidences between appearances and the state of the physical world.

We cannot here investigate the first two suppositions, which we may suppose most epistemologists, not strongly inclined to look into the metaphysics of knowledge, would be willing enough to permit. The third, however, is of direct epistemological interest and is controversial: How long a regularity of behavior does one need in order to discover the natural cause of the sensory phenomena? But even before considering that, we need a justification of a fourth and equally important presupposition of Scotus' arguments: that the experience which makes up a concurrence of sense reports is indeed applicable to cases and situations which arise later in time.

What ground is there for thinking that concurrent sense reports stretching over time and stored in the memory will at a later time provide relevant grounds to support our beliefs or that information we acquire now will support our beliefs about the future or past? This is a version of the problem of induction which we may now consider as Scotus understood it.

INDUCTION:

"As for what is known by experience, I have this to say. Even though a person does not experience every single individual, but only a great many; nor does he experience them at all times but only frequently, still, an (experienced) person knows infallibly that it is always this way and holds for all instances. He knows this in virtue of this proposition reposing in his soul: 'What occurs in a great many instances by a cause that is not free, is the natural effect of that cause.'"(26)

"Quidquid evenit, ut in pluribus, ab aliqua causa non libera, est effectus naturalis illius causae." (27)

"This proposition is known to the intellect even if the terms are derived from erring senses, because a cause cannot in most instances produce an effect that is the very opposite of what it is ordained by its form to produce..." (28)

As I said before, there are two questions; first, whether it is ever (or in general) a reliable thing to judge unobserved cases on the basis of observed ones; secondly, what degree of assurance we can have in particular judgments of that sort?

On the first, Scotus' reasoning seems to be as follows. We suppose that we have observed a fairly long run of cases; e.g., where my putting an oar in water is followed by its looking bent. Can we legitimately reason to future cases? We have a regularity of observed behavior. This regularity precludes a chance correlation between the antecedent event (my putting the oar in water) and the consequent event (its appearing bent); for to postulate a chance correlation is ex hypothesi to suppose that there is no regularity. Moreover, if there is a regularity of any length between antecedent and consequent events, it is absurd to say there is a chance correlation. Once the probability of the consequent event becomes greater than .5 given the antecedent, the hypothesis that the regularity is a "chance correlation" becomes self-contradictory because what we mean by "chance correlation" is that C and not-C are equally probable on A. There is no reason whatever to suppose that a voluntary agent arranges the correlation of the two classes of events into a regularity. Hence, we conclude that the antecedent by its very nature is related to the consequent, that is, that conditions being right, the first could not be as it is and the second not occur. Thus I have certitude that in future cases the oar will appear bent when put into water, under normal conditions; for our regular observation has disclosed the nature of the situation. But if this is so, then it is in general legitimate to judge unobserved events on the basis of observed events which disclose the nature of the events involved in the unobserved cases. To discover the nature of a thing is nothing more than to find out what kinds of behavior a thing of that sort (essence) is actually disposed to produce. You find that out first by classifying or grouping the behavior of objects; then by determining whether the behavior results from a voluntary or chance agent; then whether it results from incidental features of the thing; and lastly, if none of these, whether the regularity producing it appears to be destructive of the thing (for in that case the regularity may not proceed directly from the nature of the thing but from the corruption of a thing of a certain nature).

Scotus, as is indicated by his general empiricism conjoined with his emphasis upon the reality of natures, holds that insofar as the interactions of physical objects are neither fortuitous nor voluntary, they display the sorts of things which interact; for the sort or nature of a thing is nothing but what it is insofar as this actively disposes it to its operations. Things of the same sorts will, under similar conditions, interact similarly, since it is their natures of sorts which account for their actions. Because the unobserved cases to which a generalization applies must, ex hypothesi, be of the same sort as the observed cases upon which we base it, it follows that what we know of the observed cases in virtue of what sort they are, is also knowledge of the unobserved cases of the same sort.

The heart of Scotus' reasoning probably is as follows: since there is nothing which could account for the observed regularities beyond the natures or kinds of things or entities envolved, the regularities must be the result of what sorts of things we have perceived; whatever results from anything of a certain sort because it is of that sort, must result from everything of that sort, under suitably similar conditions. Those events which are regular perceivable consequents of antecedent events of a certain sort must be consequent-events because of the kind to which the antecedent events belong. Hence generalization to all events of that sort is not only warranted, it is such that given what we have actually perceived, the nature of the antecedent events involves active dispositions toward the consequent events, so that our generalizing to all events of that sort could not be in error or unwarranted; i.e., a contradiction would result if we suppose we know from experience the regular association of fire and heat and know that heating is an event toward which fire has an active disposition in view of what sort of thing fire is, and yet, believe that at the same time it is not true for all cases that fire tends to cause heat and will, all other things being equal, do so. For any two things of the same sort will have in common all their active tendencies to the behavior which belongs to a thing because it is of that sort.

The principle of induction, treated as a statement that it is legitimate to generalize to the natural spatio-temporal consequent of things or events of a certain sort on the basis of our experiencing regularities which indicate what sort of things they are, and what sorts of behavior are comprehended within their natures, it made a _priori_.

Scotus, without remarking on his achievement, thus reduces part of the epistemological problem concerning induction to another question: can we know the natures of things on the basis of their short-run behavior? The same reduction is performed by distinguished 20th century epistemologists as we shall we below.

The Empirical Cannon itself:

"Quidquid event, ut in pluribus, ab aliqua causa non libera, est effectus naturalis illius causae."

This proposition is known with certitude, even on the supposition that one or more of the senses is deceptive, because it is analytic: a non-free cause is unable to produce on most occasions an effect to whose opposite it is naturally ordered or to which it is not ordered in virtue of its form. And secondly, because a chance cause is ordered to the production of the contrary of its chance effect or to not producing it; so no cause is a chance cause with respect to an effect regularly produced by it; and thus, if it is not free, it is natural.

What is supposed by this argument? 1) That what happens regularly, e.g., "An oar looks bent in water," cannot be unaccounted for; 2) that, therefore, what happens regularly cannot be such that antecedent and consequent events are randomly related; hence if the correlation of A and C; C being a final cause of A and A being efficient cause of C. The natural efficient cause of C is merely that antecedent event whose nature it is to be followed by something of the same sort as C.

255

The main reason for taking the Empirical Cannon seriously is that Scotus intended to provide a basis for our inductive certitude, not so much about the actual relations of empirical events, as about the dispositions of things and events. He says, "et forte ibi non habetur necessaria cognito actualis unionis extremorum, sed aptitudinalis." (29) In the 20th century discussions of the problem of induction, such as Nelson Goodman's Fact, Fiction and Forecast, a number of traditional puzzles have been clustered around the allied question of how we come to know the dispositions of things. For example, when I say "The chair is brown" I am attributing to the chair much more than just looking brown to a normal observer under normal conditions right now; I am attributing a disposition, other relevant things remaining unchanged, to look brown to any normal observer under any normal conditions anytime. (30) How can I tell this on the basis of a short-run of experience? This is about the same as asking how can we know the natures of things on the basis of their appearances.

The problem of whether knowledge of the unobserved cases of a certain class is possible on the basis of our knowledge of the observed cases, has a direct parallel in every case where we attribute a physical property to a physical object, as Scotus and our contemporaries realize. For a physical property is a continuing disposition to produce a certain kind of sensible effect upon observers under nearly standard conditions. (To be blue is more than just looking blue; it is an active and continuing physical disposition to look blue.) Hence, every case of perception involves the very question which is fundamental to induction: how do we come to know on the basis of a limited sample, things which hold for an unlimited number of possible and actual observations? In every perceptual judgment we purport to know a proposition, (e.g., this paper is white) which involves as an empirical consequence an infinite number of statements of the form: "if a normal observer looked at the paper under normal conditions at t, it would look white to him." How can one come to know truths whose infinity of empirical consequences passes beyond actual or possible experience?

In order to know that an object has a given physical property, for example, being blue, we must know how it would appear under a very large sample of standard observations.

How are we supposed to tell that, on the basis of a short-run of sensations? The heart of our present day discussions of induction as an epistemological problem lies here. And, whatever its other merits or defects, Scotus' answer in terms of our knowledge of the natures of things is directly relevant and perceptive. But how do we get to know the natures?

We attribute the physical property of being blue to an object on the basis of concurrent and regular sense reports which indicate that it is that nature, as we have explained above. Scotus says:

> "ergo cum ab isto presente evenit ut in pluribus sit talis immutatio sensus, sequitur quod immutatio vel species genita sit effectus naturalis talis causae, et ita tale extra erit album vel calidum vel tale quale natum est representari per speciem genitam ab ipso in pluribus." (31)

The Empirical Cannon has defects; but still it directs our attention to where the fundamental answers must be sought: in what we call "physical properties" or "active dispositions to produce sensible effects."

Regularities in sensory phenomena must have their account in appropriate physical dispositions, if any account at all is possible; in fact "physical dispositions" are defined in terms of sensory and perceptual regularities. Though it may be that most sensory regularities are too short-run temporally and spatially to rule out their having resulted from chance, still some regularities are so invariant and so widespread that saying they result from chance would be equivalent to denying that there are any natures or dispositions at all. And that would be inconsistent because the hypothesis that there are no natures at all is analytically incompatible with the premise that there are widespread examples of regular correlations of phenomena.

We can only indicate some of the many problems which surround Scotus' ingenious principle: 1) Is it really analytic? 2) Are the observed regularities of natural events long-run enough to justify application of the principle? 3) Is the relation between sensation and physical objects regular enough for us to justify our ascriptions of physical properties according to this cannon?

1. When one asks whether the Empirical Cannon is analytic, one must recognize its loose relation to the principle that for what happens there is a cause, a principle many philosophers would not admit as itself analytic. But the wording of the Empirical Cannon must be interpreted so as to avoid logical commitment to that proposition: "if something happens on account of a cause which is not free, and if it happens regularly, then that cause is its natural cause." Thus the problem of whether all events are caused arises over the application of the principle and not from its strict meaning. The analytic principle applies only to cases which we have admitted to involve causation (at least in the "human" sense). This will present little difficulty because few epistemologists are willing to entertain the possibility that our sensory phenomena are entirely without causes. Separated from commitment to an empirical doctrine of causality, the principle seems obviously analytic and for the very reasons that we drew out of Scotus' text earlier. (Of course, we had not resolved pertinent questions concerning the concept of 'causality' it involves.)

2. But then, is the principle empirically applicable? Since no epistemologist short of a radical skeptic will bother to quibble over whether sensations are caused at least in large part, by external objects, that raises no problem with its applicability. But are the regularities of phenomena long enough to rule out random behavior and to disclose the natures of things? After all, in a random sequence, which is long enough, we can get a perfectly orderly sequence of events of any finite length. Although I cannot go through all the steps relevant to this question, I think most epistemologists would be willing to grant that the last supposition to be considered reasonable is that there is a purely random or chance correlation between our subjective states and the state of physical objects. Moreover, the very same Empirical Cannon can be applied to our believing states as a whole and to their subsequent justification in later experience in order to show the falsity of the hypothesis that the correlation is random. But still, we cannot deny that a large family of questions must be answered concerning the applicability of the Empirical Cannon.

3. The heart of the whole problem rests upon our being able to know the physical dispositions of things upon a short-run sensory experience. Scotus has at most indicated in general, how this matter may be approached; a detailed and precise answer, if possible at all, is yet to be produced.

Because the very best epistemologist among his successors have gained no ground by trying an array of alternative analyses, it seems to me that we should diligently develop the resources of the Empirical Cannon, along with a doctrine of perceptual sets (as developed in some recent psychology) to produce a modernized Scotist solution to the problem of perceptual knowledge. His Empirical Cannon appears to withstand initial objections well enough and to provide enough amalgamation of the problems of induction and perception to justify our developing its resources in more detail.

The length of this paper precludes further unraveling of the reasoning Scotus appears to have suggested; but I think I have shown that (i) Scotus' discussion on 'certainty' in a priori knowledge and in empirical knowledge is a remarkable anticipation of positions and arguments for which philosophers centuries later and even today have been highly praised; (ii) that Scotus' answer to the problem of induction and his realization that the same question is involved in every perceptual judgment is inherently interesting and again anticipates features of recent discussion; (iii) that Scotus' proposals, even though they are often incidental to his main essay, are initially plausible enough to justify our developing them in our contemporary context.

FOOTNOTES

(1)   A detailed comparison of the modal logic of Pseudo-Scotus and that of Lewis has been made by A. C. McDermott in her doctoral dissertation: The Assertoric and Modal Propositional Logic of the Pseudo-Scotus, University of Pennsylvania (1964).

(2)   JAAKKO HINTIKKA, Knowledge and Belief (Cornell University Press, 1962, Ithaca, New York).

(3)   Among the most elegant analytic insights of Duns Scotus was his recipe for creating an univocal predicate out of two instances of a term which are said to be irreducibly analogous in meaning; namely, disjoin the terms to create a complex disjunctive predicate applicable univocally to all instances of both analogates; this buried the oversimplified doctrine that no univocal term could serve as predicate of all things irrespective of their category or their transcatogorical status.

(4)   The entire passage is available in: Duns Scotus, John: Philosophical Writings, A Selection, translated by Allan Wolter, O.F.M., Bobbs-Merrill, LLA, 1964.

(5)   We find a contemporary epistemologist, R. Chisholm, treating this concept as one which can be elucidated. See his Theory of Knowledge, p. 22, Prentice Hall, Foundations of Philosophy Series, 1966.

(6)   See Wolter, op. cit., p. 10.

(7)   Opus Oxoniense, Vives edition, D. III, Q. 4, a. 2, vol. 9, p. 173.

(8)   Wolter, op. cit., p. 114f.

(9)   Wolter, op. cit., p. 115. (Bracketed example is my insertion.)

(10)   Oxoniense, loc. cit. supra, p. 173.

(11)   Here we stay with Fr. Wolter's translation since the
         mysteries surrounding 'conformity between terms and
         propositions' do not seem more numerous than those
         surrounding 'conformity between terms and judgment.'

(12)   Wolter, op. cit., p. 115f.

(13)   See the passages quoted below, which clearly support
         this, p. 21f.

(14)   Wolter, op. cit., p. 119.

(15)   Wolter, Ibid.

(16)   Wolter, op. cit., p. 120.

(17)   Wolter, op. cit., p. 114.

(18)   This formulation of Carneades' claim is offered by R.
         Chishol, p. 42, of his Theory of Knowledge, Prentice
         Hall, 1966.

(19)   Chisholm, op. cit., p. 53.

(20)   Ibid., p. 54.

(21)   Wolter, op. cit., p. 122.

(22)   See note 19, above.

(23)   Wolter, op. cit., p. 122.

(24)   Wolter, op. cit., p. 123.

(25)   Wolter, op. cit., p. 123.

(26)   Wolter, op. cit., p. 117. The bracketed "experienced"
         is my insertion on the basis of the Vive's text.

(27)   Oxoniense, I., d. 3, q. 4, a. 2, Vive's, Vol. 9, p.
         176.

(28)   Wolter, op. cit., p. 117.

(29) <u>Oxoniense</u>, I, d. e, q. 4, a. 2, Vives, Vol. 9, p. 177.

(30) But am I? Just how long must the chair continue to look brown to normal observers under normal conditions in order to <u>be</u> brown? The inherent vagueness of our physical object predicates is forcefully portrayed by Goodman's discussion of the "grue-bleen" problem.

(31) <u>Oxoniense</u>, I, d. 3, q. 4, a. 2, No. 11, Vives, Vol. 9 (italics mine).

Discussion

GEOFFREY BRIDGES, O.F.M., PH.D.

Professor of Philosophy
San Louis Rey College
San Louis Rey, California

Long ago Emphrem Longpre, O.F.M., developed a theme which Dr. Ross has once again illustrated. Duns Scotus, known rather commonly to the intellectual world as a voluntarist, actually proposed a pronounced intellectualism.(1) Dr. Ross has made a valuable contribution to the subject, because he develops two elements of Scotus' doctrine which Longpré simply adverts to.

Since I did not have an opportunity to give close study to the paper just presented before its reading, I will comment on just one aspect, and then I will give some of my reactions to the texts which Dr. Ross discusses, thus illustrating how differently two people of diverse background react to the same texts.

We must remember the context of Scotus' discussion. He is seeking to refute the illumination theory of Henry of Ghent. If man does not have any extrinsic aid to reach certitude, then it is through his own native power that he assents to the evidence of first principles. Scotus insists that the cause of our certitude does not lie in the terms of the proposition, nor in the conformity of the terms with reality. The origin of our certitude of self-evident or per se nota propositions is the insight or understanding of the intellect into the entailment of the predicate in the subject. In opposition to the illumination theory, Scotus holds that the mind itself is capable of perceiving that a predicate is necessarily connected with the subject. It is this insight into or understanding of the necessary relation of subject and predicate which accounts for our certitude about principles. There is no incompatibility, therefore, between what Scotus says in passing about our perception of the conformity of terms with reality and what he says about the origin of our certitude about principles.

Longpré said that it is particularly regrettable that the thought of Duns Scotus has not been studied in this matter; about the problem of certitude and knowledge, neoscholasticism would have learned a great deal from the scholastic philosophy of Duns Scotus. This judgment apparently is still true. Kenneth Gallagher, in The Philosophy of Knowledge, suggests several areas where the neoscholastic approach might be improved. He criticizes those who in their effort to ground certitude of first principles

in sense knowledge seem to lean over-heavily on the formula:
"Nothing is in the intellect which was not first in the
senses." When he emphasizes the original work of the intellect in formulating these principles, granted that the
process started in sense experience, he is proposing, with
less thoroughness and detail, what Scotus teaches in the
passage under discussion today. Similarly Gallagher takes
the neo-scholastics to task for not adequately developing
the intuition of the acts of the soul: rejoicing, hoping,
admiring, envying, and their objects, which he says are
every bit as irreducibly given as are 'sense phantasms.'(2)
Again, Scotus' doctrine of intuitive cognition includes immediate knowledge not only of our interior states but also
of the objects giving rise to these states.

        I have no intention of sounding a note of trium-
phalism: "See, we have known it all along." Rather a sober-
ing thought comes to mind. Why have these doctrines not
been proposed adequately and forcefully enough to have an
influence on neo-scholastic epistology? Longpré points to
them. Peter Vier, O.F.M. wrote his doctoral thesis on them.
Perhaps Dr. Ross' paper will help to make their contemporary
relevance appreciated.

        What Scotus teaches in the area under discussion is
not beyond criticism. In his treatment of the conceptual-
izing activity of the intellect, I believe he is overly influenced by Aristotle's theory of the abstraction of the
form from which distinct or definitional knowledge is formed.
Our experience teaches that definitions are mighty difficult
to arrive at. On the other hand, we do not know what we are
talking about before we can adequately define it. I believe
the basis of a fuller treatment of this problem lies in
Scotus' distinction between confused and distinct knowledge
and in his theory of the intuition of the singular. We
know our experiences and we know the objects of our experience prior to our definitional knowledge of these objects.
This much Scotus himself held. But I wonder if today he
would not put a higher premium on this type of knowledge
and less on the abstractive, distinct or definitional knowledge.

        When he analyzes the manner in which we form induc-
tive generalizations, I think Scotus has something to offer
a philosopher of science like Karl Popper, who speaks of the
"faith" which scientists have in the immutability of

natural processes and in the "principle of the uniformity of nature." (3) Scotus traces the genesis of our conviction and hence lays bare the basis for the scientists' faith.

Not all philosophers of science agree with Popper, however. For Stephen Toulmin, there is no uniformity of nature, only the uniformity of the scientific method. In his positivistic approach, every new instance is really a new instance; there is no justification to expect that natures will act uniformly. (4) While I would not agree with this position for the reasons which Scotus offers, I think Toulmin's arguments in seeking to establish his position points again to an excessive optimism in Scotus. Scotus says that through induction a person "knows infallibly that it is always this way and holds in all instances." (5) What Toulmin proves at least is that it is extremely difficult today, as our methods and knowledge become more refined, to say definitely (infallibly): this is the nature and so this kind of activity will hold in all instances. It is true, Scotus makes a distinction between what a nature is able to do and what it will do, to make allowance for chance interference or the intervention of God. But I do not think Scotus, if he were living today, would be so optimistic about knowing "infallibly" what the nature of anything is through the inductive method.

Despite these observations, I agree with Longpre that neo-scholastic epistemology would be better off if Scotus' insights were used to correct and improve the science.

FOOTNOTES

(1)   Cf. E. LONGPRE, La Philosophie du B. Duns Scot,
       Societe et Librairie S. Francois d'Assise, Paris,
       1924, 197-227.

(2)   Cf. K. GALLAGHER, The Philosophy of Knowledge,
       Sheed & Ward, New York, 137-140; 211-218.

(3)   Cf. K. POPPER, The Logic of Scientific Discovery,
       Basic Books, New York, 1959, p. 252.

(4)   Cf. S. TOULMIN, The Philosophy of Science, Harper &
       Row, New York, 1960, 151-154.

(5)   Oxon., I, d. 3, q. 4; tr. by A. WOLTER, O.F.M., Duns
       Scotus: Philosophical Writings, Nelson, Edinburgh,
       1962, p. 109.

FATHER CYRIN MAUS, O.F.M., since completion of
graduate studies at the Pontificium Athenaeum
Antonianum in Rome, has been Professor of
Fundamental and Systematic Theology at St.
Leonard College, Dayton, Ohio. In preparation
for publication are a paper delivered before
the Fourth Mariological Congress in Santo
Domingo in 1965: De modo, quo Paschasius
Radbertus regulam "De specie et genere" circa
Mariam et Ecclesiam usurpavit; and a major
portion of his doctoral dissertation to appear
under the title A Phenomenology of Revelation:
Paschasius Radbert's Way of Interpreting
Scripture.

The Possibility of Knowing God Naturally:

Paul Tillich and

DUNS SCOTUS-

a Contrast

CYRIN MAUS, O.F.M., S.T.L.

In view of the fact that this symposium of ours has been directed from the beginning to examining what Scotus might have to say to us today, one perhaps ought first to justify the topic he himself has chosen and committed himself thereby to defend as relevant. When I first hit upon the idea of treating the question of our knowledge of God there had already been considerable discussion of the theories of certain so-called "death-of-God" theologians. Since then the pseudo-intellectualism of our mass-produced news magazines has taken up the question, even moving it up from the religious section for one wild week as a cover story in the Easter issue. Whatever else might be said of such publicity, I at least ought to be thankful to it for guaranteeing that what I say here will not be completely-- to coin a phrase--"out of it."

Where does the present paper fit into this broader question? Although I cannot even begin to substantiate my impression here, nonetheless it does appear to me that Paul Tillich's serious philosophical theology has provided at least one major background to some of the younger Protestant thinkers and has given a certain scientific respectability to their strange notions of a "dead" God. The way that Paul Tillich came to insist on a "god above the god of theism" seems to me to be the first mile or so along the road to the proposition "God is dead."

But lest we be committed to too wide a field of discussion, it behooves us to limit the area to be covered in this paper. We shall not directly touch on such knowledge of God as we might have through revelation, although we must realize that Tillich is led to the position that it is only through what he identifies as the revelatory experience of the ultimate that one can know God truly. In other words, in regard to Tillich, we shall treat only that part of his doctrine that is prior to his analysis of "revelation," showing why he considers unrevealed and rational knowledge of God in a sense both impossible and an absurdity. It is to this position as to the impossibility of such knowledge that we contrast Scotus' doctrine of its possibility: the doctrine, that is, that real, intellectual knowledge not the result of revelation is naturally attainable to homo viator in however tenuous and indistinct a form. Our investigation will thus eventually concern itself with Tillich's and Scotus' notions of being.

272

As to sources, first of all in regard to Tillich, we limit ourselves to his _Systematic Theology_, Volume I, because it is in this work that he has expressed himself to the greatest degree of theological and philosophical precision. Elsewhere, especially in some less systematically worked out presentations, he might well have made certain statements calling into question one or the other of the more rigorous formulations preserved in this scientific work, but we must take him at his own most serious word. As for Scotus, our major source will be Distinction III of the First Book of the _Ordinatio_--not that we positively exclude other passages from our discussion, but in this place he treats the question _ex professo_ and in a text that has been guaranteed for us already by the critical edition.

I

Paul Tillich, the German-American philosopher-theologian so enamored of ontological Christianity and of what he called the "Protestant principle," once willingly accepted the designation of himself as a "dangerous man." (1) For, although he has indeed preserved most of the substance of both the _philosophia perennis_ and of the Christian Creed, he has so adapted both to provide an apology suited to the age we live in, that if his statements are understood in isolation from the whole of his system (as unfortunately he himself at times allowed them to be), they very well might lead to anything but that which he intended by them. It is with some temerity then that I try to summarize the line of thought whereby he came up with the conclusion that we possess only _docta ignorantia_ of God.

A basic aspect of Tillich's thought that must be kept in mind for fear of otherwise misinterpreting him is the very way he proceeds theologically, namely according to what he calls the "method of correlation." This method, which he admits is "ultimately...not different from the system which is built upon it," (2) seems to be a matter of analysing the content of Christian belief only in relation to and following upon an analysis of the existing situation. "It correlates questions and answers, situation and message, human existence and divine manifestation." (3)

More directly as it concerns our discussion, Tillich tells us that the word "correlation" may be used in

three ways: 1) to designate the simple correspondence one
to another of different series of data--i.e., a kind of
parallelism of elements in one series to elements in another; 2) to designate logical interdependence of concepts, as in notions that refer to each other as opposite
poles of the same relationship; 3) to designate the real
interdependence of things or events in structural wholes. (4)

It is in terms of all three ways of understanding
"correlation," but more especially of the second and third,
that Tillich develops his ideas about our knowledge of God.
All of theology, he maintains, must use the method of correlation, analysing first the human situation and then the
terms in the Christian message, to find there simple correspondence to one another. The method also, in the process
of its existential analysis of the human situation and/or
of the contents of the Christian message discerns in either
or both certain polar concepts, for instance the polarity
finite-infinite. At the same time, through these analyses,
there is called forth in the mind of the theologian an intimation of a possible correlation of question to answer
that seems to be present in the human situation (the ques-
tioning) and in the divine manifestation (the answer).
Struck with this, the theologian must then proceed to
verify if possible a further correlation, the third named
above, namely the real, not simply logical, interdependence
of the seeking human condition and the answering divine
manifestation. (5)

It is, then, in the study of the correlatives "Being" and "God" (6) that our philosopher-theologian discusses the question with which we are presently concerned,
that of man's knowledge of God. "God," in Tillich's own
words, "is the answer to the question implied in being." (7)
Or, in other words, by the awareness he possesses before-
hand within his "theological circle"--that is, by the faith-
conviction that he is attempting to illustrate but which he
thus assumes before he substantiates it (possibly to be
thus accused of arguing in a "circle"--the theologian sets
up a correlation between "Being" and "God" that at first is
but simple one-for-one correspondence, then is gradually
seen to be a logical polarity, and eventually to be discerned as a really interdependent question and answer.

I think it necessary to follow Tillich in this process in the discussion at hand. He sets up the simple correspondence of "Being" to "God" and analyses them respectively. (8) Within the analysis of "Being," that is, in Tillich's progressive breakdown of the elements of the ontological structure, or of the pattern of being itself, there are discerned a number of logical correlatives,--self and non-self, one and many, and so forth--that are found to be contrasted logically in a polar relationship. In this line-up a major polarity that especially strikes our attention is the correlation, in the cognitive order, of subject and object. The problem involved at this point (9) seems to be that of determining what connection the subject-object polarity has to the self-world polarity, chiefly whether subject and object are "correlated" in his terminology in the second sense of the word only or also in the third sense. That is, are they logically correlated or ontologically? The reason this is of some interest to us is that already at this point Tillich introduces some notions of the inability of man to know God as an object.

For Tillich, God can become an objective correlative in regard to subjective man only if the correlation is kept in the logical order. But, he says, "The danger of logical objectification is that it never is merely logical." Even in the cognitive relationship, "If God is brought into the subject-object structure of being"--that is, if the subject-object correlation is not simply logical but ontological so that the subject remains man and the object correlative to man is God--then God quite obviously"...becomes one being among others (first of all, a being beside the subject who looks at him as an object)" and indeed, "He ceases to be the God who is really God." (10) At the same time, he continues, there is the further danger that in objectifying God, one also tends to root out all subjectivity from Him who has been made object--that is, to make a "Thou" into an "It," or in Tillich's phrase, "Such an object is a 'thing,' in German, a Ding, something which is altogether bedingt ('conditioned')." (11)

Thus, in a kind of side-eddy off the main stream of his systematic development, Tillich has already hinted as to something of his objection to our considering ourselves capable of knowing God. It is time now to return to the center of his presentation.

275

In his continuing analysis of the ontological structure, our author comes upon certain correlations that are
not just the simple correspondence that was assumed from the
beginning, nor again just the logical correlation of subject-
object. There are a number of correlations in his third
sense of this word, that is, there are a number of correlatives that are ontological, really interdependent on one an-
other--thus, the correlation of individualization and participation, that of dynamics, that of freedom and destiny.

At a still deeper level in the structure of being
then, Tillich encounters the ontologically correlative
dualities that have to do with the very power to exist, being and nonbeing, finite and infinte. I simply say the
"ontologically correlative," not as if to discount the
struggle undertaken by Tillich to show their real interdependence that is verified beyond a merely logical polarity,
but so as to limit myself just to enunciating the conclusion
he arrived at. But to state the ontological character of
these two correlations brings on certain further consequences
that have repercussions on the problem of the knowledge of
God. If being and nonbeing are really correlative, that
means they are in dialectical encounter with one another,
that the one correlative depends on the other or struggles
with the other, and vice versa.

Thus, being as man knows it, is always interdependent
with nonbeing, which here is not so much the negation of being (in Greek 'ouk ou') as privation of being ('me on'). (12)
It is in this sense then that he says, "being limited by
nonbeing is finitude" (13) and thereby works into the
polarity of finite-infinite. This correlation will eventually lead him to pose the question of God that is to be answered by revelation, but before we get that far, I think it
is important to take another look at this correlation of being and nonbeing to see how it is very drastically reflected in his ideas on our knowledge of God.

"Being" for Tillich "is essentially related to nonbeing... Being is essentially threatened with disruption
and self-destruction." (14) This leads to what he considers
a necessary distinction between essence and existence, or
between essential being and existential being, in which
"essence" is both the nature and the true and undistorted
nature, while "existence" is ambiguous, both expressing and

contradicting being. (15) He says, quite notably, "Whatever exists, that is 'stands out' of mere potentiality, is more than it is in the state of mere potentiality and less than it could be in the power of its essential nature." (16)

It is obviously against this background then that we must read some remarkable statements of his concerning the existence of God, especially this: "God does not exist. He is being-itself beyond essence and existence. Therefore to argue that God exists is to deny him." (17)

This essential relation between being and nonbeing also seems to be behind Tillich's abhorrence of the referral to God as "a being" or even simply as "being"; for him this would be destructive of the very nature of God, according to which God is being-itself, or the ground of being, a prius to being. But this is to anticipate ourselves a bit, because this notion does not come out in Tillich's system until the "answer" of revelation is analysed.

The real point at issue in this reference to the being-nonbeing correlation is the insistence of Tillich that "The ground of being cannot be found within the totality of beings." (18) If this is true, this fact destroys not only the possibility of arguing to God's existence, but also, it seems, the possibility of knowing him in and through the creatures He has made. As we shall see immediately, Tillich does admit the possibility of knowing God, but not in and through those things which were made, but almost as if in spite of them.

For, with the analysis of the structure of being and the isolation of finitude, Tillich has now arrived at the juncture where the question of God begins to be framed in one's awareness--a question then that is to find its answer only in the manifestation of the divine, which is here conceived of as interdependently correlated to the question. The development of the question of God from the recognition of finitude proceeds in this way. In man's awareness of the ontological structure of finitude, that is, of the tension even within himself between essential being and its relation to nonbeing in existence, a person, Tillich says, "knows that he is finite." But in that very knowledge he also knows that "he is excluded from an infinity which nevertheless belongs to him. He is aware of his potential infinity while being aware of his actual finitude." (19)

It is precisely here, then, that the question of
God arises. It is of the nature of finite reason that it
must acknowledge the finitude of man's cognitive reason and
"its inability to grasp its own infinite ground." (20) This
is that "ignorance" of the docta ignorantia which Tillich
with his professed model Nicholas of Cusa speaks of. The
"learned" part, the docta ignorantia, also becomes apparent:

"In recognizing this situation, man is at the same
time aware of the infinite which is present in
everything finite, though infinitely transcending
it.... In spite of its finitude, reason is aware of
its infinite depth. It cannot express it in terms
of rational knowledge (ignorance), but the knowledge that this is impossible is real knowledge
(learned)." (21)

It is important to note here that Tillich's acceptance of the presence of infinitude, or of an infinite depth,
in everything finite seems to mean presence within, presence in spite of, and I think even more notably, presence
manifested, but manifested in and not because of the existent. (22) I insist on this because this seems to me a
shading of Tillich's thought that distinguishes it most
significantly from the thought of Scotus.

But first to conclude the description of Tillich's
development of the reality of God. In the experience of and
recognition of finitude, man is able to form the question
of God. At this point, Tillich seems already to admit a
certain "awareness" of God, because: "The question of God
is possible because an awareness of God is present in the
question of God. This awareness precedes the question."
(23) That is to say, "The presence within finitude of an
element which transcends it is experienced." (24) In other
words, Tillich here admits, yea rather is championing, the
experience of "the presence of something unconditional
within the self and the world." (25) Is this then a "knowledge of God" as we have projected in the title of this
paper?

As Tillich sees it, "knowledge," in its most perfect human sense, would imply that what he calls "ontologi-

278

cal reason" be in union with being-itself. (26) Now, "ontological reason can be defined as the structure of the mind
which enables it to grasp and to shape reality." (27) Or,
in other words, the structure of being (i.e. the "logos" of
the "on"--the "ontic-logos") is thought of as both received
and controlled by the reason of man, which reason can do
because it is as it were in tandem with the very structure
of being, of which it itself is a part. In this sense,
there is some real interrelation between the reason, or
mind, and the structure or logos of all being. In this
give-and-take of reason and structure, man becomes aware of
a certain "depth of reason" which is the "expression of
something that is not reason" nor the structure of being,
"but which precedes reason and is manifest through it."
And "in the cognitive realm the depth of reason is its
quality of pointing to truth itself." (28) In view of this,
we would conclude that man does not really know the unconditional, but is merely conscious of it. If I may make
a prosaic comparison, try closing your eyes and extending
your finger to your forehead. Do you not experience even
before the two touch a kind of anticipatory sensation?
This I would compare to the "awareness" of the unconditional
of which Tillich speaks. There is no real knowledge of the
unconditional, just as there is no real sense-experience of
my finger touching my forehead. Yet there is an awareness
of sorts, vague and most deceptive, but nonetheless real.
And I think that the difference between "awareness" and
"knowledge" is that the latter must be considered concep-
tual--such, that is, that the mind has formed an inner word
about what it has grasped; there is, in other terminology,
a species expressa no matter how vague and undefined it may
be.

Whatever else may be said of this "awareness," it
seems for Tillich to be the stuff of which the "question of
God" is formed. As he says himself, "The unconditional
element appears in the theoretical (receiving) functions of
reason as verum-ipsum, the true-itself...., in the practical
(shaping) function of reason as bonum-ipsum, the good-itself
.... Both (then) are manifestations of the esse-ipsum,
being-itself as the ground and abyss of everything that is."
(29) This latter, being-itself as the ground and abyss of
being, is Tillich's favorite expression for the God beyond
the God of Theism; but it should be noted that here this
"ground of being" is not known, but, as it were, pointed at

by the experience of being and its structure. To say that this is "God," the personal one God of Christianity for Tillich would be a step that is not warranted, an identification that could not be made except on the basis of a revelatory experience. Thus, one remains "naturally" in ignorance of God Himself.

There are other things one might say about Tillich's "Natural Theology," or especially about his Theology, his notion of the religious symbol particularly, or of the ultimate concern that is the constellation of the revelatory correlation. But we have limited ourselves to discussing his notion of the possibility of a knowledge of God on the merely "natural"--i.e. as opposed to "revealed"--level of man's capabilities. And we have seen that such knowledge for him must be considered impossible. We shall now look at Scotus' parallel doctrines to see how they compare to Tillich's, and perhaps might even provide for them a necessary corrective.

II

Having listened to a voice practiced in the accents of our own day, we hear now the voice of another philosopher-theologian, a voice long since stilled by death, but a voice nonetheless that for all its strangeness to our modern ear can still stir the mind that grasps for truth. Scotus speaks today, assuringly saying that in all the rigor of science our God can indeed be known. But that can be a most misleading statement, and once having made it, I would now like to so hedge it in by thorny qualification, that to reach through to take hold of it again might seem a most difficult and hardly worthwhile endeavor.

For the fact is that John Duns Scotus was quite aware that we know precious little about God other than what He Himself has told us. God was never anything but a hidden God, some interpretations of Vatican I's teaching on His knowability (30) notwithstanding. God as He is in Himself has always been confessed as incomprehensible. As Scotus would put it in his own epigrammatic way: "God-only is known naturally only to Himself." (31) And more directly in reference to the natural knowledge of the homo viator in particular:

"...I say that God is not known naturally by man in this life in particular and properly, that is under

280

the _ratio_ of God's essence as such and in itself."
(32)

So God, in a very true sense, is completely unknowable
naturally, that is, as He is in His inner-most essence.

But, while this is to be insisted upon, Scotus would
also have us be very careful why we so insist. For, above
all, we must not reason as Henry of Ghent did in saying
God's essence is incomprehensible to us because something is
known exclusively either in a particular or in a universal,
but that God's quiddity is in no way contained in a universal, nor yet by any sufficient likeness in a particular
creature. In response, Scotus would have us distinguish:
when it is argued that something is known only "per simile,"
one would have to understand "per simile" either of the
similarity of univocation or of imitation. In denying that
God is known by the similarity of univocation, Henry is
correct, Scotus says, but only provided this univocation is
understood the way Henry understands it. That is, if the
total quiddity of God--which in Scotus' theology (33) is
identified as esse infinitum--must be found univocal to some
other quiddity of a particular creature, of course this
would be impossible. But univocation must not be understood
in so absolute a sense, and thereby hangs a very long tale!

For the fact is, according to the Franciscan Master,
that we can and do know God as esse infinitum. Certainly,
it can be said that this notion of God is something that
Scotus has to begin with and that therefore he never completely comes out of what Paul Tillich has called the "theological circle," or in other words, he has never admitted
anything more than a systematic doubt. (34) All that really
says is that Scotus is here simply following the scheme proper to theology, that of fides quaerens intellectum, and in
no way of faith's having its object scientifically demonstrated with all the rigor possible.

But in that, in the fact that the essence of the
Godhead is known, if not naturally, at least as an obiectum
voluntarium, as supernaturally revealed (35), by that very
fact, there is an inherent possibility on man's part of
knowing God even in this life. Indeed, it is this very
possibility that must needs be safeguarded by any rational
theology. And this is done by Scotus through his famous

theory of the univocity of being.

Before we get into that, however, I feel it necessary to first point out that Scotus very industriously
argues against a knowledge of God that is immediate. The
proposition "Deus est" which would seem to be per se nota,
i.e. non-discursively evident, if we simply bring together
the extremes esse and esse infinitum--which is what Scotus
considers as the most perfect description of the quiddity
of the divine available to us. (36)--this proposition, I
say, is definitely not per se nota by men in this life. (37)
Granted then, that the proposition "Deus est" is not
naturally per se nota, we must now insist, on the other
hand, that it is knowable discursively. Indeed, its very
knowability hinges upon whether esse can be predicated in
any meaningful sense of God.

There is no need here to go through Scotus' proof of
the existence of God or his various discussions of the ways
of knowing God--the via negativa, the desiderium naturale
for God, and so forth. But, viewing the process of his
thought as we are in contrast with the analysis of being
engaged in by Tillich, it might be worthy of note that a
sufficient parallel exists in it up to the point where
Tillich would insist that the ground of being is present,
manifested in but not through the very structure of being.
You recall, the point at issue there was whether our knowledge of God in creatures was therefore because of the ontic
structure, or in spite of it.

On this precise point, I think a significantly
similar discussion is to be found in Bk I, Second Distinction of Scotus' Ordinatio. There the proposition that
"Aliquod infinitum esse est per se notum" (that is, Some
infinite being is known per se) is first argued affirma-
tively by an opponent, and then denied by Scotus. The
affirmative is argued with an argument based on St. John
Damascene that goes something like this: "A knowledge of
the proposition 'God is' is naturally inserted in everyone,
as is evident in the second book of the Metaphysics, namely,
that first principles, which are as it were doors, are per
se nota." Scotus' refutation takes the form of destroying
the referral to authority by explaining the quote differently. He writes: "As to the principle argument of the
Damascene, it can be (adequately) explained either as

referring to the cognitive potency naturally given to us all, whereby ex creaturis we can know that God is, at least in rationibus generalibus, or as referring to the knowledge of God (had) under rationibus communibus suitable both to Him and to creatures, which are known more perfectly and more eminently in God than in others. That (St. John Damascene) is not however speaking here of a cognition of God that is actual and distinct, is apparent from what he goes on to say, and so forth." (38)

What Scotus is thus safeguarding is the fact that we do know God ex creaturis. The thing I wish to point out is the way we do so, namely in rationes generales or in those common to both God and creatures. This is real knowledge, but admittedly most vague--the expression is cognitio non actualis vel distincta. Is this then no more than the "awareness" that Tillich speaks of? I think not, even though the expression cognitio non actualis seems to point to a kind of intuition of God, which is something of what Tillich would like to see admitted. But here, though intuition very likely is involved, it is Scotistic intuition, a most indistinct but initially conceptual intuition, not the intuition of the romantics that destroys the triadic structure of knowledge in favor of a dyadic contact of knower and known without the medium of any mental image. (39)

It is especially in this triadic sense that Scotus' themes, both of the intuition of the individual and of the univocity of "ens" or "esse," are, I think, best to be understood. One's knowledge both begins with the perception of being and reaches its highest level of abstraction in the contemplation of the same being.

Ens thus is not simply not a genus, not simply a prius to every contraction into genus, although it is that, of course, (40) and as such remains indifferent to the intrinsic modes of finite or infinite. (41) Even more so, "Being" here, the esse that is seen as common to both God and creatures, and that in this community is the basis of our real knowledge of God, is a something. To draw a more direct contrast to Tillich's notion, Scotus, in predicating "being" of God is first of all not saying that God is essentially related to nonbeing, in the sense that His existence is to be thought of as mixed with or bounded on either side by nonebeing--that would be to make of "esse" a genus, a contraction of ens into the modality of finiteness; but Scotus has "esse" as a reality prior to such determination. Secondly, and here the going becomes much rougher, Scotus is not so objectifying God as to make of Him some thing: where Tillich used the German noun "Ding" and the adjective "bedingt," I would suggest the German word "etwas" for what Scotus thinks of as "being"--God is some thing, not some thing, and is grasped conceptually as something, most vaguely, certainly, and not at all distinctly, but nonetheless conceptually.

It may help to refer this discussion to one passage from Scotus' own writings in order to at least exemplify these notions in his words. The passage is, however, quite difficult and requires close attention. As against a forementioned opponent, in the question whether God is the primum cognitum by us naturally in this state, John Duns Scotus asks (42) us not to make a distinction between the knowledge of God's essence (the "Quid est") and the knowledge of his existence (the "Si est"), because in this question he is merely seeking a simple concept about which "esse" might be known through an act of judging intellect. For one never knows about the "si est" of something unless he has some concept of that about which he knows the "esse." This almost sounds like Tillich's statement to the effect that "The question of God is possible because an awareness of God is present in the question of God." Except that Scotus uses the word "concept" where Tillich refers to "awareness."

Scotus continues in a note appended to his text and speaks more at length about the "what" in the "Quid est." He writes: "The 'What' that is said through name is a 'what' that is of the reality and is something that includes the 'si est'; as Aristotle says, 'the ratio signified by the word 'name' is a definition.' Still, the 'esse-quid' (that is, the 'to be something') of the name is more common than either the 'esse' or the 'quid' of the thing, because it is suitable to more things to be signified by (this) name than by 'esse.'" In other words, the most common concept of all, is "to be something," "esse quid," a concept that is more common, because less determined, than either "to be" or "something." To this most common ratio entis there is at the same time a true concept, or name of the thing known, and a truly univocal concept applicable to both

God and creatures. With this common ground, no longer is that concept of esse merely equivocal which is composed in the esse infinitum of our theologically determined notion of the quiddity of God and which is the basis of our whole analysis of the structure of being whereby we come to a vague and indistinct, an intuitional but conceptual, and eventually a discursive knowledge of God.

In closing, I hesitate to claim too much, but from my limited understanding of both the theorizations of Tillich and Scotus and of the formulation of the current question of the existence and life of God, I think that Scotus' theory of univocity of ens in the sense posited above is a real contribution. He does not perhaps say the final or the only word on the question of our knowledge of God, but he does say a word worth listening to.

In this way, Scotus truly can speak to us today.

(1)   D. MAC KENZIE BROWN (ed.), <u>Ultimate Concern: Tillich in Dialogue</u>, New York, 1965, 188-193.

(2)   PAUL TILLICH, <u>Systematic Theology</u>, I, Chicago 1951, 8.

(3)   <u>Ibid</u>.

(4)   <u>Ibid</u>., 60

(5)   Note should be taken already here of the objection against this step that some theologians much concerned with safeguarding the transcendence of God have had: see Tillich's own recognizance of their uneasiness: <u>Ibid</u>., 61.

(6)   This is Part II of his System, following on the first part that dealt of the correlation of reason (question) and revelation (answer). Part I thus dealt more with the very structure that the method of correlation was based on, whereas Part II concerns itself with the one single correlation that is really most at the center of all the further individually abstracted correlations adduced subsequently.

(7)   <u>Op. cit</u>., 163.

(8)   <u>Ibid</u>: the analysis of the first correlative, "being"; 163-174; of the second, "God," 211-235.

(9)   <u>Ibid</u>., 171-174.

(10)   <u>Ibid</u>., 172.

(11)   <u>Ibid</u>., 173.

(12)   <u>Ibid</u>., 188.

(13)   <u>Ibid</u>., 189. See also his <u>Love, Power and Justice</u>, New York, 1954, 38-39; "Being which includes non-being is finite being. 'Finite' means carrying within one's being the destiny not to be. It designates a limited power of being, limited between a begin-

ning and an end, between non-being before and nonbeing after."

(14)   Systematic Theology, I 202.

(15)   Ibid., 203.

(16)   Ibid.

(17)   Ibid., 205. The larger context reads: "Both the con-
        cept of existence and the method of arguing to a con-
        clusion (i.e. in 'arguments' for the existence of
        God) are inadequate for the idea of God. However,
        it is defined, the 'existence' of God contradicts
        the idea of a creative ground of essence and exis-
        tence. The ground of being cannot be found within
        the totality of beings, nor can the ground of
        essence and existence participate in the tensions
        and distruptions characteristic of the transition
        from essence to existence."...

        "It would be a great victory for Christian apolo-
        getics if the words 'God' and 'existence' were very
        definitely separated except in the paradox of God
        becoming manifest under the conditions of existence
        that is in the Christological paradox."
        It is here then that Tillich makes the statement
        quoted in the text.

(18)   Ibid.

(19)   Ibid., 206.

(20)   Ibid., 81.

(21)   Ibid.

(22)   Ibid., 155.

(23)   Ibid., 206.

(24)   Ibid.

(25)   Ibid.

(26)   Ibid., 75.

(27)   Ibid.

(28)   Ibid., 79.

(29)   Ibid., 207.

(30)   Denziger-Schoenmetzer, 3004-3005, 3026.

(31)   "Solus Deus est sibi soli naturaliter notus"--
         Ordinatio, Prol., p. 3, q. 3 (I. Duns Scoti, Opera
         Omnia, I 102-103: The critical edition will be cited
         subsequently only by volume and page: I 102-103.)

(32)   Ordinatio, I, d. 3, p. 1, q 1-2 (III-38).

(33)   That is in his theologia in nobis, as it is had by
         the human intellect, not necessarily as it is in
         theologia in se. In other words, by speaking of
         "quiddity of God' he is not contradicting what we
         just noted about the incomprehensibility of God.

(34)   Note, for example, the beginning of his De primo
         principio, where the initial thoughts are prayerful
         aspirations to a God already recognized.

(35)   Eg. Ordinatio, I, d, 3, p. 1, q. 1-2 (III 39).

(36)   Cf. Ordinatio, ibid. (III 40).

(37)   Ordinatio, I, d. 2, p. 1, q. 2 (II 137): "...Pro-
         positio illa est per se nota quae coninngit extrema
         ista, esse et essentiam divinam ut haec est, sive
         Deum et esse sibi proprium, quo modo Deus videt
         illam essentiam et esse sub proprissima ratione qua
         est in Deo hoc esse, quo modo nec esse a nobis nunc
         intelligitur nec essentia, etc...."

(38)   Ordinatio, I d. 2, p. 1, q. 2 (II 128-129, 145).

(39)   Cf. JOHN F. BOLER, "Scotus and Intuition: Some Re-
         marks" in The Monist, 49 (1965) 551-570.

(40)   I. Duns Scoti, Quaestiones Subtilissimae super libros

<u>Metaphysiconum Aristoteles</u>, IV, q. 1, Schol. 1 (Vives VII 149).

(41)   <u>Ordinatio</u>, I, d. 8, p. 1, q. 3 (IV 205-206).

(42)   <u>Ordinatio</u>, I, d. 3, p. 1, q. 2 (III 6ss).

Discussion

WILLIAM O'MEARA, PH.D.

Professor of Philosophy
University of Chicago
Chicago, Illinois

Father Cyrin has presented an admirably clear paper on a difficult and important subject. The paper deserves a more systematic critique than I am prepared to give. I merely wish to raise some points for discussion in order to clarify some of the issues.

Fr. Cyrin places his technical discussion of the doctrines of Scotus and Tillich in a setting provided by contemporary discussions on the nature of God, and he refers to the so-called "God is dead" school. It appears that Fr. Cyrin does not actually blame Tillich for fostering such ideas but he does seem to suggest that Tillich's ideas were a first stage along the road to these "strange notions." "The way that Paul Tillich came to insist on a 'god above the god of theism' seems to me to be the first mile or so along the road to the proposition 'God is dead.'" It is hard to say just what or how much he means by this. I would like to suggest, on the other hand, that undeniably orthodox Christian theologians have always been alert to the dangers of anthropomorphism and of claiming too much for human knowledge of God. As. Fr. Cyrin says towards the end of his paper "...the fact is that John Duns Scotus was quite aware that we know precious little about God other than what He himself has told us." "God, as he is in himself has always been confessed as incomprehensible." Now surely statements such as these could also be interpreted, however incorrectly, as a stage "along the road to the proposition 'God is dead.'" On the same point, if we look at some of the supposedly dangerous statements of Tillich, e.g., that too much of a claim to know God makes God "become one being among others" and "He ceases to be the God who is really God," must we not say that orthodox theology agrees? To say with Tillich, that God is not a being, seems entirely acceptable to me. God does not enter into any class--is not in any category.

A prime theological rule, guiding both the philosopher and the theologian, is for him to make sure that nothing he says would seem to convey the idea that human knowledge of God could be taken to mean that our knowledge of God is other than unique. I think both Tillich and Duns Scotus observe this rule and that for both of them we may properly say that our knowledge of God is always non-standard. Let me take a particular text in Fr. Cyrin's paper, which, I think, does not sufficiently recognize this. Quoting Tillich: "The ground of being cannot be found within

the totality of being," Fr. Cyrin goes on to say, "If this
is true, this fact destroys not only the possibility of
arguing to God's existence, but also, it seems, the possibility of knowing Him in and through the creatures He has
made." In my interpretation, Tillich's assertion amounts
to holding that God, as the ground of being, is wholly other
than any or all of the beings, in the plural, of which we
may have standard knowledge. Again, a little farther on, in
attempting to show that our knowledge of God is possible,
according to Tillich, but not "in and through creatures but
almost as if in spite of them," Fr. Cyrin gives a dubious
interpretation of a text in Tillich. The text is

> "In recognizing this situation, man is at the same
> time aware of the infinite which is present in
> everything finite, though infinitely transcending
> it.... In spite of its finitude, reason is aware of
> its infinite depth. It cannot express it in terms
> of rational knowledge (ignorance), but the knowledge
> that this is impossible is real knowledge (learned)."
> (Tillich, S.T. I:81)

This is interpreted as follows: "It is important to
note here that Tillich's acceptance of the presence of infinitude, of an infinite depth, in everything finite seems
to mean presence within, presence in spite of, and I think
even more notably, presence manifested, but manifested in
and not because of the existent. (N.B. footnote 21, at this
point, referring to S.T. I:155 does not seem to be correct.)
I insist on this because this seems to me a shading of
Tillich's thought that distinguishes it most significantly
from the thought of Scotus." My comment is this. I do not
at all contend that there is no difference between the
thought of our two theologians. But I fail to see that when
Tillich says "in spite of" he means anything which would
count against saying that we know God in and through those
things which were made. "In spite of" in the context means:
"We realize, become aware of, the reality of God exactly by
going beyond, or through, if you like, creatures-not resting
in them as final terms of our knowledge but precisely recognizing that the finitude of ourselves and other creatures
calls for an acknowledgment of their lack of self-sufficiency,
and thus, in spite of the temptation to stop short in knowing beings, we push on to affirming the reality of the
ground of being."

Along the same line, Fr. Cyrin contends that
Tillich's "awareness" of God does not count as knowledge of
God. In one statement, he seems to wish to claim that man
really knows the unconditional beyond being merely conscious
of it. It is not clear to me that this distinction is anything more than a matter of terminology and context.
Tillich does not express himself in such terms as species
expressa, etc. For Fr. Cyrin, there is a difference, in
such terms, between awareness and knowledge in that the
latter is conceptual and the former is not. But then he
concedes that although there must be a concept it doesn't
matter how vague and undefined it may be. It is difficult
for me to see how a highly vague and highly undefined concept constitutes knowledge as importantly different from
awareness.

To repeat, when Tillich claims that the ground of
being is not known, I take him to mean what we all grant,
that God is not known in the standard way in which other
beings are known. Surely this is not significantly different from Duns Scotus' insistence that we do not know God as
this essence. In Scotus' language God can indeed be known,
but this is certainly a non-standard sense of knowledge.
The knowledge is also conceptual but the concepts involved
are constructed from our concepts of finite things and although they are about God they are not from God in the sense
that the concepts whereby we know creatures are both about
and from creatures.

In conclusion, I would like to refer to a text which
seems difficult to reconcile with Fr. Cyrin's interpretation
which apparently claims some positive or standard character
for our knowledge of God according to Duns Scotus. According to Fr. Cyrin "Even more so, 'Being' here, the esse that
is seen as common to both God and creatures, and in this
community is the basis of our real knowledge of God, is a
something." There are further details in which, as Fr.
Cyrin says, the going becomes rougher, but I will keep it
simple and call attention to just one difficulty. The
univocal concept of being which is common to God and creatures is one of our concepts and, of course, is a finite
one. There is a concept, then, in which, one may properly
say, Deus et creaturae conveniunt. But this does not mean
for Scotus that there is any corresponding reality in which
Deus et creaturae conveniunt. Cf. Ordinatio I, d. 8, p. 1,
q. 3, #82, Ed. Vat., t. IV, p. 190: "...Deus et creaturae

non sunt primo diversa in conceptibus; sunt tamen primo
diversa in realitate, quia in nulla realitate conveniunt..."

As I see it, the knowledge claim is slight, the
knowledge is definitely non-standard, and there is not such
a great degree of difference between Duns Scotus and
Tillich as has been alleged. Of course, the differences
are great and far-reaching--this is inevitable given the
facts of time and history. But my opinion remains that
both theologians had essentially the same goal in mind--to
claim a genuine knowledge of God without making God in any
sense a being among other beings.

FATHER ROBERT R. BOYLE, S.J., made graduate
studies at the University of St. Louis and Yale
University. On the faculty at Regis College,
Denver, since 1955, he is at present Professor
of English there. He is well known for papers
and articles on James Joyce and Gerard Manley
Hopkins in collections and journals. He recently contributed the article on Hopkins to
the New Catholic Encyclopedia. He is author of
the book Metaphor in Hopkins, University of
North Carolina, 1961.

DUNS SCOTUS
in the Poetry of Hopkins

ROBERT R. BOYLE, S.J., PH. D.

Christopher Devlin ends his splendid essay, "Hopkins and Scotus," with the following sentence: "GMH's central identity with Scotus is in Scotus' theology of the Incarnation." (1) I accept fully Father Devlin's conclusion, and my task in this paper will be to show the wisdom of beginning with this fact, if one is to see clearly the effect of Scotism in Hopkins' poems, and to demonstrate in some of the poems how that effect operates.

Critics tackling the problem of Scotus' influence in Hopkins normally have begun elsewhere. W. H. Gardner, the dean and still the best of Hopkins' critics, started an unfortunate trend in his pioneer efforts to deal fully with this difficult matter himself and to apply what he learned from the theologians he consulted and from the article or so Fr. (then Mr.) Devlin had up to that time written. He states:

> To demonstrate clearly the influence of this School-
> man on the poetry of Hopkins we must give some
> account of three of his chief doctrines--his meta-
> physical formalism, his intuitionalism, and his
> voluntarism. On all these questions Scotism dif-
> fers from Thomism, the system taught by the Jesuit
> theologians. (2)

Since "Thomism" can mean many things, and since Jesuit theologians have never been noted for unity of doctrine, a dark foreboding might well shadow the mind of Gardner's reader. And indeed it could not be too dark, since Gardner's brief account, not well based on either Thomist or Scotist metaphysics, cheapens Thomism (of any kind) and falsifies Scotism, making the first a closed, neat system which can deal adequately only with clear quiddities, (3) and making the second an intuitionalist, mystical, dreamy surge into mystery. (4) The words of Scotus (or of his students) appear, mostly in translation, but the meaning in context, a most difficult matter, does not. And the parody of Thomism, used here as a mere foil for the broad statements about Scotism, would surely offend Hopkins himself, to say nothing of Scotus.

Many other critics developed this sad beginning, recently John E. Keating, (5) who centers his discussion of Scotistic influence in Hopkins' understanding and use of "really distinguishable attributes" in God and of God's closeness to creation, involved in the univocity of the concept of being. All the virtues that Mr. Keating attempts to attribute to Scotism can at least equally well be attributed to the Thomism of St. Thomas, where God's attributes and His closeness to creation are in no sense less profoundly or satisfactorily treated than in Scotus. Scotus' doctrine on these points may have supported Hopkins' faith, indeed, but it could do no more for his poetry than could the doctrine of Thomas. Indeed, in a review of Mr. Keating's generally excellent study, I wrote the following opinion (which, as will appear, I have since found occasion to qualify):

> What is clear is that Hopkins used what he thought Scotus was saying to shoal up favorite attitudes and conclusions of his own. More than that should be left in the realm of the unattainable, I judge, or at least dealt with as mere speculation, not safe ground for critical conclusions. (6)

Mr. Keating does make efforts to arrive at Scotus' thought. More destructive by far are those critics who work confidently from a large and tolerant ignorance of the subject or who attempt to wrest Scotus' (and Hopkins') thought to an anti-Christian dogma of their own. An example of the first is Elizabeth W. Schneider, (7) who wishes to persuade us that the nun on the Deutschland really did have a vision of Christ, like St. Paul or, perhaps better, Bernadette in her vision of the Blessed Virgin, and that Hopkins, intuiting this fact, saw therein a sign of the conversion of England--not really probable, even had such a vision occurred, since if anything it would more likely have signified, among numerous possibilities, the conversion of Germany. Miss Schneider, moreover, takes visions far more seriously than any Catholic priest is likely to do. "Miraculous healing," which she finds Hopkins eagerly seeking, along with "other miraculous signs of grace," is not, after all, a vision. And her bald assumption that Hopkins here dwelt, "with somewhat abnormal personal intensity," or "the suggestion of a new miracle" (p. 113), needs considerable proof, which she does not and could not supply. Her attempt to make "fectch" prove her point (p. 118), while clever, is not convincing.

But the main point here is Miss Schneider's discussion of Hopkins' Scotism. She has well learned from Fr.

Devlin that Hopkins' central influence from Scotus is his
treatment of the doctrine of the Incarnation. She repeats
Devlin's explanation accurately enough at first, though she
clearly fails to perceive the significance of Hopkins'
discussion of "aeonian time." She supposes that in Hopkins'
thought the Incarnation "is in fact coeval with time itself." (p. 115)

We had better, I suppose, at this point look at the
text under discussion. Hopkins is discussing the nature of
sacrifice, and he searches back into the prime intention of
God in creating, the "first" Incarnation of Christ before
our time had begun, and the reason for such an incarnation:

> The first intention then of God outside himself or,
> as they say, _ad extra_, outwards, the first outstress
> of God's power, was Christ; and we must believe that
> the next was the Blessed Virgin. Why did the Son of
> God go thus forth from the Father not only in the
> eternal and intrinsic procession of the Trinity but
> also, by an extrinsic and less than eternal, let us
> say aeonian one?--To give God glory and that by
> sacrifice, sacrifice offered in the barren wilder-
> ness outside of God, as the children of Israel were
> led into the wilderness to offer sacrifice. This
> sacrifice and this outward procession is a conse-
> quence and shadow of the procession of the Trinity,
> from which mystery sacrifice takes its rise; but of
> this I do not mean to write here. It is as if the
> blissful agony ox stress of selving in God had
> forced out drops of sweat or blood, which drops
> were the world, or as if the lights lit at the
> festival of the 'peaceful Trinity' through some
> little cranny striking out lit up into being one
> 'cleave' out of the world of possible creatures
> (S, p. 197). (8)

Hopkins clearly opposes himself to any notion that
the cosmos itself was God's first intention, with the Incarnation coming along later in view of man's fall. He holds,
with Scotus as Hopkins understands him, that God's first
intention and His first creative product is the humanity of
Christ, by virtue of which the Son, the second divine Person, becomes Christ, the anointed one. All else would thus
be created through and for Christ, not through and for the

Divine Word alone. Then Hopkins wants to consider the "aeonian" procession of incarnation, not yet the temporal one which took place in our time. This aeonian incarnation would be for the angels, who could thus, if they chose, join in the Great Sacrifice and be raised to a share in divine life. The Great Sacrifice stems from the complete and loving, personal self-giving within the Trinity, and this loving sharing of personal being is the essence of true sacrifice. In the Trinity it is infintely blissful.

Now Hopkins embarks on an image which throws Miss Schneider completely off Hopkins' Catholic track into Freudian quicksands. Hopkins, perhaps feeling safe in his image because he has not yet brought in Christ's actual temporal incarnation, glances forward (or, perhaps, since we deal with different dimensions of time, outward) into the Garden of Gethsemane, where Christ exercised his bloody sacrifice (which sacrifice should have been, in God's first intention, unbloody, an uncomplicated reflection of sacrifice in the Trinity, a blissful giving and fulfillment on Christ's part and on ours), and speaks now of God's "blissful agony" which, as it were, forces into time drops, analogous to the drops of Christ's blood. These drops symbolize creation, both angelic (which is here under discussion) and, later, our own cosmos. (9) It is an involved image, but surely, to one who grasps Hopkins' context, a manageable one, suggesting that if all had worked out according to God's first intention, only blissful self-giving in love would have prevailed and sweat and blood themselves could only have been symbols, not of labor and suffering, but of divine sharing of life.

Not so for Miss Schneider. Before she quotes the image on sweat and blood, she states, "He added, significantly . . ." (p. 115) Should anyone be in any doubt about what she thinks the image is significant of, she, confidently rushing in where the Angelic Doctor himself would tread fearfully, goes on to say:

> This Scotist doctrine, with its undeniably masochistic implications, had found immediate response in the corresponding temperament of Hopkins. To conceive Christ's sacrificial incarnation, as well as the concomitant "storms" of nature, not as solely redemptive of man and therefore not as spiritually

301

practical or functional for man's good but rather a
free supernatural sacrifice for its own sake, is to
conceive both sacrifice and storms as exquisite, to
be rejoiced in for themselves (not simply endured
for the good they may be thought to produce), the
pleasure-in-pain sour-sweet of the sloe raised to
the highest pitch of emotional and spiritual intensity. The image is exact though I should think
to most people somewhat repellent. (pp. 115-6)

Miss Schneider's concept of perverse seeking of pain
for its own sweet-sour sake--and we need not try to deny, she
feels, that both Scotus and Hopkins were clearly masochists--
is sufficiently repellent, indeed, but Scotists and most (I
should think) readers of Hopkins will judge that she pro-
jects the concept into the text. She understands, like
many who have written on "The Windhover: to Christ our
Lord," that "sacrifice" for a Christian, at least a
Catholic, necessarily involves some desire for pain and
bloody self-destruction. Hopkins conceives sacrifice as perfect in the Trinity, where each Person gives Himself in infinite fulness to two other Persons in the perfect union of
one infinite act of Being. The Great Sacrifice which so
seized Hopkins' imagination in The Deutschland, "The Windhover: to Christ our Lord," in "Alphonsus," and, indeed,
in most of his poems, is this loving act of self-forgetful-
ness, like the nun on the swamped ship, in the interests of
another person:

> Let him ride, her pride, in his triumph, despatch
> and have done with his doom there (Deutschland,
> stanza 28).

Miss Schneider could have profited from more study
of page 109 of S. Here Fr. Devlin states once more the
effect of Scotus' theory of the Incarnation on the thought
and poetic imagination of Hopkins: "He saw creation as dependent upon the decree of the Incarnation, and not the
other way around." And he discussed with admirable clarity
Hopkins' view of sacrifice:

> But he did not see God the Son's descent into crea-
> tion merely or primarily as the reparation for sin.
> He saw it as an act of love which would have taken
> place in one form or another whether or not there

had been any sin. Since He was God himself He could
not perform the act of an inferior nature; so from
all eternity He willed to become a creature so as to
express that aspect of his love which was impossible
to Him as God alone. This is 'the great sacrifice';
a sacrifice of joy and adoration, which only incidentally, as it were, became one also of sorrow and
reparation. (p. 109)

"Incidentally," owing to the sins of men, sacrifice
comes to involve suffering. But in Hopkins' thought redemp-
tion or sacrifice is designed in its essence "to give an
opportunity for love by free choice." (S, p. 110)

A more intelligent and profound probing of Hopkins'
dealing with Scotus than Miss Schneider's we find in J.
Hillis Miller's The Disappearance of God. (10) Mr. Miller
has done his best to bring his impressive knowledge of
Hopkins' texts to the Scotistic tribunal for thorough examination, but the judges, I fear, have been bribed. His intent, as he states clearly on the final page (p. 359) of his
own text, is to demonstrate that man should "reject twenty-
five hundred years of belief in the dualism of heaven and
earth." Then man could "come to see that being and value
lie in this world . . ." With such a dogma determining his
own vision, a critic could scarely be expected to see clearly the operation of Hopkins' imagination.

Mr. Miller does his best, though, and many of his
comments and insights on Hopkins' theologizing are brilliant
and helpful. But, like Miss Schneider, he does not understand the Catholic theology involved, and he thus inevitably
misreads Hopkins' imaginative expression of his vision of
reality.

Mr. Miller's lack of grasp of Catholic theology
appears in such statements as ". . . the Trinity, in which
the Persons are one and yet three." (p. 351) He uses this
obvious contradiction, which he supposes that Hopkins and
other Catholic theologians hold, to explain how Hopkins
could hold another contradiction, that the self can be altogether changed and yet remain the same self. It is not surprising that Mr. Miller could be confused by theological
discussion of the quasi-substantial change brought about in
the human person by the substantial accident of divine

grace. And though it is a human failing to which all of us engaged in the confusing and difficult field of literary criticism are subject, I wish more of my colleagues would try better to realize that Catholic theology is, in its own procedure and its own exacting terminology, at least as complicated as the science of micro-biology (in which none of us is tempted to pontificate). Why not inquire of one or more Catholic theologians before publishing? Is it possible that, even with the best will in the world, some literary critics judge Catholic theology to be, after all, merely myth, wishful thinking, and "point of view?" If so, such judgments will surely make for difficulty in dealing with a literary artist--like Chaucer, or Dante, or Shakespeare, or Crashaw, or Hopkins, or Joyce, or J. F. Powers--who takes Catholic theology seriously, and who knows it well.

In any case, Mr. Miller unfortunately does not perceive any need to distinguish between the Word, the second divine Person, and Christ, whose human nature justifies the name of the Anointed One. This prevents him from seeing the main point of Hopkins' centering in Christ rather than in the Word throughout his poetry. Many Catholic theologians, and, as I understand and have experienced the matter, most Catholics, following the main stream of Scholastic teaching, have imagined the universe reflecting the Word, as is stressed in the opening of St. John's gospel, widely-known, since it was formerly read after each Mass; but they did not think of each thing in the universe reflecting the humanity of the Word. In very recent years, I understand, this trend has changed, and the Scotist view is in general favor. At any rate, Hopkins thought of every creature, birds, weeds, bells, and men, reflecting and, each in its own perfection of act, completing its own nature in the humanity of Christ, not only in the divine Word.

In this point, as I see the matter, we will find the most profound influence of the Scotist view in Hopkins' poems. A glance at a few of the poems may clarify my contention. I will consider first "Duns Scotus' Oxford," in which Hopkins' love for Scotus and his teaching merges with his love for his alma mater:

Towery city and branchy between towers;
Cuckoo-echoing, bell-swarmèd, lark-charmèd,
  rook-racked, river-rounded;
The dapple-eared lily below thee; that country and
  town did
Once encounter in, here coped and poisèd powers;

Thou hast a base and brickish skirt there, sours
That neighbour-nature thy grey beauty is grounded
Best in; graceless growth, thou hast confounded
Rural rural keeping--folk, flocks, and flowers.

Yet ah! this air I gather and I release
He lived on; these weeds and waters, these walls
  are what
He haunted who of all men mos t sways my spirits to
  peace;

Of realty the rarest-veinèd unraveller; a not
Rivalled insight, be rival Italy or Greece;
Who fired France for Mary without spot.

Hopkins first pictures the lovely city, its towers
and trees, then hears the sounds of birds and bells, all
charming except the raucous rooks, a racking counterpoint
to the lovely harmony. He sees, and no doubt feels, the
Isis flowing in a verdant half-circle around Oxford. He recalls the city's history, in which the lily played not only
a real but an heraldic, symbolic role; the struggle of the
rural beauty and the medieval town producing the lovely com-
promise which makes up Oxford. The ugly brick utility of
the modern town seems to be making progress against the grey
beauty of the stone buildings.

But most of all, the beauty of Oxford focuses on
another past beauty, not now of architecture and of nature
but of mind, and an Oxford student and teacher, the great
Franciscan Duns Scotus, brings all that intellectual beauty
into clear view. Like the brickish architecture, inferior
philosophers threaten that beauty with modern vagaries. (12)
Scotus, however, towers above them, as Purcell towers above
Sullivan, or Shakespeare above Browning. Scotus dealt with
the real; he could unravel "being's dread and vacant maze"

of which Hopkins had written when he was a student at Oxford
("Nondum," No. 22). Not Aquinas nor Aristotle (certainly
not Hegel) could surpass him.

Scotists will know more than others how triumphant
that last line of the sonnet sounded in Hopkins' mind.
Scholastics had troubled themselves over the belief, held
throughout the Church, that the Mother of God could never
have been under the influence of sin. Then how explain the
revealed truth that all children of Adam required redemp-
tion? At Paris Scotus, or so Hopkins believed, (13) argued
with successful subtlety that one who was prevented, by the
foreseen merits of Christ, from falling into original sin,
would be most of all redeemed. Hence the Virgin, who would
otherwise have suffered the fall with the rest of us, was
prevented from so doing by a special privilege. Thus
Scotus did for the glory of Mary and of the Church what even
Aquinas could not do. And the fires Scotus started in
France blaze throughout the Church yet.

Hopkins' deep interest in Mary's role and his
Scotistic view of it appear more clearly in his exquisite
"May Lines" (Poems, No. 139), written probably while he was
teaching at Stonyhurst, four years or so later than "Duns
Scotus' Oxford":

MAY LINES

Ab initio et ante saecula creata sum et usque ad
futurum saeculum non desinam

O PRAEDESTINATA bis
            Quo fuisti
A saeculorum saeculis
            Mater Christi,
Post praevisa merita
            Innocentis,
Iterum post scelera
            Nostrae gentis,
Quamvis illa purior
            Sit corona
Magis haec commendat cor-
            di Dei dona.
Utique deiparam
            Te mirarer,
At non pastu tuo tam

```
              Delectarer;
        Confiterer virginem
              Matrem factam,
  At non inter omnes sem-
              per te intactam,
  Sed bifronti gloriae
              Tibi erunt
  Haec quae stant et illa quae
              Conciderunt--
  Et redempta scelera
              Nostrae gentis
  Et praevisa merita
              Innocentis. (14)
```

As the note in Poems indicates (p. 272), the "iterum"
of line 7 indicates a second predestination for Mary, following upon that of Christ. As Christ was first predestinated
to be the Head and Source of the universe, so Mary was predestinated to share that role with Him. After He was predestinated to be Saviour of our fallen race, she was again
predestinated, as among all women immaculate, to be associated with Christ in that role. Thus Hopkins' profound insight into and overwhelming interest in the nature of the
Incarnation once more appears.

About this same time Hopkins wrote "As kingfishers
catch fire" (Poems, No. 57), which gains in meaning if we
see it in a Scotist light:

        As kingfishers catch fire, dragonflies draw flame;
        As tumbled over rim in roundy wells
        Stones ring; like each tucked string tells, each
        hung bell's
        Bow swung finds tongue to fling out broad its name;
        Each mortal thing does one thing and the same:
        Deals out that being indoors each one dwells;
        Selves--goes itself; myself it speaks and spells;
        Crying What I do is me: for that I came.

        I say more: the just man justices;
        Keeps grace: that keeps all his goings graces;
        Acts in God's eye what in God's eye he is--
        Christ--for Christ plays in ten thousand places,

Lovely in limbs, and lovely in eyes not his
To the Father through the features of men's faces.

Each of the things mentioned has a characteristic act which belongs to it alone, and which is sometimes expressed in its name: kingfishers flash reflected flame as they dive, dragonflies shimmer, stones tell of themselves when dropped in wells, strings vibrate their quality, great bells clang out their names. All of us do this, and we are made to do so, to speak that act central to us, to our nature if we are not spirits, to our person if we are.

The quotation of Christ's words before Pilate--". . for this I came" (John, 18:37)--suggests that every single creature is made to do the same thing that Christ did, to speak out that which it is and, in so doing, to reflect Truth Himself.

But "I," the person, as we are accustomed to speak of the person in Theology, do more than speak my own name if I am just. I, too, speak Truth, Justice. I live by grace, which is my own sharing in the divine nature along with Christ. Hence my "I" is no longer just mine but also Christ's, which is Hopkins' paraphrase of Paul's, "I live now, not I, but Christ lives in me." (Galatians, 2:20) And my act is not just mine, but Christ's too, an idea Hopkins somewhat more generally expresses in "The Soldier" (Poems, No. 63). Thus God, when, as "a father and fond" (Poems, No. 40), he casts his eye to see at what we are playing, (15) sees not only us but the beauty of His own Son in us. Scotism adds to the glory of this concept the special union we have by nature with the humanity of Christ. Not that Thomism or other orthodox philosophical views neglect that union when they speak of persons, but Scotism does place more wholehearted emphasis upon its operation throughout the cosmos and upon its universal necessity. (16)

Finally, I would like to consider one of the best-known of Hopkins' early sonnets, "The Windhover: to Christ our Lord," in order to see if a Thomist view could fail to see something that would be obvious in a Scotist view. For me it was so, since while I always saw in the poem a union between creature and the Word which both the bird and the Christian speaker share, I did not see, as I do now, that they shared an intimate union with Christ. First, the poem itself:

THE WINDHOVER

To Christ our Lord

I caught this morning morning's minion, king-
    dom of daylight's dauphin, dapple-dawn-
    drawn Falcon, in his riding
Of the rolling level underneath him steady
    air, and striding
High there, how he rung upon the rein of a
    wimpling wing
In his ectasy! then off, off forth on swing,
As a skate's heel sweeps smooth on a bow-
    bend: the hurl and gliding
Rebuffed the big wind. My heart in hiding
Stirred for a bird,--the achieve of, the
    mastery of the thing!

Brute beauty and valour and act, oh, air,
    pride, plume, here
Buckle! AND the fire that breaks from thee
    then, a billion
Times told lovelier, more dangerous, O my
    chevalier!

No wonder of it: shéer plód makes plough
    down sillion
Shine, and blue-bleak embers, ah my dear,
    Fall, gall themselves, and gash gold-
    vermillion.

The name of the bird indicates that characteristic act by
which it reaches the completion of its nature, its mastery of
the wind. And here Hopkins says of it obliquely what he said
more pointedly of the bluebell in his Notebooks, "I know the
beauty of our Lord by it." (17) And "To Christ our Lord"
does not merely dedicate this poem to Christ, in my opinion.
Hopkins dedicated his every act to Christ, and thus I would
be surprised at his supposing his inferior poems were not so
dedicated. Further, the colon, exercising the act proper to
colons, ties the phrase to the original title, "The Windhover," as it does elsewhere when an explanation is helpful,
e.g. "Spring and Fall: to a young child" (Poems, No. 55).
Here in "The Windhover: to Christ our Lord," I take it, the
second phrase tells us to whom the poem is addressed, and

might well be tied in with the "through Christ our Lord"
which ends all our liturgical prayer, and above all with the
Preface of the Mass, where all praise comes to God, from
angels and men, through Christ our Lord. Lower creation,
too, thus praises Christ, as Hopkins understood Paul to be
saying in Romans viii. 19. (18)

Then the bird is described in knightly terms. At
the end of the Deutschland, Hopkins describes Christ as
"King. . .Pride, rose, prince, hero of us, high priest. . .
fire. . .Lord." In "The Windhover: to Christ our Lord" the
bird is dealt with as minion or favorite of the King, as
dauphin or prince, and as master of the wind. The bird
deals with the wind as a chevalier deals with his horse, and
in terms which do recall, as Mr. Gardner points out in his
Penguin edition, Henry V, III, 7. (19) Hopkins employs all
the technique of a master poet in producing in the sound and
rhythm of his words the movement and sound and feel of the
bird in the wind. But his enthusiasm surpasses that of the
most dedicated Aubonite. He sees something beyond the
bird itself, as he had done with the bluebell.

His own heart, in Jesuit imagery drawn from The
Spiritual Exercises, is indeed his chevalier, and should be,
in the spirit of "the Kingdom of Christ" meditation, gallant-
ly marching after his Lord, as his thoughts do in the last
words of the Deutschland: "...our thoughts' chivalry's
throng's Lord." But his heart is hiding, unlike the knightly bird. It admires the bird, however, and envies its
achieve, its fulfillment of its own nature ("a bird," not
"that bird"). It admires a bird's mastery, or, in the meaning the word had in knightly times, its dangerousness.

Now, in the sestet, more as a Scotist than a Thomist,
with an imagination of qualities different from that of many
Thomists, he calls upon his heart to buckle on, as armor on
a knight, the qualities of the bird--the intrinsic beauty and
valour and act, with their respective extrinsic attributes,
the knightly air, the pride in valour (like the popular re-
cruiting ad for our Navy, which features that one word,
"Pride," over two men in Navy uniform, or like the word
applied to Christ in the Deutschland, Stanza 28, line 8, and
stanza 35, line 7), and the plume which symbolizes knightly
act. When the heart has so buckled on this knightly armor,
a new fire will break from it, not only the fire of his own

natural ("brute") act, but also the infinitely more beauti-
ful fire which is personal to Christ, which the bird cannot
share. In the last line of the Deutschland, Christ is called
"Our heart's charity's hearth's fire," and Hopkins is surely
thinking of a devotion central in his own thought, the devotion to the Sacred Heart of Jesus. For him this devotion was
not the sentimental horror it has become in much of modern
practice (and in literature, as in Joyce's Dublin), but a
human treatment of the incomprehensible beauty of the
Incarnation. (20) He held that the hearts of Christ's
followers were aflame with the fire that came from the
divine coal, in Christ's vivid image, dear in tradition to
Jesuits and to the devotion to the Sacred Heart. (21) And
this would be so whether sin had entered the picture or not,
he as a Scotist would unequivocally assert. So that his
heart, his chevalier, becomes infinitely more lovely and
more masterful than the bird can be, a new echo of Paul's
"I live now, not I, but Christ lives in me."

But in the present order, sin has entered in, and
labor and suffering and death cloud the picture. Yet there
is no wonder that the triumph still comes; the divine reflection and inner fire still operate. Two symbols darkly reveal the truth, based on objects that have only a humble
act, the plow, and, seemingly, no act at all, the embers.
The plow was a favorite symbol, for Christ, of the Christian.
Here the rusty plow, in its sheer act of plodding down the
sillion or communal field not only plows up the earth but
shines in unexpected beauty at the end, a symbol of the
laboring Christian reflecting at the end the divine beauty
of Christ. And the seemingly dead embers, symbols of Christ
on the cross (hence "ah my dear" in loving sympathy), have
yet an act of bursting open, not only to reveal the unexpected beauty of the shower of sparks, but, as in Christ's
scriptural image, to spread their fire throughout time and
space.

A Scotist will see, as another philosopher or theologian might not, the union here between the speaker and the
bird based upon the humanity of Christ as the first product
of God's creative act, the source of all perfection and fulfillment for creatures. For all Catholic theologians,
Hopkins and the bird share an intrinsic relationship to the
Word who gives them being, and both reflect, in their differing finite orders, the Word's infinite perfection. But not

for all theologians need Hopkins and the bird share an intrinsic relationship to Christ based on Christ as the
universal goal of every good act and of every moral assent
to good. For Scotists, as Hopkins understood and imagined
the matter, this is necesarily so. Hence the qualities of
the good acts of the bird nature and of the good acts and
the moral assents to good of human nature can be dealt with
in some sort of univocity alien to Thomistic imaginings,
without supposing a pantheistic unity of existence. The
created human nature of Christ enters into the picture of
creation immediately for a Scotist, and for this reason any
notion of pantheism, some communal sharing of pieces of the
universal existence, which some confused critics have
attributed both to Hopkins and to Scotus, is immediately
prevented. Christ shares his infinite personal existence
with those capable of sharing in it according to their
limited capacities, namely spirits, but he shares with all
things, in their good acts, the beauty of his created human
nature. Thus "The Windhover: to Christ our Lord" expresses
Scotistically the way in which both bird and man reflect,
not only the perfection of the divine Word, but also the
perfection of Christ in his human nature, and the infinitely
greater sharing of man and Christ in the personal union of
spirits.

Obviously, in the discussion of the effect of
Hopkins' Scotism on his poems, there is no question of discussing whether Scotism is a better theological approach to
God's revelation than is Thomism. Such a discussion, as I
pointed out at first, is irrelevant here. Whatever may be
the truth in this matter, for this discussion it is important
to know only that Hopkins preferred Scotism and acted on that
preference. (22)

Nor does a poem care what its maker believes or
thinks. A poem is not a man. It is a being made out of intelligible sound, and, like music, comes into being not in
the mind but in the ear-drum. The poem demands that the intellect descend from the lofty heights of intelligibility
and sink into (and remain in) the ear-drum and the sounds
and rhythms which actuate it. Intelligibility is not the
prime concern of the poem's being, as it is not of music's.
The poem aims at being a sensible object of contemplation
for the mind by way of ear, in Hopkins' excellent definition. (23) And the things which make a poem good are more

immediately the sensible rather than the intelligible.

Furthermore, the "meaning" the poem first of all cares about is not that which proceeds from organized thought or belief, but the intuitive vision which precedes those. If the poet can remain faithful to that prime vision, what Hopkins, referring to the penetration of the mind by reality in the image of sexual union, calls "the fine delight that fathers thought" (Poems, No. 75) and what Joyce's Stephen Dedalus calls an "epiphany," then the poet may believe and think anything at all, true or false, and still produce a living poem. It is the intuiting spirit of the seeing maker which gives life to the poem.

But the poet's thought and belief will condition the poem, since the imagination will be affected, often profoundly, by them. And it is so in Hopkins' case. We can better see his poems as they are if we see that their Christ-centeredness stems from his Scotistic imagining of Christ in his humanity as the first-born of all creatures, for all creatures "Their ransom, their rescue, and first, fast, last friend." (Poems, 34)

FOOTNOTES

(1) The Sermons and Devotional Writings of Gerard Manley
     Hopkins (London: Oxford University Press, 1959), p.
     351. Hereafter this work will be cited in the text
     as S.

(2) Gerard Manley Hopkins (1844-1889): A Study of Poetic
     Idiosyncrasy in Relation to Poetic Tradition (London:
     Oxford University Press, 1949, reprinted 1961), I, p.
     22. Hereafter cited as Gardner.

(3) Cf. Gardner, II, p. 328: "a finished and finite
     dogmatism."

(4) Ibid.

(5) The Wreck of the Deutschland: An Essay and Commen-
     tary (Kent State University Bulletin, 1963), pp. 36-
     44.

(6) Journal of English and Germanic Philology, Vol.
     LXIII, No. 3 (July 1964), pp. 537-8.

(7) "The Wreck of the Deutschland: A New Reading" PMLA,
     LXXXI, No. 1 (March 1966), pp. 110-122.

(8) Father Devlin discusses this passage, S, pp. 110-
     114. The main center of confusion, for most of us
     conventionally educated priests as well as for
     English teachers like Miss Schneider, will be
     Hopkins' supposition that Christ was from the first
     instant of creation materially present, not only in
     some kind of understanding or vision in angelic
     minds, but in the flesh, or in a "condition of
     matter": "Christ, he (Hopkins) thinks, was material-
     ly present in the same sort of way that he is pre-
     sent in the Eucharist: a material substance, but
     without actual extension." (S, p. 112) Devlin
     thinks that Hopkins based his notion on such state-
     ments of Scotus as: "I say then, but without in-
     sisting on it, that before the Incarnation and 'be-
     fore Abraham was,' in the beginning of the world,
     Christ could have had a true temporal existence in a
     sacramental manner." (S, pp. 113-4) Thus Hopkins

can, and does, imagine everything in the cosmos flowing out from and returning to God through the humanity of Christ, which is, as it were, the one door
for existence and final fulfillment for all creatures. Thus an imaginative element different from
the one common in Scholastic tradition is introduced. Commonly the human nature of Christ has been
imagined as the door through which sinful humans can
enter the divine sheepfold. For Hopkins it is the
door through which all creatures pass to existence
and toward which they tend to find their natural
and, if they have the spiritual capacity, supernatural fulfillment.

(9)   Hopkins used a similar image to express the ubiquity
        of God's presence in love: "The First is that all
        God gives us or does for us He gives and does in
        love and therefore all we do towards God we should
        do in love . . . . Suppose God showed us in a vision
        the whole world enclosed first in a drop of water,
        allowing everything to be seen in its native colors;
        then the same in a drop of Christ's blood, by which
        everything whatever was turned scarlet, keeping
        nevertheless mounted in the scarlet its own colour
        too." (S, p. 194) Water and blood, the symbols of
        the life-giving sacraments of baptism and the
        Eucharist, do not suggest masochism to a Christian
        imagination.

(10)   Cambridge: Harvard University Press, 1963.

(11)   Poems of Gerard Manley Hopkins, Third Edition, ed.
        by W. H. Gardner (London: Oxford University Press),
        No. 44. Hereafter this work will be cited in the
        text as Poems.

(12)   "After all I can, at all events a little, read Duns
        Scotus and I care for him more even than Aristotle
        and more pace tua than a dozen Hegels." (Feb. 20,
        1875). The Letters of Gerard Manley Hopkins to
        Robert Bridges, ed. by Abbott (London: Oxford
        University Press), 1955, p. 31.

(13)   "It is a comfort to think that the greatest of the
        divines and doctors of the Church who have spoken

315

and written in favor of this truth (the Immaculate
Conception) came from England: between 500 and 600
years ago he was sent for to go to Paris to dispute
in its favor. The disputation or debate was held in
public and someone who was there says that this wise
and happy man by his answers broke the objections
brought against him as Samson broke the thongs and
withies with which is enemies tried to bind him."
(S, p. 45) Hopkins' chauvinism was one of the elements, no doubt, which led him to perceive Scotus
and Purcell as the greatest in their respective
fields.

(14) The translation printed in Poems, p. 272, is as
follows: 'O doubly predestinated, in that from all
eternity thou wert Mother of Christ, (predestined)
after the foreseeing of the merits of the Innocent
One, again (predestined) after (the foreseeing of)
the sins of mankind;--though the former privilege is
the purer crown, yet it is the latter which the more
readily brings home to the heart the gifts of God.
In all truth I should marvel at thee as God's mother
(deiparam); yet I should not savour thee so sweetly:
I should confess a virgin made mother, but not in
thee one--the only one--for ever unsullied. But to
thy two-fold glory there will always be those things
which stand fast and those which have fallen away--
both the redeemed sins of mankind and the foreseen
merits of the Innocent One.'

(15) "For grace is any action, activity, on God's part by
which, in creating or after creating, he carries the
creature to or towards the end of its being, which
is its selfsacrifice to God and its salvation. It
is, I say, any such activity on God's part; so that
so far as this action or activity is God's it is
divine stress, holy spirit, and, as all is done
through Christ, Christ's spirit; so far as it is
action, correspondence, on the creature's it is
actio salutaris; so far as it is looked at in esse
quieto it is Christ in his member on the one side,
his member in Christ on the other. It is as if a
man said: That is Christ playing at me and me playing at Christ, only that it is no play but truth;
that is Christ being me and me being Christ." (S, p.

154)

(16)   Devlin's speculations on space travel and the desir-
         ability of having the first missionaries in space to
         be Scotists, at least in respect to the Incarnation,
         stress this Scotist emphasis: "The second thing is
         on the supposition that Hopkins' distinction between
         ensarkosis and enanthropesis were allowed as tenable,
         it might have an important bearing on the future.
         Space travel and the discovery of other planets are
         now possibilities that have to be taken into account.
         In the event (however unlikely) of some form of
         rational life being found on another planet, the
         question of the redemption would be bound to arise.
         If Hopkins' distinction were valid, one would not
         have to suppose that the creatures of another planet
         had been deprived of the light of the Incarnation
         because they had had no historical knowledge of
         Christ's life and death on earth. The whole affair
         is too vague and problematical to be worth discuss-
         ing further. But perhaps just that much was worth
         saying." (S, pp. 114-5)

(17)   The Journals and Papers of Gerald Manley Hopkins, ed.
         by Humphrey House, completed by Graham Storey (Lon-
         don: Oxford University Press), 1959, p. 199. The
         entry was written in 1870, two years before Hopkins
         began seriously to read Scotus. His enthusiasm for
         Scotus was undoubtedly in part the result of his
         finding a solid Catholic theological base for the
         imaginings he already had, perhaps stemming from the
         Platonic tradition popular at Oxford in his under-
         graduate days.

(18)   "For the created universe waits with eager expecta-
         tion for God's sons to be revealed. It was made the
         victim of frustration, not by its own choice, but
         because of him who made it so; yet always there was
         hope, because the universe itself is to be freed
         from the shackles of mortality and enter upon the
         liberty and splendour of the children of God."
         Hopkins wrote "Ribblesdale" (Poems, No. 58) specifi-
         cally on this text, stressing that Earth's eye,
         tongue, and heart yearn to speak to God, and can do
         so only through the just man, not the thriftless

heir, the unregenerate Prodigal. One of his loveliest curtal sonnets, "Ashboughs" (Poems, 111), unfortunately relegated to the "fragments" section,
expresses the theme of Earth groping for God as a
woman might grope in the dark for her husband.

(19)   Gerald Manley Hopkins: A Selection of his Poems and
        Prose by W. H. GARDNER, Penguin Books, 1953 (reprint-
        ed 1956), p. 221.

(20)   Cf. Hopkins' sermon on the Sacred Heart, S, pp. 110-
        114.

(21)   Christ's image, "I am come to cast fire . . ." from
        Luke 12:49, operates throughout the tradition which
        flowers in the modern liturgy honoring the Sacred
        Heart (where the plow image also operates) and in
        the Mass of St. Ignatius on July 31. I treat of
        this matter in detail in my Metaphor in Hopkins
        (Chapel Hill: University of North Carolina Press),
        1961, pp. 98-104.

(22)   Hopkins' preference is clear. Indeed, he became al-
        most truculunt in dealing with the subject. Writing
        to Coventry Patmore of the fact that Patmore's
        poetry was not appreciated by his contemporaries,
        Hopkins says: "And so I used to feel of Duns Scotus
        when I used to read him with delight: he saw too
        far, he knew too much; his subtlety overshot his
        interests; a kind of feud arose between genius and
        talent, and the ruck of talent in the Schools find-
        ing itself, as his age passed by, less and less
        able to understand him, voted that there was no-
        thing important to understand and so first mis-
        quoted and then refuted him." Further Letters of
        Gerard Manley Hopkins, second edition, ed. by Abbott
        (London: Oxford University Press), 1956, p. 349.
        The feud between the genius of men like Thomas and
        Scotus and the talent of men like Suarez and Cajetan
        led, in this fallen world, to the development and
        triumph of the "ruck of talent" in the seminaries
        and to the academic abuse of the men of genius. It
        is this admirable but intransigent attitude, I take
        it, which supports whatever authenticity may lie be-
        hind the quotation which Devlin gives from A Page of

Irish History: Story of University College, Dublin
(1883-1909) by Fathers of the Society of Jesus
(Dublin: Talbot Press), 1930: "Guardedly but not altogether accurately the historian of University
College, Dublin, wrote of 'the strains of controversy' which had 'marred his earlier years,' and
added more explicitly: '. . . as a theologian his
undoubted brilliance was dimmed by a somewhat obsti-
nate love of Scotist doctrine, in which he traced
the influence of Platonist philosophy. His idio-
syncracy got him into difficulties with his Jesuit
preceptors who followed Aquinas and Aristotle!" (S,
xiii)

(23)   "Poetry is speech framed for contemplation of the
mind by way of hearing . . ." *The Journals and
Papers*, p. 289. I have a detailed discussion of
this definition in the final chapter of *Metaphor in
Hopkins* and in *The Modern Schoolman*, 31 (May 1954),
247-280, and 34 (May 1957), 283-98.

Discussion

JAMES P. CAINE, S.J., M.A.

Professor of English
Chairman of Theatre Department
University of Detroit
Detroit, Michigan

Father Boyle's paper is an excellent example of an up-to-date problem in critical analysis: the influence of theology on the imagination of an artist, the relationship between theology and literature. Within that large perspective, and with an expert's knowledge of both analogues, he shows how a central point in Scotus' theology on the Incarnation influenced the poetry of Hopkins.

Some critics may regard the average study of literature as little more than a waste of time. And yet such studies are necessary when we wish to see literature (or theology) as a continuous whole or as an important development. Hopkins, a Victorian, illustrates the development of some "modern" qualities in poetry. One of these is the Incarnation, studied so much in contemporary criticism because it has a place in so many artistic creations. Its place in Hopkins is central to his life as a priest and to his total vision as a poet. That central inspiration in its particular effects on him as a poet, he drew from Scotus.

Father Boyle's scholarly presentation gives the details of those particular effects. The usual account of Scotus' influence tends to stress his principle of individuation, and there is no doubt that it is an important influence. However, Father Boyle clearly demonstrates how much more central is Scotus' view of creation as dependent upon the decree of the Incarnation, and not the other way around; how Hopkins thought of every creature in the universe as reflecting the humanity of Christ, and how that is intrinsic to the poetry itself.

Some theologians--assuming their knowledge of poetry as well as of the Incarnation--may not agree with all of Father Boyle's interpretations, and part of their disagreement may well follow from their system of theology. But no one can find fault with the evidence for his position, nor with his vital, knowledgeable use of it.